International Political Economy Series

General Editor: **Timothy M. Shaw**, Professor and Director, Institute of International Relations, The University of the West Indies, Trinidad & Tobago

Titles include:

Hans Abrahamsson
UNDERSTANDING WORLD ORDER AND STRUCTURAL CHANGE
Poverty, Conflict and the Global Arena

Morten Bøås, Marianne H. Marchand and Timothy Shaw (*editors*)
THE POLITICAL ECONOMY OF REGIONS AND REGIONALISM

James Busumtwi-Sam and Laurent Dobuzinskis
TURBULENCE AND NEW DIRECTION IN GLOBAL POLITICAL ECONOMY

Bill Dunn
GLOBAL RESTRUCTURING AND THE POWER OF LABOUR

Myron J. Frankman
WORLD DEMOCRATIC FEDERALISM
Peace and Justice Indivisible

Barry K. Gills (*editor*)
GLOBALIZATION AND THE POLITICS OF RESISTANCE

Richard Grant and John Rennie Short (*editors*)
GLOBALIZATION AND THE MARGINS

Graham Harrison (*editor*)
GLOBAL ENCOUNTERS
International Political Economy, Development and Globalization

Patrick Hayden and Chamsy el-Ojeili (*editors*)
CONFRONTING GLOBALIZATION
Humanity, Justice and the Renewal of Politics

Axel Hülsemeyer (*editor*)
GLOBALIZATION IN THE TWENTY-FIRST CENTURY
Convergence or Divergence?

Helge Hveem and Kristen Nordhaug (*editors*)
PUBLIC POLICY IN THE AGE OF GLOBALIZATION
Responses to Environmental and Economic Crises

Jomo K.S. and Shyamala Nagaraj (*editors*)
GLOBALIZATION VERSUS DEVELOPMENT

Adrian Kay and Owain David Williams (*editors*)
GLOBAL HEALTH GOVERNANCE
Crisis, Institutions and Political Economy

Dominic Kelly and Wyn Grant (*editors*)
THE POLITICS OF INTERNATIONAL TRADE IN THE 21st CENTURY
Actors, Issues and Regional Dynamics

Sandra J. MacLean, Sherri A. Brown and Pieter Fourie (*editors*)
HEALTH FOR SOME
The Political Economy of Global Health Governance

Craig N. Murphy (*editor*)
EGALITARIAN POLITICS IN THE AGE OF GLOBALIZATION

John Nauright and Kimberly S. Schimmel (*editors*)
THE POLITICAL ECONOMY OF SPORT

Morten Ougaard
THE GLOBALIZATION OF POLITICS
Power, Social Forces and Governance

Jørgen Dige Pedersen
GLOBALIZATION, DEVELOPMENT AND THE STATE
The Performance of India and Brazil since 1990

Markus Perkmann and Ngai-Ling Sum
GLOBALIZATION, REGIONALIZATION AND CROSS-BORDER REGIONS

Marc Schelhase
GLOBALIZATION, REGIONALIZATION AND BUSINESS
Conflict, Convergence and Influence

Leonard Seabrooke
US POWER IN INTERNATIONAL FINANCE
The Victory of Dividends

Timothy J. Sinclair and Kenneth P. Thomas (*editors*)
STRUCTURE AND AGENCY IN INTERNATIONAL CAPITAL MOBILITY

Fredrik Söderbaum and Timothy M. Shaw (*editors*)
THEORIES OF NEW REGIONALISM

Susanne Soederberg, Georg Menz and Philip G. Cerny (*editors*)
INTERNALIZING GLOBALIZATION
The Rise of Neoliberalism and the Decline of National Varieties of Capitalism

Ritu Vij (*editor*)
GLOBALIZATION AND WELFARE
A Critical Reader

Matthew Watson
THE POLITICAL ECONOMY OF INTERNATIONAL CAPITAL MOBILITY

International Political Economy Series

Series Standing Order ISBN 978–0–333–71708–0 hardcover
Series Standing Order ISBN 978–0–333–71110–1 paperback

You can receive future titles in this series as they are published by placing a standing order. Please contact your bookseller or, in case of difficulty, write to us at the address below with your name and address, the title of the series and one of the ISBNs quoted above.

Customer Services Department, Macmillan Distribution Ltd, Houndmills, Basingstoke, Hampshire RG21 6XS, England

---

The Politics of Housing Booms and Busts

Edited By

Herman M. Schwartz
Professor of Politics, University of Virginia, USA

and

Leonard Seabrooke
Professor in International Political Economy, University of Warwick, UK

First published 2009 by
PALGRAVE MACMILLAN

Palgrave Macmillan in the UK is an imprint of Macmillan Publishers Limited, registered in England, company number 785998, of Houndmills, Basingstoke, Hampshire RG21 6XS.

Palgrave Macmillan in the US is a division of St Martin's Press LLC, 175 Fifth Avenue, New York, NY 10010.

Palgrave Macmillan is the global academic imprint of the above companies and has companies and representatives throughout the world.

Palgrave® and Macmillan® are registered trademarks in the United States, the United Kingdom, Europe and other countries.

ISBN: 978–0–230–23080–4 hardback
ISBN: 978–0–230–23081–1 paperback

This book is printed on paper suitable for recycling and made from fully managed and sustained forest sources. Logging, pulping and manufacturing processes are expected to conform to the environmental regulations of the country of origin.

A catalogue record for this book is available from the British Library.

A catalog record for this book is available from the Library of Congress.

10 9 8 7 6 5 4 3 2 1
18 17 16 15 14 13 12 11 10 09

Printed and bound in Great Britain by
CPI Antony Rowe, Chippenham and Eastbourne

Contents

Illustrations

Figures

Tables

Acknowledgments

This book is not an exercise in ambulance-chasing or *schadenfreude*, but has evolved with the housing booms and busts of recent years. Len had previously worked on the everyday politics of credit access for housing, as well as how mortgage securitization had permitted Freddie, Fannie, and Ginnie to spur growth and recycle international capital (in *The Social Sources of Financial Power*, Cornell, 2006). Herman had worked on how a prominent feature of American hegemony in the world economy was its capacity to suck up East Asian capital and put it into areas like housing. Our mutual interest in linking up comparative political economy and international political economy made sense when it came to housing.

We first discussed this project in 2005 and then organized a series of papers on "The New Politics of National Economic Growth: Global Capital Flows and Local Housing Markets" for the International Studies Association (ISA) conference in 2007. This was the only discussion of housing within the international political economy at that conference, and also the first on the topic to our knowledge. The American Political Science Association's annual meeting, held at the height of the crisis in August 2008, was similarly devoid of papers or panels on the housing bubble. As we reflected on what was driving the economy within many Organisation for Economic Cooperation and Development (OECD) member states, and transforming their growth models, it struck us that housing was very high on our list but had no place within comparative and international political economy literature. Such an omission was all the more odd given that for most citizens in the OECD the family home is their main store of wealth, and that mortgages and mortgage-backed securities account for a substantial share of bank assets and securities markets.

Housing, though, is about more than just money. In each of our countries fights over resources and ideas about whether housing is a social right or a means to wealth informed the kind of welfare system and the kind of housing finance system that developed. Transnational trends towards financial deregulation eventually reached the markets supporting housing credit, causing new conflicts with path-dependent national welfare and housing systems. We could see these dynamics as property booms peaked in many OECD economies and then went bust prior to, or at the same time as, the subprime crisis and international credit crunch (for the particulars, see Schwartz, *Subprime Nation*, Cornell, 2009). Our workshops and scholarly exchanges on the politics of housing markets evolved as the crisis dynamics kicked in, requiring all the contributors to this volume to watch carefully how states and markets were responding.

This volume documents the comparative politics of housing booms and busts as they occurred in "real time." The character of these politics differs according to each case and can be understood only through comparison. As the subprime crisis demonstrates, housing finance systems can have large international economic effects, but discussions on how to change them tend to remain national and between competing domestic political and economic interests. We note that at the 2009 ISA conference there were five panels related to the subprime crisis. While the property boom is over, we hope that interest in the political economy of housing markets and housing finance will flourish.

We would like to thank a number of colleagues who offered their thoughts and comments on draft papers and chapters. We would like to thank Gerard Alexander, Randall Germain, Richard Leaver, Lars Mjøset, Peter Nedergaard, Gregory P. Nowell, Ove K. Pedersen, Kasa Sjur, Gunnar Trumbull, and Jane Zavisca for their feedback and criticism. Errors remain ours. Many of the chapters in this collection are significantly revised and updated versions of articles that appeared in a Special Issue on "The Political Cost of Property Booms" in *Comparative European Politics*, Vol. 6, No. 3, 2008. Our sincere thanks go to Ben Rosamond and Colin Hay, two of the editors of *Comparative European Politics*, for their keen interest in the project. Our thanks also go to Mark Blyth for his excellent commentary piece in the same Special Issue. We also thank the Norwegian think tank Res Publica for funding an extremely productive workshop on "The Subprime Housing Bubble and the Crisis in Financial Capitalism" in April 2008, and the Bankard Fund for two summers of research funding for Herman. Our special thanks also go to Trygve Lie for his excellent research assistance. And as all politics is local, we would also like to thank our palindromic spouses, Eve and Anna, for making our houses pleasant places to be.

HERMAN M. SCHWARTZ
LEONARD SEABROOKE

Contributors

Manuel B. Aalbers, a human geographer, sociologist, and urban planner, is a post-doctoral researcher at the Amsterdam Institute for Metropolitan and International Development Studies at the University of Amsterdam. His main research interest is in the intersection of finance, the built environment, and people. He is preparing a type-script for a book titled *Place, Exclusion and Mortgage Markets*.

André Broome is Lecturer in International Political Economy in the Department of Political Science and International Studies at the University of Birmingham. His research explores the changing role of the International Monetary Fund in the global political economy as well as the comparative politics of taxation and monetary reform, and includes journal article publications in *Comparative European Politics*, *Contemporary Politics*, *Global Society*, *Journal of International Relations and Development*, *New Political Economy*, *Review of International Political Economy*, and *The Round Table*.

Jens Ladefoged Mortensen, Ph.D. is an Associate Professor in the Department of Political Science at the University of Copenhagen, Denmark. He has published on trade and WTO-related topics in various books and journals, including a contribution to *Political Economy and the Changing Global Order* (edited by Richard Stubbs and Geoffrey Underhill, 3rd edition, 2005) and *The European Union and International Organisation* (edited by Knut Erik Jørgensen, 2009). Apart from an growing interest in global finance and property politics, his current research includes the framing power and analytical capacity of IOs in trade and emerging climate governance.

Julie Pollard is a Doctoral Candidate at the Centre of Political Research of Sciences Po (CEVIPOF) in Paris, France. Her research concentrates on housing policies, interest groups, policy instruments, and political regulation and has published on these issues in *Politiques et Management Public* and *Flux*. She also teaches courses on French Politics, Sociology, and Policy Analysis at Sciences Po Paris and at Sciences Po Grenoble.

Herman M. Schwartz is Professor of Politics at the University of Virginia. His other publications include *In the Dominions of Debt* (1989), *States versus Markets* (1994, 2000, 2009), *Employment Miracles* (co-editor with Uwe Becker, 2005), *Crisis Miracles and Beyond* (co-editor with Albaek, Eliason, and Norgaard, co-editors, 2009), and most recently *Subprime Nation: American Power, Global Capital and the Housing Bubble* (2009).

Leonard Seabrooke is Professor in International Political Economy in the Department of Politics and International Studies, and Director of the Centre for the Study of Globalisation and Regionalisation, at the University of Warwick. His other publications include *The Social Sources of Financial Power* (2006), *US Power in International Finance* (2001), *Everyday Politics of the World Economy* (co-editor with John M. Hobson, 2007) and *Global Standards of Market Civilization* (co-editor with Brett Bowden, 2006).

Bent Sofus Tranøy is a Senior Researcher at the Institute of Labour Research (Fafo) and Associate Professor at the Department of Political Science, University of Oslo. He holds degrees in political economy and political science from the London School of Economics (MSc) and the University of Oslo (PhD). He has published on macroeconomic governance, globalization, European Integration, and financial instability. In 2006, Tranøy was awarded the Brage Prize for best non-fiction Norwegian book for a study on market power and market fundamentalism.

Matthew Watson is Associate Professor (Reader) in Political Economy at the University of Warwick. He is the author of almost thirty articles in refereed academic journals and two single-authored monographs with Palgrave Macmillan. They are *Foundations of International Political Economy* (2005) and *The Political Economy of International Capital Mobility* (2007).

1
Varieties of Residential Capitalism in the International Political Economy: Old Welfare States and the New Politics of Housing

Herman M. Schwartz and Leonard Seabrooke

Introduction

Comparative and international political economy (CPE and IPE) are justifiably obsessed with finance as a source of power and as a key causal force for domestic and international economic and political outcomes. Yet both CPE and IPE ignore the single largest asset in people's everyday lives and one of the biggest financial assets in most economies: residential property and its associated mortgage debt. This volume argues that residential housing and housing finance systems have important causal consequences for political behavior, social stability, the structure of welfare states, and macroeconomic outcomes. Put bluntly, home equity and social equity are often at odds. The individual country chapters and paired country comparisons show specific instances of these outcomes, while Chapter 9 considers the origins and responses to the 2007–08 crises. This introductory chapter has broader aims.

First, we argue that housing finance systems are as politically central as systems of industrial finance. The kind of housing people occupy and the property rights surrounding that housing constitute political subjectivities and objective preferences not only for the level of public spending, but also for the level of inflation, the level of taxation, and the nature of that taxation. Different kinds of housing finance systems thus produce different political subjectivities influencing the core issues on which IPE and CPE typically focus. Our concern is not simply a reaction

1

to the global financial crisis that emerged from the subprime mortgage bond crisis of 2007 and 2008 (for analyses of its sources and effects, see Seabrooke, 2006 and Schwartz, 2009), but also with understanding how housing finance systems – what we refer to as "varieties of residential capitalism" – are important for national economic systems and stability and order within the international political economy.

Second, we argue that housing finance systems also have important institutional complementarities with the larger national political economy. This comports with arguments in the varieties of capitalism (VOC) literature (Hall and Soskice, 2001). But we diverge from the VOC approach in four ways. First, sorting countries by the degree of financial repression – systematic state control over the volume, direction and price of credit – in their housing finance systems produces groupings that do not correspond one-to-one with the liberal versus coordinated market economy (LME vs. CME) distinction at the heart of the VOC approach. Second, where VOC is concerned with explaining the structure of manufacturing and export specialization and largely eschews causal arguments about macroeconomic outcomes, housing market finance systems are much more connected to macroeconomic outcomes than to what is being produced. Moreover, as Schwartz's and Watson's chapters show, housing finance systems mattered for the distribution of global growth in the past two decades, and growth largely favored one specific variety of residential capitalism. As Pollard's chapter, too, demonstrates, the supply of housing within national systems reflects both prior institutional systems for supplying housing and political aspirations for economic change. Third, divergent macroeconomic performance, combined with the fact that housing finance is a substantial portion of domestic investment everywhere, suggests serious limits to the VOC approach insofar as it tries to explain outcomes on the basis of *domestic* complementarities alone (see also Blyth, 2003). Financially repressed and financially liberal systems are globally interdependent, and the deregulation of national housing finance systems has largely been a transnational phenomenon, often tied to processes of globalization and Europeanization. As Mortensen and Seabrooke point out in this volume, the impetus for change is often political and regional, such as with Denmark's compliance with, or anticipation of, European Commission financial directives. More informally, external institutions such as the Organization for Economic Cooperation and Development (OECD), primarily through their policy reports, as well as lobby groups such as the European Mortgage Federation (EMF) also pressure national policymakers. As a method of study, VOC deals poorly with transnational processes, but the varieties of residential capitalism we identify do not operate in a transnational political vacuum. However Pollard (this volume) disagrees, pointing out that the construction industry is still substantially local in nature. Fourth, the degree of financial repression in housing directly affects the degree of social stratification. In repressive systems, housing finance tends to reinforce existing patterns of stratification, while in liberal systems housing finance enables a reordering of intergenerational wealth transfers with corresponding political effects. Finally, convergence and divergence in housing finance may also be a matter of external political influence, an element that is missing from the VOC approach.

Our third major point is that housing finance systems have ballot-box consequences because, among other things, they affect voters' preferences for the level of public spending, taxation, and interest rates. The institutional structure surrounding housing thus has important political consequences paralleling those of welfare institutions. Houses and welfare programs both confer rights to a stream of income or services onto people. But unlike welfare programs, houses are potentially tradable assets – the income stream or service can be sold, and the value of that stream rises or falls with interest rates and demand pressure on the housing market. The political effects emanating from housing thus depend on specific conjunctural combinations of prices, interest rates, and homeownership patterns.

In an economy with unevenly distributed ownership of assets, sharply rising housing prices rise will exacerbate existing inequalities of wealth. Access to new kinds of housing loans can provide the means to defer payment on such loans or help owners to hide assets from tax authorities while they transfer property ownership to the next generation. These effects will vary according to differing institutions, interests, and norms within a society – producing distinctly political varieties of residential capitalism. In societies with a strongly developed norm of "asset-based welfare" the distribution of wealth over generations is likely to become a hot political topic, particularly for housing affordability (see Schwartz, Watson, Broome, and Mortensen and Seabrooke this volume). In societies where the state has provided generous supplements to support access to public or private housing, property booms may encourage citizens to reconsider how well their welfare monies are being distributed (see Tranøy, and Mortensen and Seabrooke, this volume).

The degree of decommodification and stratification we find in housing markets diverges from the patterns which the traditional welfare state[1] literature would predict. In contrast to the apparently stable welfare state configurations Esping-Andersen (1990) typologizes as liberal, conservative, and social democratic welfare regimes, deregulation of housing finance systems has enabled considerable divergence with respect to preferences, incentives, and consumer behavior. In many countries perceptions of self-interest in relation to housing markets have been dramatically realigned away from communal wealth and towards increasing individual wealth, even within countries in which property was commonly considered a social or communal right. This makes understanding changing everyday behavior particularly important (Aalbers, 2008; Langley, 2008; Seabrooke, 2006, 2007).

We offer some speculation about the current conjuncture: how will pocketbooks drive politics when housing prices fall globally and homebuyers face further stretching of already strained budgets to cover living expenses and mortgage payments? Put simply, we argue two things. First, because the current conjuncture combines high housing price levels and thus high levels of mortgage debt with relatively low interest rates, the constituencies for a low-tax, low-inflation policy package are much larger than they would otherwise be. Much as Margaret Thatcher hoped, but for different reasons, today's housing market has conscripted more manpower for the trenches defending parts of the neoliberal policy line of the past two decades. Second, because more liberal housing markets seemed to deliver better macroeconomic outcomes in terms of Gross Domestic Product (GDP) and employment growth, politicians and policymakers in financially repressed housing markets faced pressure to introduce the elements that make housing finance systems "liberal," particularly the securitization of mortgages (the bundling of hundreds of individual mortgages into one bond for sale into capital markets). But the current crisis will inevitably prompt a backlash against U.S.-style financial engineering everywhere. How will this affect the degree of complementarity or coherence characterizing financial institutions in coordinated and liberal market economies? Will they each become more hybridized? The contributions by Tranøy and Mortensen and Seabrooke demonstrate that even before the 2007–08 crises, the politics of housing had become extremely sensitive politically. Even high-income, high-welfare societies, like Norway or Denmark, that traditionally had low levels of residential owner-occupation saw fights between political parties and among social groups over the types of housing loans and tax burdens. Many overtly socialist political parties now blush at any suggestion of increasing property taxes, fearing that such a policy would make them unelectable. And within more liberal systems some political parties have made a great deal of headway by trumpeting the crisis in housing affordability for ordinary workers.

In the following sections we first locate housing finance within extant CPE and IPE literatures. We then show the lack of correspondence between the types of OECD housing systems and the usual welfare systems and VOC typologies. We then discuss the importance of framing and discourse in understanding why homeowners within the countries discussed do not simply respond to market incentives but change their attitudes and conventions towards housing in a manner that realigns what they consider their material self-interest to be and their own role and responsibilities within economy and society. We conclude by briefly highlighting how the chapters in this volume speak to our key themes and conclude with a call for further research on varieties of residential capitalism within the international political economy.

1.1 Houses, housing finance systems, and political economy

Do housing and housing finance matter politically? The supply side orientation of traditional CPE and IPE gives them few answers to this question, although as Pollard (this volume) shows, a supply side understanding of housing does matter. In IPE literature, research on finance largely examines aggregated flows of capital, foreign direct investment, and the effects of liberalization of capital markets on national policy autonomy (Singer, 2007). Pride of place goes to analyses of deregulation, pure financial flows, and speculation-driven financial crises. CPE literature largely attends to manufacturing, which now accounts only for between one-sixth and one-fifth of most advanced economies. Analytic pride of place goes to employment and training systems, collective bargaining regimes, production systems, and financial systems understood in relation to the supply of capital to manufacturing. Financial analyses thus tend to look at aggregated stock and bond markets as providers of investment capital for, and oversight of, manufacturing firms, with occasional detours into the role of block-holders (institutions, like banks or pension funds that own a controlling portion of a firm's shares) or other institutional investors (e.g. Gourevitch and Shinn, 2005). CPE's attentiveness to finance generally dissipates once it has considered the relationship between industrial policy and finance (e.g. Hall and Soskice 2001; Zysman, 1983). The usual point of intersection between the IPE and CPE research domains is typically a debate about the allegedly homogenizing effects of globalization, or consideration of issues of comparative competitiveness (which largely ask, *"who's doing it better?"*), rather than trying to assess the articulation of financial flows at different levels in the global economy (Germain, 1997; cf. Seabrooke, 2001).

Even before financial crises cascaded out of dodgy mortgage-backed securities, IPE and CPE's analytic neglect of residential property markets was odd. In many advanced industrial economies the family home is *the* key asset in a given household's portfolio. In 2004, the median net worth of the bottom 90% of U.S. households was approximately $40,000. Yet for the homeowners who bought housing between 1999 and 2005, median net worth jumped from $11,000 to $88,000 in real terms, driven largely by rising home equity (Harvard University Joint Center for Housing Studies, 2008, 16). Key international institutions agree on the macroeconomic centrality of residential property. The International Monetary Fund (IMF) and the World Bank have been interested in residential property markets as means to revenue stability and economic development in emerging markets. The Organisation for Economic Cooperation and Development (2005b) has specifically criticized member states' governments for permitting property booms potentially to rob from further wealth creation, and has strongly advocated the removal of implicit government subsidies that sustain public residential property markets.[2] Given the importance of economic growth and well-being in people's and parties' electoral calculations, it is odd that IPE and CPE largely ignore houses while favoring narrower policy areas. Finally, while labor disputes in the late 1960s and early 1970s clearly helped to terminate the Bretton Woods or Fordist period of growth, housing helped to start and stop the current period of growth (Schwartz, 2009).

Our point here is not that IPE and CPE's extant foci are wrong, but rather that each ignores a major source of political behavior and macroeconomic outcomes and this leads to omitted variable bias. Nor is our point that the usual analytical tools of CPE and IPE cannot be applied to understanding changes in residential property markets. On the contrary, this volume uses some of the traditional IPE and CPE tools to understand the politics and economics of residential property markets in a comparative, international, and transnational context, albeit in ways that force a reassessment of those tools. This chapter, and Schwartz's Chapter 2, also show how that understanding sheds light on some persistent problems explaining the core macroeconomic outcomes of employment and growth.

We pose three broad questions to open up a discussion of housing related to *ownership, credit access,* and *welfare redistribution.* First, what is housing in any given society, how do people think about it, and who owns it? Housing may be understood as a consumption good, as a social right, or as an investment vehicle. Ownership may be understood as private, public, communal, cooperative, or familial. Tracing how commodified housing systems are provides some insight into these dynamics (commodified is the degree to which people's access to housing depends on their market incomes and market-based transactions rather than a socially guaranteed access). Second, how are houses financed? What access is there to mortgage credit within a system? This includes access to first-time homeowner grants and subsidies, the determination of fixed or variable interest rates, the deposit requirements for a loan, whether the contractual terms favor the creditor or debtor, the role of nonbank financial intermediaries, and the extent of mortgage securitization. Third, how is housing treated within the national welfare regime for tax purposes? What taxes are paid, or tax breaks given, on housing-related matters? Whether systems favor mortgage interest deductibility, property taxes, taxes on capital gains from housing sales, state subsidies for rental payments, or tax breaks for investors in social housing will all affect the national economy. All three of these issues also generate everyday politics about what is appropriate and legitimate as regards who owns, who has credit access, and who is paying which taxes in a given country.

The answers, put bluntly, are that housing finance systems can connect people to global capital flows and interest rates in a more direct way than tax systems, public debt, or employment. But the degree of decommodification and stratification this connection produces varies by the level of owner-occupancy and the structure of housing finance markets. In turn, because housing is often people's key asset, housing creates immediate and different partisan and policy effects over tax resistance, preferences for cash in hand over social services, orientations towards inflation, and preferences for the party that best protects property or property values regardless of which party that happens to be. Housing creates durable, structural effects on politics, much like pension systems. Because the big political questions often revolve around structural or institutional issues, housing finance systems have substantial and long-term political consequences.

1.2   Housing and the welfare trade-off

We can break housing systems up along two major dimensions, both of which are objective, but which in turn give rise to different subjective understandings about housing. The first objective dimension is the degree to which people are owner-occupiers rather than renters, measured by owner-occupation rates. This tells us something – but not everything – about how decommodified housing might be. The second is the degree to which housing finance is "liberal" or "controlled," measured both by the level of mortgage debt in relation to GDP and the degree of mortgage securitization. As we will see, this reveals how stratified homeownership is and also suggests the potential macroeconomic consequences of different housing market finance systems. These two objective dimensions are convenient because they are suggested by the welfare state literature's traditional typology as well as that of the VOC literature. We amend these typologies better to reflect the role of state developmentalism which refers to state efforts to promote industrial development using targeted investment subsidies (in which "late development" can place barriers on welfare claims, see Uzuhashi, 2003), as well as the role of the family in mediating welfare concerns and protecting intergenerational equity (see, for example, Hemerijck, 2002).

Subjectively, commodified markets with large numbers of indebted owner-occupiers are clearly liberal in nature, and people are likely to see housing as a form of investment to a greater degree than in systems dominated by socially provided rentals, where housing is more likely to be perceived as a social right, or in self-help systems where families build their own housing. Between the poles of housing as an investment vehicle and housing as an object of family consumption, mixed systems obviously have their own dynamics where housing is perceived as a social right. High levels of ownership but low commodification indicate a familialist mentality. By contrast, low levels of ownership are not necessarily associated with less market pressure on individuals, because renters do not necessarily have flexibility in their housing choices. The degree of commodification rises with rising mortgage debt, since debt service requires cash income.

Breaking housing systems up by owner-occupation and financial structure creates a four-cell table. Figure 1.1 displays the degree to which the 19 OECD member countries for which we have data deviate from the average OECD level of owner-occupied dwellings as a share of all dwellings (a measure of relative exposure to markets and thus the potential for commodification) and from the average level of mortgage debt in relation to GDP (a measure of the financial structure and the potential for stratification). To provide some analytical coherence, we label our four different housing finance systems in ways that correspond to

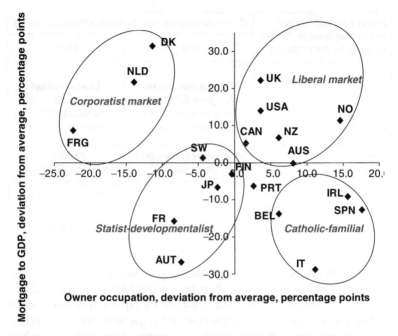

Figure 1.1 Relative deviation from average OECD levels of mortgage debt to GDP and owner-occupation prevailing 1992 to 2002 (percentage points)

the common distinctions made in the welfare states and VOC literature even though there is no one-for-one correspondence.

What makes these groupings coherent? By capturing the interaction of owner-occupancy and financing regimes, Figure 1.1 suggests the four ideal-types displayed in Figure 1.2. The groupings are not distinct enough to make an extremely robust causal argument. However a plausible explanatory logic links two or possibly three causal forces: the interaction of pensions and owner-occupation, competition for investment capital, and the level of urbanization or new settlement in the postwar period. Again, we can look to the welfare states and VOC literature to explain some of these dynamics, although it is already clear that we will have to modify each.

First, does owner-occupation or high mortgage debt expose people to market pressures or inhibit welfare state development? Gøsta Esping-Andersen used the degree of decommodification in social policy to typologize welfare states as social democratic, conservative, and liberal ideal-types (Esping-Andersen, 1990). Francis Castles argued for a "wage

(Figures in each box are unweighted average % level for group for the indicator)		*Owner-occupation rate* (average of 1992 and 2002)	
		Low	High
Mortgages as a % of GDP (average of 1992 and 2002)	High	**Corporatist market** Mortgage::GDP: 58.3 Owner-occupation: 47.0 Social rental: 20.7	**Liberal market** Mortgage::GDP: 48.5 Owner-occupation: 70.1 Social rental: 9.4
	Low	**Statist-developmentalist** Mortgage::GDP: 28.2 Owner-occupation: 58.3 Social rental: 16.8	**Familial** Mortgage::GDP: 21.6 Owner-occupation: 75.5 Social rental: 5.5

Figure 1.2   An analytic understanding of Figure 1.1 for 19 OECD countries

earner" variant, encompassing Australia and New Zealand and possibly Ireland and Finland, and then later a southern European variant (Castles and Mitchell, 1992). But in Figure 1.1 Esping-Andersen's social democratic and corporatist/conservative groups both break up. While the northeastern "high-high" (high commodification, high ownership) "liberal market" group includes most of Esping-Andersen's liberal cases, and also Castles' wage-earner states, it also includes Norway, a social democratic welfare state (Tranøy, this volume, suggests reasons why this occurs). These countries combine early homeownership, a liquid market for houses, and mortgage securitization.

By contrast, social democratic Denmark ends up among what we call "corporatist-market" neighbors in the high-low northwest quadrant. These countries combine relatively large public/social rental sectors with substantial mortgage securitization or large nonbank holdings of mortgages. Sweden and Finland occupy an ambiguous position close to the origin, but their nearest neighbors are countries in the southwest quadrant that share state targeting of industry or a high level of public industry, which is why we call them "statist-developmentalist." Sweden aside, they lack any substantial mortgage securitization, increasing the state's leverage over financial markets and thus its ability to target sectors. These countries also tend to have low rates of homeownership. The southeast quadrant is a set of familialist countries that lack both social housing and securitization but do have high levels of homeownership. This quadrant should be closest to Esping-Andersen's conservative type, but does not encompass all his cases.

Esping-Andersen's categories ultimately rest on an explicit causal model and not just a measure of decommodification. For Esping-Andersen, different configurations of class power produced different sets of policies characterized by different degrees of decommodification, stratification, and universality. All other things being equal, more power for labor should produce a correspondingly higher level of decommodification and universality. This is roughly – but only roughly – borne out by Figure 1.1, because high levels of political power for labor are associated with a general tendency to have below the average level of owner-occupancy. Indeed, Esping-Andersen's first book (1985) explicitly linked variation in Scandinavian housing policies to social democratic parties' desire to prevent a split from emerging between homeowning white collar workers and blue collar renters. Yet by the 1990s homeownership levels in three cases no longer reflected his assessment of labor's relative strength, with Sweden intermediate to high rental Denmark and homeowning Norway.

Our categorizations could diverge from Esping-Andersen's simply because his ideal-types are *regimes* that will always encompass some deviant programs. And, as Esping-Andersen noted many times in response to his critics, not all cases conform tightly to his ideal-types. This could indicate that the discrepancy between where countries fall in Esping-Andersen's categories and ours might be meaningless. Nonetheless, we think our categories have some degree of internal coherence that suggests both causal and consequential logics. The causal logic however is somewhat at odds with Esping-Andersen's argument. Putting aside whether labor naturally seeks decommodification, the issue here is whether a higher level of power for labor produces greater decommodification in housing markets, as measured by the levels of owner-occupation and mortgage debt. If our housing groups share similar causal forces this would force us to reconsider Esping-Andersen's regimes. The classic debate between Jim Kemeny (1980) and Frank Castles (1998) over the salience of owner-occupied housing for the development of the welfare state suggests this kind of reconsideration (see also Malpass, 2008).

Kemeny (1980) argued that a trade-off existed between owner-occupation of residential property and the quantity and quality of welfare state benefits. This trade-off did not arise from differences in the total life cycle cost of housing across societies but rather its temporal distribution. The total life cycle cost of owner-occupied or rented housing was the same at any given level of income for a society or a specific individual. What varied was the distribution of costs over a given individual's life cycle. Renters spread the housing costs over their entire lifetime, making essentially level payments each year. The arrival of children in the middle of renters' life cycles would push up housing costs at roughly the same time that their incomes rose; symmetrically, as income fell at the end of the life cycle, children would depart and housing costs would fall.

By contrast, would-be purchasers of owner-occupied housing face a front-loaded schedule of payments. Buying a house compresses the bulk of the life cycle cost of housing into a household's early years. First, households have to save for a down payment. In the early and middle part of the twentieth century, when welfare regimes were forming, these down payments were considerably larger than they are today as a percentage of the purchase price, but even today 20% is a fairly common requirement in most countries. Second, the normal mortgage term is typically less than 30 years and in many countries mortgages have 15-year terms. Consequently, a household might spend its lower-income twenties accumulating a down payment and then its thirties and forties paying off a mortgage. Italy, where a 50% down payment and a ten year amortization schedule were common until recently, provides an extreme example of this kind of compression.

Kemeny argued, all other things being equal, that this front-loading of housing costs made homeowners a natural constituency favoring a smaller welfare state. Young, lower-income households faced a sharp trade-off between cash income for home purchase and taxes for social welfare services. They would also not favor extensive government borrowing, since this would inevitably raise interest rates and thus the monthly cost of a mortgage (Watson, this volume). By contrast, renters would face a less sharp trade-off between taxes and cash income because renting did not crowd housing expenditures into one of the lowest income periods of life. Kemeny's key insight thus was that the level of homeownership was not a natural outcome of rising or high per capita income levels, but instead reflected political choices by voters and parties. High-income economies like Denmark and Germany could exhibit low levels of homeownership if politics and policy favored social spending, including social housing, over private homeownership (Kemeny, 2005, 60).

Frank Castles' (1998) critique of Kemeny and Esping-Andersen provided a more compelling and focused causal argument with a more precise micro-foundation for homeowners' relative hostility to welfare spending. More recent research by Dalton Conley and Brian Gifford (2006) confirms Castles' intuitions. Castles noted that countries with low levels of old-age pension provision also typically had high rates of private homeownership. Housing generally constitutes not only the greatest single item in most retirees' budgets, but also, with food, one of the least substitutable or dispensable. Castles thus argued that the imputed income from homeownership substituted for public pension income, a point consistent with his broader argument about "social policy by other means" in the wage-earner welfare state. For Castles, housing choices specifically affected pensions, but not necessarily other aspects of the welfare state. Countries or individuals could trade off homeownership against robust public pensions. Causally, settler societies with high levels of homeownership prior to the emergence of public pension systems would be less likely to develop robust public pensions, because freehold ownership of housing sharply reduced the income requirements of the homeowning elderly. Echoing Kemeny, Castles also noted that better off parts of the elderly population were more likely to own houses and thus were less favorably disposed towards higher taxes to provide cash income to elderly renters. In addition, while both renters and owners bear the cost of property taxes, these taxes are most visible to owners, and it is visible taxes that always draw the most resistance (Martin, 2008). As such, homeownership split the natural elderly constituency for expanded pensions.

While Castles and Kemeny disagree somewhat on details, they agree on the central premise about private homeownership: down payments and mortgages have important political consequences because they crowd out taxes early in a voter's life cycle. The level of homeownership shapes citizen attitudes on the extent of commodification or decommodification of housing markets and time-horizons about welfare maximization. But the critical dimension with respect to decommodification is not simply the degree to which housing is socially or privately rented, and the degree of rent control. Societies with high levels of homeownership and (as we will see) liberal mortgage markets are just as likely to have large socially rented sectors as those with controlled mortgage finance. Thus in Denmark, Britain and the Netherlands, socially rented housing accounts for more than 20% of the entire housing stock and in excess of half of the rental stock. Indeed, even after Margaret Thatcher, British social housing accounted for roughly 70% of the rental stock (making Britain an exception in this regard to the broader liberal trend). By contrast, in high owner-occupier Italy, Spain, and Ireland, the social rental sector accounts for less than 10% of all dwellings and less than half of an already relatively smaller rental stock (European Central Bank, 2003). Simply looking at the level of owner-occupancy does not tell us whether homeowners are exposed to the market. Do we really think that Italians or Spaniards, who on average are more likely to own their own home free of a mortgage than Americans or the Dutch, are more exposed to the market? These considerations suggest looking more closely at the level of and access to mortgage debt.

1.3   Varieties of residential capitalism and institutional complementarities

Above we discussed how housing forces us to adjust the common ideal-types in the welfare state studies, while suggesting the political importance of housing. Can we integrate housing finance systems with the VOC literature and the broader work on comparative capitalisms? Our first cut into this literature is to assess to what degree housing finance systems are liberal or repressed/controlled, because this affects how owner-occupied housing articulates with global markets, which, in turn, affects the stratification of owners by wealth. The degree of financial repression ultimately boils down to the degree to which mortgages are securitized and the depth and internationalization of mortgage pools.

The VOC literature splits the world into liberal and coordinated market economies (LMEs and CMEs), depending in part on the degree of financial repression and the presence of coordinating block-holders or actors in capital markets. VOC argues that the institutional ensembles constituting LMEs and CMEs produce specialization in different kinds of export goods, with repression and block-holding characterizing CMEs. Housing finance markets also clearly vary in the degree to which financial repression is present, but with types and outcomes that differ from VOC's. The critical differentiating *outcome* with respect to these segmented markets is the level of mortgage debt in proportion to GDP. The scale of mortgage debt matters for macroeconomic outcomes, not export specialization. Consistent with VOC literature, this outcome is a function of the degree to which states practiced financial repression, not in general, but in their specific housing market.

Mortgages matter macroeconomically because they provide a significant drain on savings, and may also stimulate housing-related consumer demand (Schwartz, 2009). All OECD member states thus have clear regulations for housing finance systems, including limits on lending and deposit interest rates, quantitative limits on mortgage credit, and strict limits on loan-to-value (LTV) ratios for mortgages (Girouard and Blöndal, 2001).[3] Table 1.1 displays the predominant features of the major OECD cases.

In addition, many OECD member countries have created specialized and varied public, private, and quasi-public financial institutions to manage housing finance within a national economic policy framework (Seabrooke, 2008). These different financial institutions and regulations distribute risk differentially among borrowers and lenders. While legal systems matter here with respect to foreclosure and collateral, the single most important characteristic is the possibility for banks to shift risk onto third parties by selling mortgages into the general market for securities. We will call mortgage systems *"liberal"* if this kind of securitization is legal and widespread and *"controlled"* if securitization is not possible or minimal. Countries with financial systems characterized by control and state direction of finance obliged the savings system to park small savers' capital in the central bank or other state institutions so that it could then be loaned onward to industry. By contrast, in non-repressive financial systems mortgage banks freely recycled savings back into mortgages, and, eventually used securitization to move mortgages off their books and into the hands of long-term private investors like insurance and pension companies. Table 1.2 displays household debt and interest burdens for 15 OECD countries.

The differences in securitization show that country/housing types deviate from their typical VOC category as much as they do from Esping-Andersen's welfare state categories. Securitization allows banks to refresh their capital and shift interest rate risk off their books and onto the buyers of mortgage-backed securities (MBS). This allows banks to originate yet more loans and earn the bulk of their income from transaction fees. It also shields banks from the maturity mismatch between short-term time deposits and long-term mortgages. This contrasts with the model in which banks hold mortgages to maturity and make money off the interest rate spread between deposits and loans. Securitization can also remove credit risk, depending on the kinds of guarantees banks must make when selling loans on. Buyers of MBS are typically pension and insurance funds matching predictable long-term assets against their equally predictable long-term liabilities. Thus Castles' observation about houses and pensions returns full force: there is not only a causal harmony between private homeownership and private pension funds but also a direct institutional complementarity: because his archetypical owner-occupier societies often have securitization, they also have larger *private* pension systems as well, and use MBS rather than taxation as the conduit for intergenerational transfer of income.

After the Second World War, only the U.S. and Denmark had non-repressive housing finance systems, because they were the only systems

Table 1.1 Housing market characteristics, 19 OECD countries

	Owner-occupation, % households*	Social rental, % of households*	Private rental, % of households*	Change in Owner-occupation as % of households, 1980-latest*	Residential mortgages as % of GDP (1992)**	Residential mortgages as % of GDP (2004)*	Typical loan-to-value ratio (%) (2002)***	Maximum loan-to-value ratio (%) (2002)***	Typical loan term (2002)***	Mortgage securitization possible?	Home equity release possible?	Absolute change in number of women working, 1980-2004, as % of 1980
Austria	56	21	20	+6	-5.0	20.3	60	80	20-30	No	No	42.8
Belgium	74	7	16	+9	19.9	31.2	83	100	20	No ****	No	36.2
Denmark	51	19	26	-2	70.1	88.4	80	80	30	As covered bonds	Yes	18.9
Finland	60	14	16	0	37.1	37.8	75	80	15-18	No (?)	Yes	4.4
France	54	17	21	+9	21.2	26.2	67	100	15	Yes but limited	Not used	33.5
Germany (West)	43	7	50				67	80	25-30	As covered bonds	Yes, but not used	
Germany (all)	40^			+5	41.0	52.2				As covered bonds	No	57.2
Ireland	78	9	16	+1	20.3	52.7	66	90	20	Yes but limited	Yes but limited use	131.4

	(1)	(2)	(3)	(4)	(5)	(6)	(7)	(8)	(9)	(10)	(11)	(12)
Italy	69	5	11	+16	3.2	15.3	55	80	15	Only recently	Not used	34.2
Netherlands	53	36	11	+13	43.2	111.1	90	115	30	Yes	Yes	128.8
Norway	78				46.1	56.0	83	80	15–20	No	No	38.6
Portugal	64	3	25	+23	c. 20.0	52.5	83	90	15	No	No	55.5
Spain	85	1	10	+9	12.9	45.9	70	100	15	New but rising	Yes but limited use	110.0
Sweden	41	27	13	+4	50.8	51.6	77	80	<30	Yes but limited	Yes but limited use	6.3
United Kingdom	69	22	9	+11	52.8	75.3	69	110	25	Yes	Yes	28.6
Australia	72				78.0	301.0	65		25	Yes	Yes	86.7
New Zealand	70				146.0	267.0				No	Yes but limited	116.5
Canada	64				42.7^	43.1^	75		25	Yes	Yes but limited use	71.8
United States	68				45.0	65.0	78		30	Yes	Yes	53.7
Japan	60				25.3	36.8	80		25–30	No	No	22.1

Sources: * Allen 2006, European Central Bank, 2004, plus Catte, Girouarde, Price, and Andre, 2004: 138 for non-EU countries; ** Hypostat 2006; *** based on MacLennan, Muellbauer, and Stephens, 1998: 70 and OECD, 2004b; ^ Catte et al., p. 138. Empty cells reflect unavailable data. **** We have coded 'No' where securitization is permitted but an insignificant share of the market.

Table 1.2   Households' mortgage debt and interest burden, by housing market type

	% of household disposable income						Variable interest rates as a % of all loans
	Mortgage debt			Interest payments			
	1992	*2000*	*2003*	*1992*	*2000*	*2003*	*2002*
Australia	52.8	83.2	119.5	4.8	6.4	7.9	73
Canada	61.9	68.0	77.1	5.9	5.7	4.9	25
New Zealand	67.0	104.8	129.0	6.9	9.3	9.4	n/d
UK	79.4	83.1	104.6	4.4	3.7	3.0	72
US	58.7	65.0	77.8	4.9	5.2	4.5	33
Average*^	*61.1*		*82.9*	*4.9*		*4.5*	
Denmark	118.6	171.2	188.4	10.6	9.9	8.3	15
Germany	59.3	84.4	83.0	3.9	4.0	3.0	72
Netherlands	77.6	156.9	207.7	5.0	8.4	8.2	15
Average*	*65.3*		*107.4*	*4.4*		*4.1*	
Finland	56.7	65.3	71.0	7.1^^	2.9	1.9	97
France	28.5	35.0	39.5	1.7	1.4	1.1	20
Japan	41.6	54.8	58.4	2.5	1.3	1.4	n/d
Sweden	98.0	94.4	97.5	5.0	4.2	3.3	38
Average*	*40.7*		*55.2*	*2.5*		*1.4*	
Ireland	31.6	60.2	92.3	2.3	3.0	2.5	70
Italy	8.4	15.1	19.8	0.7	0.8	0.7	56
Spain	22.8	47.8	67.4	1.6	2.2	1.7	75
Average*	*14.0*		*38.1*	*1.1*		*1.1*	

Notes: * weighted average for this group using share of OECD GDP in 2003; ^ Data for Norway unavailable; ^^ reflects GDP crash after collapse of Soviet Union

Source: Compiled from OECD, 2005b, 131.

that permitted the creation of securities from housing loans and thus relatively long-term mortgage instruments. They also grew out of unique institutional arrangements that followed state-led and community-led responses to widespread economic crises (Seabrooke, 2008). They also did not systematically limit the volume of credit going into housing. But by the 1990s, most of the countries in the upper half of Figure 1.1 had created either long-term mortgages, a covered bond market based on housing loans, or MBS. By contrast, countries with short-duration mortgages or no MBS mostly populate the lower half of Figure 1.1, although in some MBS issues skyrocketed after EMU (Aalbers, 2006, 17; Stephens, 2000).[4]

However, countries with financially repressed housing finance markets do not display a one-to-one correspondence to VOC's CMEs, where block-holders and financial repression characterize industrial credit. Germany, the Netherlands, and Denmark – all CMEs for VOC – all permit mortgage securitization. Indeed, these three countries accounted for 70% of covered bonds in the European market in the late 1990s, with the Danes relatively speaking the most securitized, although their "mortgage bond system ... can be thought of as a variant of a securitization, somewhere in between an MBS and a German pantbrief system" (Davidson et al., 2003, 487). In the past 15 years the Danes have been able to double foreign investment into their mortgage bond system while not altering the "balance principle," which is that all residential property loans must be supported by bonds that must, in turn, be supported by existing mortgages (this system also keeps risk with the borrower and provides only a "pass through" securitization service, see Seabrooke, 2008). In general, the European pool of securitized mortgages was only half the size of the U.S. pool; indeed, in 2005 Australian MBS issues exceeded German issues (Aalbers, 2006, 17; Hardt, 1998, 7). In other words, not all CMEs have CMF (controlled mortgage finance). However these three countries also had substantial social rental sectors, which insulated non-homeowners somewhat from housing market pressures.

By contrast, all of VOC's LMEs have LMF (liberal mortgage finance). In LMEs, securitization enables banks to shift interest rate risk onto the ultimate purchaser of the MBS. This permits banks to make large, long-term, fixed-interest loans. In turn this permits borrowers to take on quite large amounts of debt because the fixed interest rate cushions borrowers against balance-sheet risk (the risk that rising interest rates will trigger higher mortgage payments and throw them into default). This leads to high levels of mortgage debt in proportion to GDP. While these levels of debt are actually lower than those in our corporatist market economies, this reflects the combination of higher average inflation levels in liberal economies and stricter land-use policies in crowded northwestern Europe.

When banks cannot shift interest risk onto some other entity, and instead must hold mortgages to term, they ration lending and borrowers avoid debt in order to control their balance-sheet risks. Banks that cannot securitize mortgages typically shift the bulk of risk to the borrower through higher interest rates, variable interest rates, prepayment penalties, and big down payments. Thus Italy and Austria, which lack securitization, have the highest effective mortgage interest rates in Western

Europe, the lowest levels of mortgage debt to GDP, and loan-to-income (LTI) ratios that are half the average European level. Before European Monetary Union (EMU), Italian borrowers were also confronted by punitive interest rates as a result of high inflation. And foreclosure in Italy also typically takes an excruciating (for creditors) six years, followed by Portugal, France, and Belgium at around a still lengthy two years (Catte et al., 2004, 144; Hardt, 1998; Neuteboom, 2004). Where banks ration lending most housing is financed from personal savings, which compresses consumption.

Securitization and long-term mortgage loans interact with the commodification of housing through owner-occupation. The more mortgage resources are available, the bigger the market for housing will be. And the greater the possibility of borrowing, the more reliant the average buyer will be on early-life-cycle income to service that mortgage. By contrast, where banks must carry the credit and interest rate risk, mortgages tend to be small and buyers rely on their own resources to finance houses. Thus one of the consequences of Italy's specific mortgage system is that much housing is self-provided, with families and friends pitching in weekend labor and pooled savings to expand dwellings as families grow. Families live together as intergenerational units for longer periods of time. In addition, housing also serves as a sink for income and capital generated in the black market (Castles and Ferrera, 1996, 178, 180–1). The open market for dwellings is thus thin.

VOC's CMEs require not just financial repression but also large block-holders to act as monitors for firms. Is this also true of mortgage markets? Europe's socially rented housing is mostly controlled by powerful block-holders, who act like the controlling shareholders in VOC's CMEs (Gourevitch and Shinn, 2005). But it is easy to overstate their influence on the market. Even in the LMEs, powerful institutions or organizations exert tremendous influence precisely because of the risks involved in pricing and floating mortgage bonds and the economies of scale involved in the servicing of mortgages. The sheer size of the U.S. market and an alleged orientation towards free markets might suggest an unstructured and competitive market. But in fact a few giant players structure the MBS market. Two government sponsored (but private) agencies, "Fannie Mae" and "Freddie Mac," set the rules for most mortgage origination and also did most of the securitization of mortgages until 2005 (Schwartz this volume; Seabrooke, 2006, 125–9; Aalbers, 2008, 157–8). The private market is also concentrated. One U.S. mortgage giant, Countrywide, accounted for 8% of all *global* private asset-backed securities (ABS) originations in 2005, while the top ten private issuers accounted for 38.1% of all ABS issues in this nearly $2 trillion market.[5] Similarly, pension funds loom large in the Danish private rental market, which accounts for about 20% of all dwellings, just as real estate investment trusts (REITs – a kind of real estate mutual fund) loom large in U.S. commercial and residential rental markets.

What matters, then, is not the presence of block-holders, but rather their orientation towards the market. This is why socially constructed ideas about the purpose of housing and the logic of appropriateness governing housing block-holders matter. So while we suggest that the institutional complementarities literature provides important analytical tools for mapping varieties of residential capitalism (once amended), not all can be explained by the economic fundamental or by exploring the logic of institutional frameworks. Indeed, within this volume we also point to the importance of understanding how political and economic elites can use "ideas as weapons" to frame change in residential property markets (Blyth, 2002; Campbell, 2004), as well as how more broadly changing attitudes and conventions about these markets can provide clear impulses to those in power (Seabrooke, 2007).

1.4 From complementarities to consciousness

In the countries examined in this book, housing is seen either as a social right or as a means to wealth. No individual country presents a pure form, but social ideas about what is legitimate, fair, and appropriate for behavior in relation to residential capitalism vary between these poles. These attitudes provide a means to trace social change as they inform and respond to the political framing of residential capitalisms. Within LMF systems the "financialization" of everyday life with regard to residential property markets has been extensive, providing new constraints and opportunities for the fulfillment of social wants and desires (Aalbers, 2008; Langley, 2008). In systems where there is a "sea change" in thinking about the role of housing, we should expect to see some political conflict, not only in formal politics but also in society. Mortensen and Seabrooke's description (this volume) of the rapid transformation of Danish housing cooperatives (*andelsbolig*) from a system based on socialist principles to a system based on capitalist principles within a five-year period provides a case in point. In general, citizens' understanding of their economic and, given the "welfare trade-off," social choices shapes the framing of political debates about the transformation of residential capitalism within national political economies, and within regional institutions (Rosamond, 2005).

These choices create strong possibilities for stratification. Esping-Andersen's social democratic welfare type is marked by the absence of programs that stratify citizens by income (like liberal welfare states) or status (like conservative welfare states). But housing in liberal mortgage markets is inherently stratifying because housing is most households' largest asset. By permitting high levels of mortgage debt, liberal housing finance systems also permit households to leverage their housing investment by committing only a small amount of purchase money (down payment) while borrowing the bulk of the house price. When housing prices are rising strongly, these households can accumulate assets much, much faster than unleveraged households. Wealth inequalities thus cumulate more rapidly as prices rise. However, this price rise also exposes borrowers to global interest rate shocks and the abrupt de-leveraging and loss of unrealized wealth that we now see occurring in housing markets everywhere.

This wealth accumulation shows why the Castles and Kemeny arguments do not provide a clear road map for exploring today's housing politics. Kemeny and Castles provided plausible interpretations of the effects of different levels of owner-occupation on the *formation* of welfare states. But both missed the interaction of growing asset accumulation not just by the middle classes but also by slices of the working class. Nearly 30 years ago Peter Drucker noted the growing political importance of funded pensions, which were accumulating large shares of the equity market on behalf of workers. Because housing finance systems characterized by high levels of homeownership and particularly by securitization make houses into assets, they create the same dynamic for a broader range of households. Castles and Kemeny also ignore the macroeconomic consequences of housing. Asset prices are not only vulnerable to changing interest rates but they also help to create macroeconomic swings, which in turn affect tax revenue and spending through the level of employment and output. All this means they have less to say about the politics of housing now than they did about the politics of housing two generations past. We sketch out those politics in Figure 1.3.

Those politics are strongly affected by the economic conjuncture of the past 20 years, but they affect countries in the different quadrants differently. The past 20 years have seen the following trends: secularly declining nominal interest rates; rising homeownership; rising housing prices (with considerable country-by-country variation); integration of global financial markets; and the rise of neoliberal discourses emphasizing the self-management of assets and justifying market-driven income

		Owner-occupation rate (reflects size of social rental sector and thus commodification; partial disconnect from global capital markets as a consequence)	
		Low	High
Mortgages as a % of GDP (reflects securitization as a cause and stratification as a consequence; but also a stronger connection to global financial markets)	High	**Corporatist market** Housing (but not houses) as social right, but strong stratification of the market: Owner-occupiers vs. renters; plus defamilialization; plus public organizations control rented housing. Low property tax revenues. Problems of intergenerational equity as housing market outsiders are priced out of accommodation.	**Liberal market** Highly commodified: Houses as assets; strong stratification of the market: Owner-occupiers vs. renters. Market based self-help. High property tax revenues. Problems of intergenerational equity as housing market outsiders are priced out of accommodation. Many of these economies were also 'Frontier' societies.
	Low	**Statist-developmentalist** Housing (not houses) as social right, but financial repression reduces market segmentation/ stratification (?); plus private organizations control rented housing. Low property tax revenues.	**Familial** Noncommodified but not de-commodified: Houses as a familial social good, but not as a social right. Stratification from access to formal sector employment. Nonmarket self-help. Low property tax revenues.

Figure 1.3   A political understanding of Figures 1.1 and 1.2

and wealth disparities. How have these influences filtered through each type of housing system?

Falling nominal interest rates since 1991, abetted by financial integration, have created a strong potential for increased stratification in liberal housing markets. Because houses are effectively assets in liberal financial markets, falling interest rates bestow capital gains on housing market insiders. (Houses behave like bonds – falling interest rates push their price over par.) In liberal mortgage markets, banks have an incentive to extend as much credit as consumers demand, and face little risk for doing so. Instead risk is passed on to investors buying those mortgages as MBS, or retained by homebuyers using flexible rate loans, as in the Britain, or term loans with frequent balloon payments, as in Canada, where payments are due every five years (in balloon payments, the entire mortgage is due at one time). Because most people buy houses based on a monthly payment they can afford, falling interest rates mean that people can "afford" a higher purchase price. This leads to a normal asset style re-pricing of dwellings as people bid up the cost of housing based on their target monthly payment. This re-pricing conveys windfall gains on housing market insiders, while burdening new entrants with increased debt. Because on net nearly all insiders are older established households while new entrants are younger households, re-pricing creates a massive transfer of wealth upwards in both age and income terms. And where incumbents cash out and spend home equity, as in the U.S., intergenerational inequality can become even more extreme as inheritances disappear.

Re-pricing also will increase the share of housing in the average person's portfolio unless other financial assets appreciate at the same rate. This makes housing market incumbents more sensitive to any change in interest rates that might decrease the value of their house. New entrants are also sensitive to rising interest rates. If they have bought using a variable rate mortgage, any increase in rates can be doubly crippling, increasing their monthly debt burden while decreasing the value of a house in which they have little equity. The only hedge new entrants have is to increase their work burden. This explains part of the pressure towards dual income households over the past two decades.

The level of homeownership mediates the effects of falling interest rates. The larger the pool of homeowners, the bigger the effect of falling interest rates. We would expect that intergenerational or insider-outsider stress would be greater in the northeastern "liberal market" quadrant than in the "corporatist-market" quadrant. The positive macroeconomic effects of rising housing prices might ameliorate this stress, if owners can tap into their equity to finance new consumption and thus spur rapid economic growth (Schwartz's first chapter explains this phenomenon for the U.S.). However the public in the corporatist market quadrant is less tolerant of the rising inequality that accompanies this kind of "barrister-barista" (well-paid professionals vs. low-paid service personnel) growth.

Our archetypical case for these phenomena is the Netherlands. Although conventional accounts credit the Wasenaar wage-restraint accord for the Dutch employment miracle, the reality is much less clear.

Wiemer Salverda has argued that much of the increased labor participation came from the substitution of part-time youth employment by older, married female workers. Salverda argues that "[t]he number of two-earner households increased by 1.5 million while at the same time the number of one-earner households was more than halved, falling by one million" (Salverda, 2005, 50). Meanwhile the share of work hours going to women older than 25 increased by nine percentage points at the expense of workers under 25. Both processes occurred simultaneous with changes in Dutch mortgage markets permitting second incomes to qualify for loan-to-income limits, and allowing new mortgage products that used long-term appreciation in equities (shares) to fund the principal balance on mortgages. Dual income couples could bid for more expensive houses; doing so increased the pressure on married women to enter the labor market to make housing more affordable. The U.S. market, where both incomes have always been counted in LTI ratios, saw an even sharper increase in the number of hours worked after 1982. Housing trends thus exacerbated the trends towards increased polarization of income, wealth, and work hours between established well-to-do dual income couples and younger, unmarried entrants into labor and housing markets.

These stratifying effects were muted in countries with repressed housing finance. Banks that are unable to shift risks off their books are unlikely to abet borrowers buying up in the market. This dampens housing prices, slows stratification by wealth, and puts less pressure on married women to enter labor markets. Housing-market-driven stratification is slower as household income is not polarized between dual income owning and no income renting households. Italy and Austria again are archetypical of a familial model combining high levels of self-provided housing with very low levels of mortgage debt. Italian banks cannot externalize the risks from mortgage lending; the Austrian state diverts a considerable volume of saving toward a large, state owned industrial sector. Falling interest rates have little effect on people carrying relatively small mortgages and little consumer credit in general. Given less pressure to generate more income to fund housing, these societies also generally have lower female and especially married female labor force participation.

Tentative conclusions

This volume aims to demonstrate that residential property markets must be included as both a major causal driver of the [macroeconomic?]

outcomes that CPE and IPE analyze and a constitutive factor for political preferences. This is not simply because the houses that *The Economist* celebrated as saving the world in 2002 turned around and destroyed, if not the whole world, certainly its financial system in 2008. It is not simply because the family home is normally *the* store of wealth for citizens in OECD member states and a place where people spend an enormous amount of time. Rather, residential property markets also matter for understanding ongoing processes of commodification and decommodification in dynamic capitalist economies. Residential property's imbrication in financial markets means that it can serve as a prism diffracting the otherwise homogenous concept of neoliberalization into discrete wavelengths.

During the Bretton Woods era, houses were largely delinked from markets even though construction generated a substantial macroeconomic stimulus. Massive programs for building social housing in Europe produced shelter in forms that were largely isolated from open financial markets and totally isolated from global capital markets. Even in the U.S., where the bulk of housing construction and transaction took place in private markets, houses functioned as a form of forced pension saving, and their occupants largely understood them in those terms. Privately held housing (and regulated social housing) constituted one leg of a pension stool whose other two legs were the basic pension and various forms of earnings related pensions. During this period, new labor market entrants also became new housing market entrants within a short time and with little difficulty.

The post-Bretton Woods shift in homeowners' perceptions of houses away from literal and figurative shelter in old age toward houses as a perpetual ATM or cash-point machine is a telling indicator of a massive shift in the political and macroeconomic significance of housing. The following chapters detail those shifts. Aalbers (the Netherlands and Italy), Broome (New Zealand), Mortensen and Seabrooke (Australia and Denmark), Tranøy (Norway), and Watson (Britain) show how mortgage finance markets and political attitudes towards taxation and inflation changed in tandem in as houses left the shade of Bretton Woods for the sunlit fields of the neoliberal market. Pollard shows how the same process played out on housing's supply side in France and Spain, with the state shifting resources from direct provision towards private construction. Schwartz's chapters bookend these case studies by laying out the macroeconomic consequences flowing from different housing finance systems beginning in 1991 and ending with the housing induced financial crisis of 2007.

Many participants in this brave new world of residential property markets willingly accepted a greater risk of long term financial insecurity in exchange for the hope of greater self-governance and long-term wealth. Nonetheless, as the framing devices above suggest and the chapters below show, the initial starting conditions either tempered or exaggerated households' ability to treat their houses like an asset or credit card, just as they tempered or exaggerated the macroeconomic stimulus emanating from housing. Similarly, the structure of residential property finance either enabled or inhibited financial innovation in different countries, allowing banks and nonfinancial firms to shift risks in unexpected ways. The essays below attempt to detail these divergences.

Notes

1. Decommodification refers to the degree to which people have access to housing and other basic necessities by virtue of a social right, rather than as a function of their market income. In addition, because more liberal housing markets seemed to deliver better macroeconomic outcomes in terms of Gross Domestic Product (GDP) and employment growth, politicians and policymakers in financially repressed housing markets faced pressure to introduce the elements that make housing finance systems "liberal," particularly the securitization of mortgages.
2. On the former see the OECD 2004a argument about the Netherlands; on the latter see Erlandsen, Lundsgaard and Huefner, 2006 on Denmark.
3. The pervasive regulatory laxity of the second Bush administration is an obvious exception.
4. EU-wide MBS issues increased tenfold from 1995 to 2005, and tripled in 2001–2005.
5. http://www.abalert.com/Public/MarketPlace/Ranking/index.cfm?files= disp&article_id=1044674725

2
Housing, Global Finance, and American Hegemony: Building Conservative Politics One Brick at a Time

Herman M. Schwartz

Introduction

What role did capital flows into and out of the U.S. play in both the global housing boom and bust and the new politics this bubble produced? This chapter provides an international context both for U.S. domestic housing developments and the more domestically oriented analyses in the other chapters. The international context matters for three reasons. First, the U.S. housing finance system was one of a few crucial conduits for the international capital flows that drove down the nominal cost of borrowing globally over the past 20 years. Second, because housing finance systems differ across countries, declining nominal interest rates differentially stimulated growth across the developed countries. Third, the politics of housing is closely connected to the politics of U.S. "hegemony" by creating a more market-friendly domestic politics globally. These are different but overlapping phenomena.

There are thus three parts to this argument. Section 2.1 argues that the U.S. operated a system of financial arbitrage at the global level 1991–2007. The U.S. systematically borrowed short term at low interest rates from the rest of the world and then invested back into the rest of the world long term for a higher return. Arbitrage worked because the liquidity created by the U.S. Federal Reserve system flowed back into U.S.-dollar-denominated instruments that set benchmark interest rates for mortgages, while capital flows from the U.S. flowed into instruments that did not affect benchmark rates. Housing finance markets linked the system of claims on the future circulating in global financial markets to local political and economic behaviors that affect the security of those claims. At the beginning of this period inflows to the U.S. were predominately private, but after 2004 they became overwhelmingly public, making U.S. arbitrage simultaneously more robust and more fragile.

Section 2.2 shows how this system of arbitrage connected *differentially* to housing markets and thus produced heterogeneous outcomes with respect to employment and Gross Domestic Product (GDP) gains over the past 20 years. Falling global nominal interest rates should have reflated all developed economies. But differences in housing finance markets caused markedly different employment and GDP gains across those nations. Those benefits have electoral consequences for incumbents and challengers who can claim credit for good outcomes. Consequently, politicians in economies characterized by financial repression, rather than the U.S.-style financial free for all, began introducing some elements of the U.S. housing finance system, particularly securitization of mortgages. Housing-led differential growth advantaged the U.S. and similar economies while creating political pressures to liberalize repressed financial systems.

Section 2.3 specifically considers the U.S. housing politics case. U.S. housing market developments produced a specific variety of the conservatizing politics found in the other cases. In the current conjuncture, the combination of large mortgages at low interest rates changes voter preferences at the margin toward a politics hostile to inflation and increases in tax-funded collective services. The current housing market structure thus shifts the median voter toward a more conservative local politics. Because microlevel behaviors and preferences limit what occurs at the macro level they also affect global politics. To rework an old phrase, cheap mortgages are financing the trenches defending against new demands for social protection in the U.S. and some other countries.

The central narrative message in this chapter is that the disinflation of the 1990s combined with the operation of global capital markets differentially to produce increased aggregate demand in countries characterized by widespread homeownership, high levels of mortgage debt relative to GDP, easy refinance of those mortgages, and mortgage securitization. In turn, this increased aggregate demand produced a self-fulfilling increase in employment and output that benefited politically critical cohorts in those countries. The increased housing costs those cohorts face gives them a stronger interest in cash income over collective social services and in keeping inflation, and thus nominal interest rates, low. Housing outcomes and the financial structures for housing thus have important political consequences.

2.1   U.S. arbitrage in global financial markets

All politics are local, and real estate is even more local. Nevertheless, local housing markets in the U.S. and some other countries are tightly connected to global capital markets. The usual literature on global financial markets sees them as a *constraint* on government policy and spending that might shelter people from the market, as in the typical argument that globalization constrains welfare state provision. This constraint operates by limiting politicians' fiscal resources. Other versions see financialization as a *constraint* on the "real" economy and particularly manufacturing, which then secondarily affects average people through the kind of employment they can obtain. This constraint operates through high real interest rates.

By contrast, this section argues that global capital flows in the 1990s and 2000s also created *opportunities* for growth, rather than just constraints on organizational or collective behavior. These opportunities in turn affected people's behavior by providing a combination of incentives and disincentives toward additional consumption based on the specific housing market financial structures in which they found themselves. Put simply, during the 1990s the U.S. operated a huge system of financial arbitrage that led to above average GDP and employment growth relative to the average for members of the Organization for Economic Cooperation and Development (OECD). While this process ultimately created new constraints via homeowners' economic preferences and the subsequent housing bust, it shows that financialization has ambiguous consequences.

My starting point is a well-known paradox: while the U.S. has been a large net foreign debtor since the early 1990s, it receives net positive international investment income. As Gourinchas and Rey (2005) have shown, from 1960 to 2001, U.S. overseas assets earned an annualized rate of return 2 percentage points higher than U.S. liabilities to foreigners, at 5.6% vs. 3.6%. Furthermore, the gap expanded after 1973, as U.S. overseas assets yielded 6.8% while its liabilities to foreigners cost only 3.5%. This is one reason why, despite five more years of cumulating trade deficits, U.S. net foreign debt was the same 20% of GDP in 2007 as it had been in 2002. Indeed, from 1999 to 2007 net income rose faster than both U.S. inward and outward payments, indicating a widening gap in returns. While a smart individual plausibly could borrow money, invest only part of it, and still show a net profit, it is implausible that at an economywide or global level all Americans are systematically better investors than everyone else. Instead, the U.S. operated a global system of financial arbitrage to produce this odd outcome.

Arbitrage occurs when an intermediary exploits price differences between similar commodities on two different markets, buying and selling that commodity at the same time. At the macroeconomic level, the U.S. systematically borrowed short term, at low interest rates, from the rest of the world, and then turned around and invested back in the rest of the world in longer term, higher risk, higher return, active investment vehicles. Space constraints prevent a detailed analysis of U.S. global arbitrage (but see Schwartz 2009).[1] But a simple breakdown of inward and outward foreign investment stocks presents the essentials. Table 2.1 disaggregates foreign investments into four broad categories: Foreign Direct Investment (using the U.S. Department of Commerce 10% threshold for control), portfolio equity holdings (i.e., passive holdings of equity below the 10% threshold for control), portfolio debt (i.e., bonds), and bank loans. Aside from the obvious large U.S. net debt position, what emerges from this first cut is the long-term versus short-term distinction noted above.

Approximately three-fifths of U.S. overseas assets take the form of foreign direct investment and holdings of equities ("stocks" in U.S. parlance). These relatively active holdings have the potential for capital appreciation and for the capture of profits if firms are well managed.

Table 2.1 Relative share of FDI, portfolio equities, portfolio debt, loans, and derivatives in international holdings, year end 2006

	FDI*	Portfolio equities	Portfolio debt**	Loans	Derivatives	*Total*
$ billion						
US to world	2855	4252	1181	3938	1238	13,754
World to US	2099	2539	5408	4356	1179	15,930
% shares						
US to world	20.8	30.9	8.6	28.6	9.0	100.0
World to US	13.2	15.9	33.9	27.3	7.4	100.0

Notes: * Current Cost Valuation; ** omits holdings of currency and official US government holdings totaling $292 billion.

Source: BEA website, *International Investment Position*.

By contrast, almost over three-fifths of foreign investment in the U.S. occurs as passive holdings of bonds and loans. Let us put aside one implication of this crude data, which is that at a macroeconomic level the world subsidizes the global expansion of U.S. corporate capital and financial intermediaries, in favor of a detailed examination of a second, important connection to mortgage markets.

Fifty-nine percent of foreign investment in U.S. bonds as of December 2005 occurred as purchases of U.S. government and government-guaranteed agency debt. At that time, foreign investors held 51.7% of outstanding marketable U.S. Treasury securities and 14.1% of outstanding "agency" mortgage-backed securities (MBS) (U.S. Department of the Treasury, 2005, 13; U.S. Department of the Treasury, 2007, 3, 5). A mortgage-backed security bundles discrete mortgages into one or more bonds that can be sold in the open market. Agency debt refers to MBS originated by "Fannie Mae" – the Federal National Mortgage Agency – and "Freddie Mac" – the Federal Home Loan Mortgage Corporation. Outsized foreign holdings of Treasury and agency debt helped to drive down interest rates on U.S. mortgages during the 1990s. Current estimates suggest that recycling of Asian trade surpluses during the late 1990s and early 2000s depressed yields on ten-year U.S. Treasury debt by about 90 basis points, or almost 1 percentage point, and as much as 150 basis points in 2005 (Warnock and Warnock, 2006). The interest rate on the ten-year Treasury bond (T-bond) serves as the reference rate or benchmark for nearly all U.S. mortgages. Changing interest rates for T-bonds thus immediately affect interest rates on new mortgages.

Foreign purchases of agency debt from Fannie Mae and Freddie Mac – the "Frannies" – have an even more direct effect on mortgage interest rates. The U.S. federal government created Fannie Mae in 1938 as a government agency that would make housing more affordable by nationalizing the flow of funds in the mortgage market. While Fannie Mae was privatized in 1968–70, the market behaved as if it had an implicit government bailout guarantee, because it was still considered a government sponsored enterprise (GSE).[2] Savings and loan banks (i.e., the U.S. version of *sparkassen* or building societies) got their own version of Fannie Mae, Freddie Mac, in 1970; it was fully privatized in 1989. The market's belief in an implicit government guarantee gave the Frannies an advantageous position in their business, which is the creation of MBS. The U.S. government bailout of the Frannies in summer 2008 validated the market's belief in a guarantee.

Fannie Mae essentially invented the MBS in 1981. Freddie Mac invented the CMO, collateralized mortgage obligation, a derivative that slices up principal and interest payments so that investors can buy bonds of varying maturities. CMOs and MBS are thus different, if simpler, flavors of the larger category of CDOs, or collateralized debt obligations, which includes receivables from car loans, student loans, credit cards, and other forms of debt. Fannie Mae issues about 50% of U.S. MBS, representing about 1.3 trillion in mortgages, and held a further $0.8 trillion in its own portfolio as of year end 2003 (Fannie Mae, 2003, 12). Freddie Mac issues about 45% of U.S. MBS, representing about $1.6 trillion in mortgages at year end 2005 (Freddie Mac, 2005, 19). The Frannies are the pipe connecting international credit markets to the domestic U.S. housing market via the sale of securitized mortgages.

Securitization allows banks to move mortgages off their books by selling those mortgages in the open market and thus refreshes their capital. Then banks can originate yet more loans while earning the bulk of their income from transaction fees. This contrasts with the older model in which banks held mortgages to maturity and made money off the interest rate spread between deposits and loans. Securitization shifts interest-rate risk off banks' books and onto the buyer of the MBS or CMO. The Frannies are both intermediaries and principals in this process. They buy residential mortgages from original mortgage lenders (banks), pool and securitize those mortgages, and sell them directly or as derivatives to the secondary market. Pooling mortgages averages out the risks of default and prepayment, creating a predictable stream of payments. In addition, mortgages with similar risk characteristics can be packaged and sold at interest rates that reflect those risks. Securitization allows investors to buy a bond whose income stream is defined by the aggregated principal and interest payments made by individual homebuyers. The primary domestic purchasers of agency debt are insurance funds and pension plans seeking to offset predictable long-term liabilities with equally predictable long-term assets.

While foreign purchases of securitized agency debt are *relatively* lower than their purchases of Treasury debt, in terms of the total foreign share of outstanding securities, the *absolute* amounts are nearly identical because there was usually about twice as much agency debt in circulation than Treasury debt until the vast expansion of the federal government deficit after 2008. Indeed, agency debt typically represented a full one-third of all marketable U.S. debt securities, public and private, until 2008. This reflected an increase in the aggregate value of U.S. personal mortgage debt from roughly $2.5 trillion in 1990 to about $9.5 trillion in mid-2006 (Federal Reserve Bank). Foreign purchases thus directly depressed yields on U.S. mortgages by lowering the reference rate for mortgages and by absorbing mortgages in the form of MBS. U.S. arbitrage in global capital markets thus stimulated its domestic housing market by providing relatively low interest rates to existing homeowners wishing to refinance their mortgages and to new homebuyers.

2.2   Differential effects of housing market financial structures

Of course, U.S. Treasury debt is the reference rate not only for the U.S. market, but also for many global markets, including indirectly the Euro market. Why didn't foreign purchases of U.S. Treasuries depress yields and lending rates in other countries, and thus redound to everyone's benefit? After all, long-term nominal interest rates fell everywhere in the 1990s, a period of profound disinflation. Euro-area long-term interest rates fell from 11.2% in 1990 to 4.7% in 1999. U.S. long-term rates similarly fell from 8.7% to 4.0% between 1990 and 2003, almost halving the average new mortgage interest rate (Harvard University Joint Center for Housing Studies, 2008, 36; Organisation for Economic Cooperation and Development, 2005 *Factbook*).

Disinflation and subsequently lower nominal interest rates should have increased aggregate demand everywhere, even if real interest rates remained high. But as disinflation filtered through different housing market finance systems it produced different degrees of increased aggregate demand and thus different employment gains. Put bluntly, the more housing was socialized and the more impediments there were to consumer access to housing-related credit, the smaller the aggregate demand "bang" a given economy got from a "buck" of disinflation. This is why the U.S. system of global financial arbitrage largely benefited the U.S. and those economies with similar housing market institutions. Housing market financial systems more like those in the U.S. were better at translating 1990s disinflation into increased demand.[3] Thus the liberal housing market economies identified in Chapter 1 did best in terms of employment and GDP growth, while the familialist ones did worst. Note that the point here is *not* that housing alone drove the U.S. and other economies. Rather, differences in housing finance systems are associated with the *net* difference in growth rates. While all rich economies shared growth impulses from the internet boom, the supply chain revolution, and the mobile telecoms revolution, only some rich economies also got growth from housing. Why?

Disinflation in the 1990s could have released additional purchasing power as debtors' interest payments potentially fell with falling nominal interest rates, and as consumers' dollars went farther in goods markets. Yet disinflation had to be translated through housing finance market institutions into additional purchasing power. Countries with housing finance markets most like those in the U.S. received the greatest increment to purchasing power, causing rising employment through normal Keynesian multiplier mechanisms. The familialist countries with housing finance market institutions least like those in the U.S., and which in addition stifled growth of aggregate demand through wage restraint, did not experience rising aggregate demand and employment. The corporatist market and state developmentalist countries with mixed institutions had mixed outcomes.

Four key features characterize U.S. housing finance markets:

1. relatively high levels of private homeownership
2. relatively high levels of mortgage debt in relation to GDP
3. easy and relatively cheap refinance of mortgages as well as "cash out" of home equity
4. securitization of mortgage loans.

These four features enabled a relatively straightforward process of Keynesian demand stimulus to operate in the U.S. economy in the late 1980s and even more so in the 1990s. As nominal interest rates fell, homeowners refinanced mortgages, shifting considerable purchasing power away from rentier interests and toward individuals with a higher propensity to consume goods, services and housing. This consumption in turn generated new employment through standard Keynesian multiplier effects, sustaining the expansion by helping shift the U.S. federal budget into surplus and thus enabling the Federal Reserve to continue lowering interest rates.

Falling interest rates also flowed through liquid housing markets to create fictitious capital that also boosted employment and growth. Nominal interest rates matter for asset valuation. As nominal interest rates fell, the same nominal dollar income could be used to service a larger and larger mortgage. People entering the housing market thus bid up housing prices because they could enjoy more "housing" at the same monthly mortgage price. Much the same happened in equity markets. But retrospective analyses confirm that the release of home equity mattered much more than rising share markets for the net increase in real personal consumption in the OECD from 1996–2001, both because the propensity to consume new home equity is much higher than for rising capital gains and because home equity bulks larger in the average person's portfolio (Borio, 1995; Case et al., 2001; Ludwig and Sløk, 2002).

However, in the absence of any easy way to tap home equity, this latent additional purchasing power remained exactly that: latent. This is why countries needed to combine widespread ownership with high levels of mortgage debt, easy refinance, and securitization. Widespread ownership without mortgage debt, as in familialist Italy, meant that there was no way to reduce the carrying costs of housing and free up purchasing power. While France had widespread homeownership, the difficulty and cost of refinancing their mortgages prevented French homeowners from translating falling interest rates into a smaller interest burden. Shallow homeownership and difficult refinance meant renter interests prevailed over debtor consumption, as in corporatist Germany. And without securitization, banks would not be willing to refinance loans and thus pass disinflation along to consumers.

Figure 2.1 and Tables 2.2 and 2.3 characterize most developed economies into winners and losers based on the degree to which those countries had U.S.-style housing markets and their employment and

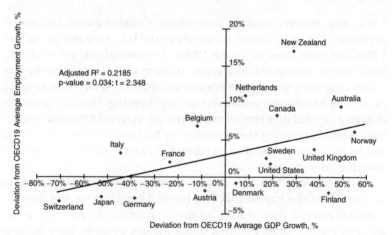

Figure 2.1 Deviation from the average per capita increase in employment and GDP 1991–2002, selected countries

Interpretation: Countries to the RIGHT of the X axis have above-average gains in employment after adjusting for population growth. Countries NORTH of the Y axis have above-average gains in GDP per capita expressed in constant 2000 US$. Thus France combined average employment growth with slightly below-average GDP per capita growth. The chart thus assesses changes in *relative* growth.

Table 2.2 Deviation of growth of indicator from unweighted average of growth for selected countries (%), 1991–2005

	USA	UK	Australia	Netherlands	Sweden	Denmark	France	Italy	Japan	FRG
Employed (#)	7.06	-2.56	9.24	12.50	-1.79	-3.47	0.15	-5.12	-8.34	-7.68
Unemployed (#)	16.26	-23.98	-10.54	-19.96	-40.81	-36.61	24.58	-2.37		93.43
Gross value added	4.79	28.30	13.85	-0.91	-1.74	-3.85	-7.65	-9.84	-13.91	-9.03
Manufacturing GVA	9.60	5.96	2.67	-5.97	32.30	-2.99	13.82	-13.04	-18.89	-23.46
Gross fixed capital formation	27.83	6.15	45.24	-10.64	8.76	20.45	-16.29	-16.89	-35.58	-29.04
GFCF-housing	41.04	10.03	49.33	7.90	-67.80	33.62	-15.14	-13.96	-37.92	-7.11
GFCF metals, machinery	71.15	n/d	n/d	-12.48	0.47	26.09	0.55	-17.43	-32.29	-36.05
Gross Domestic Product	10.9	3.8	17.5	2.7	0.3	-0.6	-4.3	-8.1	-12.9	-9.4

Notes: # = percentage change in absolute number of people employed (or unemployed) in 2005 vs. 1991, as compared to the average change; positive numbers for employed indicate an increase in employment; positive numbers for unemployed indicate an increase in the number registered unemployed. It is possible to have an increase in both numbers because of increased labor force participation.

Source: OECD National Accounts at www.sourceOECD.org.

Table 2.3 Housing finance market characteristics and economic growth in selected countries

	USA	UK	Australia	Netherlands	Sweden	Denmark	France	Italy	Japan	FRG
Transaction costs for property/mortgage acquisition, % of total cost	1.9	1.9	2.4	8.6	2.4	3.3	7.8	11.8	5	4.5
Is mortgage securitization possible? (1 = yes; 0 = no or rare)	1	1	1	1	0	1	0	0	0	0
Home Equity Withdrawal 1990–2002 (as % of GDP *10)	5	7	7	8	4	4	0	1	1	0
Mortgage debt as % of GDP, 2002	58	64.3	50.8	78.8	40.4	74.3	22.8	11.4	36.8	54
Owner occupied housing, 2002, %	69	68	70	53	61	51	55	80	60	42
Synthetic housing indicator*	7.22	7.72	7.41	6.78	4.42	6.75	2.23	2.03	3.29	3.16
Un-misery index^	9.0	0.6	13.4	7.6	–0.8	–2.0	–2.1	–6.6	–10.6	–8.6

Notes: * = constructed from data above by normalizing values to get a 0–10 scale; higher values equal a greater ability to generate aggregate demand from falling interest rates; ^ = from Table 2.2, (row 1 + row 8)/2 to get a –10 to +10 scale.

Sources: OECD National Accounts at www.sourceOECD.org, Kostas Tsatsaronis and Haibin Zhu, "What Drives Housing Price Dynamics," BIS Quarterly Review March 2004, 69–70; Pietro Catte, Nathalie Girouarde, Robert Price, and Christopher Andre, "The Contribution of Housing Markets to Cyclical Resilience," OECD Economic Studies #38, 2004/1.

GDP growth in the 1990s. Figure 2.1 graphs the *relative* growth in absolute employment and GDP per capita. It does not graph absolute percentage changes in those two items, but rather, the degree in percentage terms by which a given country either *outperformed* or *underperformed* the average level of performance for the indicated countries. GDP per capita is used because it controls for the very different rates of population growth across these countries. Absolute employment is used because it captures job creation better than does the unemployment rate. Figure 2.1 shows an unsurprising but nonetheless meaningful correlation between employment performance and growth in GDP per capita. Countries that outperformed the OECD average on employment growth also typically outperformed on GDP growth, allowing us to categorize countries as growth winners or losers in the 1990s.

Table 2.2 shows that GDP and employment gains were neither solely the consequence of financial manipulation nor solely about housing construction. Winners not only had above-average growth for those two indicators, but also typically had even stronger above-average increases in economywide gross value added (GVA), manufacturing gross value added (GVA-M), gross fixed capital formation (GFCF), housing GFCF (GFCF-H), and GFCF in metals and manufacturing (GFCF-MM). While housing construction surely played a strong role in the winners' economic booms, in almost all of the winners the evolution of the absolute level of GFCF-H was smaller than overall growth of GFCF, although in the U.S. GFCF-H was relatively stronger than in many other countries, and definitely above historical norms in 2005–06. Moreover, in most of the winners, the share of housing and all construction in GFCF fell; in the U.S. for example it fell from roughly 65% of GFCF in 1991 to 49% in 2002. Housing had strong multiplier effects but was not the sole driver in the economy. Instead, the housing-led economy spurred outsized increases in real production and investment. In turn, this undoubtedly boosted productivity as throughput increased.

Table 2.3 characterizes countries using the four salient housing market financial characteristics noted above. It creates a synthetic housing index to capture the degree to which a given housing finance market facilitates the translation of falling nominal interest rates into additional purchasing power. This index combines the rate of homeownership, the ratio of mortgage debt to GDP, the availability of home equity withdrawal, the level of transaction costs involved in mortgage refinance, and the degree to which mortgage securitization occurs. Table 2.3

also presents a synthetic index that combines the degree of deviation from the average evolution of per capita employment and GDP gains 1991–2005 – a kind of reverse misery or "Un-misery" index. Figure 2.2 combines these two indices to relate graphically how housing market characteristics map onto employment and GDP gains. Figure 2.2 shows that countries with U.S.-style housing finance systems benefited with respect to employment and GDP growth relative to those without, and that the relationship is not random.

The housing-growth connection was somewhat self-sustaining. Without income and employment growth, housing prices could not rise. Rising prices would have quickly priced income-short buyers out of the market, leading to falling or stable prices. Instead, home equity withdrawal and refinance enabled consumers to increase their consumption across the board, generating faster employment and income growth. In turn, this growth both validated housing prices, enabling lenders to advance ever larger mortgages, and helped profitability in the rest of the economy, promoting job growth and a rising share market. A virtuous (but not eternally so) cycle of rising home prices, rising consumption, rising income and employment, and rising profitability drew in yet more foreign capital seeking assets with increasing

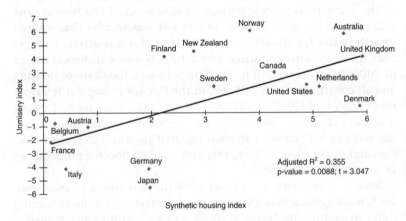

Figure 2.2   Synthetic housing index vs. "Un-misery" index

Note: The synthetic housing index measures the degree to which we would expect housing related increases in aggregate demand. The Un-misery index is sum of the deviation from the average per capita increase in Employment and GDP 1991–2002.

Interpretation: The chart assesses the connection between housing finance market arrangements and *relative* growth.

values. Because foreign central banks as well as private entities chan-neled much of this investment into Treasury and Agency securities, this in turn reduced interest rates, providing a further boost to housing prices and aggregate demand. This in turn further motivated investors in relatively slowly growing economies to continue to invest in other economies with housing booms. Once the U.S. economy ran out of employment gains and potential new buyers in the 2000s, though, the boom turned to bust.

This section argued that the benefits of the 1991–2004 disinflation were felt unevenly in the rich countries. While other factors surely also mattered, one important factor was the degree to which hous-ing finance systems could translate falling nominal interest rates into increased aggregate demand and thus into increased employment and GDP. This increased demand was *not* solely housing related, but also deeply affected the core parts of the nonhousing economy, including manufacturing. What consequences did the housing boom have on individual interests and politics? This was the task set forward at the beginning of the paper, and it is to this task that we now turn.

2.3   The old and new politics of homeownership

The current combination of historically low nominal interest rates, high rates of homeownership, and high, but falling, housing prices should incline core groups in the U.S. voting public toward a pref-erence for low inflation and low taxes. All other things being equal they will favor more conservative politics benefiting long-term credi-tor interests and groups with strong private incomes. Thus this sec-tion makes three related arguments: First, that in the abstract, private homeownership produces more conservative politics; second, that the current conjuncture makes these preferences even stronger; third, in the U.S., the core cadre that dominates electoral politics has a substan-tial economic interest in housing that meshes with a similar orienta-tion in lower income groups. This core group and similar groups in other countries are the soldiers who man the trenches in defense of private incomes and against greater public spending. The ramparts of these trenches are the local governments and neighborhood associa-tions these people dominate.

As the introductory chapter noted, the classic arguments about housing by Kemeny and Castles made a theoretical and an empiri-cal case that widespread private homeownership inhibited a uni-versal welfare state. Both agreed on a central premise about private homeownership: mortgages crowd out taxes. Kemeny argued that homeownership crowded housing expenses into the early part of a typical homeowner's life. Homeowners' need to accumulate a down payment and then to service a mortgage would incline them against higher taxes for public services. Castles demonstrated a statistical link between high rates of homeownership in the first half of the twentieth century and low rates of public pension provision, arguing that homeownership and larger pensions were functional equivalents. Conditions in the current American housing market reinforce both Kemeny and Castles' dynamic, while also inclining people against higher inflation and higher nominal interest rates.

Although the structure of the U.S. housing market did not change much during the 1990s, conjunctural conditions did change. The U.S. housing market, as noted above, is characterized by relative high levels of homeownership (generally more than two-thirds of households), relatively easy mortgage refinance, relatively easy access to home equity, and widespread securitization of mortgages (Table 2.3). Transaction costs for mortgage refinance are low, generally around 1% of the principal, and are often capitalized into the mortgage. This means that U.S. homebuyers can often make a one-way bet on mortgages by taking out a fixed-rate mortgage. If rates rise, debtors are protected for the duration of what is typically a 30-year loan. If rates fall, debtors can take advantage of this by refinancing the mortgage at a new, lower rate, because most loans do not have prepayment penalties. That said, marginal buyers, or those who anticipate having to move in the near future, often take out adjustable (variable) rate mortgages (ARMs) because the introductory rate on ARMs are often lower than for fixed-rate mortgages, albeit higher after the inevitable rate reset. ARMs were not invented until the late 1970s and not widespread until the 1980s. Today in the U.S. they typically constitute 20–35% of new mortgage originations in any given year, up from about only 10% in the late 1990s, although at the housing bubble's peak they constituted around half of new mortgage originations (Freddie Mac, 2005, 2).

By the same token, home equity – the difference between the house's market value and the residual mortgage principal – is easily (clearly too easily) tapped in the U.S. Transaction costs for a loan secured by home equity are low – less than 1% and often waived for owners with substantial equity – and interest rates are generally the prime rate or LIBOR plus 1–2%. Because mortgage interest is tax deductible in the U.S. and because home equity loans are considered mortgages, households not only generally use home equity lines of credit (HELOCs) to finance home improvements but also cars, college, and the retirement of (much more expensive) credit card debt (McConnell et al., 2003, 6). HELOCs are widespread (see below). Americans' ability to do this kind of credit arbitrage encourages consumption.

Finally, the bulk of U.S. mortgages are securitized. Up until the late 1990s this had beneficial effects, unless you were a bad credit, no/low down payment borrower. The Frannies set criteria for "conforming" loans that made them easier to package into an MBS: 30 year maturities, 10–20% down payments (i.e., purchase money), household housing-related debt payments no higher than 28% of gross income and total debt payments no higher than 36% of gross income. Banks in turn imposed these criteria on buyers, providing lower interest rates in return for a lower probability of default.

But by the late 1990s, new nonbank mortgage lenders began aggressively offering "Alt-A" and "subprime" mortgages to households with bad credit history, no or miniscule down payments, and quite high debt-to-income ratios. Not all this subprime lending went to poor households. Much also went to over-leveraged higher income groups. These mortgages accounted for 32% of all originations in the U.S. by 2005 (JCHS, 2008, 39). Banks packaged these risky mortgages into MBS and then tried to control for their inherent riskiness by pooling slices of these MBS as CDOs. This risk-reduction strategy turned out to be totally misguided. When housing prices decelerated and buyers proved unable to either handle their housing payments or refinance their way into a lower-interest-rate prime mortgage, the subprime and Alt-A loans backing these MBS and CDOs began defaulting in large numbers. Their dispersion into multiple CDOs made all CDOs suspect. The central point in the arguments below is that cash-constrained households are also often households that have ARMs – so if inflation drives up their interest rates this puts them in a precarious position with respect to their housing costs. Secondarily, foreclosures of defaulting homeowners affect even stable ones, as housing prices fall everywhere, taking the local property tax base with it. While debtors normally welcome some inflation, American homeowners with ARMs have strong reasons to fear inflation in the short run.

Three households and the core of civil society

How did this affect actual people? Let us consider three different American families – recent young homebuyers, a middle age household, and a near retirement age household – to show how the current conjuncture induces each to fear high inflation, higher nominal interest rates, and higher taxes. Imagine a young family in their early thirties whose $37,000 post-tax income puts them in the middle quintile of the income distribution (U.S. Bureau of Labor Statistics, 2004). Half of these families have bought a house (see Table 2.4). New homebuyers in this group were confronted by a 90% increase in housing prices in 2000–06, which means they probably will be devoting approximately one-third to half of their income on mandatory housing-related payments for mortgage principal and interest, taxes, and insurance (i.e., "PITI"). Overall, the middle 50% of the U.S. income distribution devotes about 20% of total income to debt service, but more than 10% of this quintile faced housing payments in excess of 50% of their income in 2006 (Federal Reserve Bank; Fellowes and Mabanta, 2007, 4–7, 13; JCHS, 2008, 40). This family precisely fits Kemeny's ideal-type. With such a high proportion of income devoted to housing, this family will be hostile to additional tax burdens. This is even truer for households in the bottom quartile, with household incomes under $22,000. There, 40% of households had a mortgage, and of these 42% had housing costs in excess of 50% of their income (JCHS, 2008, 40).

Rising inflation creates a triple threat to the financial security of this family, particularly if they have an ARM. First, inflation increases the nominal interest rate on their ARM. While inflation also erodes somewhat the long-term cost of carrying that loan, the change in PITI payments triggered by upward interest-rate adjustments subjects this family to immediate financial stress. Second, a rising interest rate also puts downward pressure on housing prices. In liberal housing systems, houses are assets, and their price rises and falls as interest rates change,

Table 2.4   Homeownership and mortgage debt by age of household head, 2004

Age group	Percent home-owners	Median home value	"Mortgage free" owners, % of group	Median mortgage value	Median mortgage as % median home value
25–34	49.9	$137,000	9.1	$108,000	78.8
35–44	68.3	160,000	8.0	110,000	68.8
45–54	77.3	170,000	16.3	97,000	57.1
55–64	79.1	200,000	35.6	83,000	41.5
65+	83.3	140,000	69.6	43,000	30.7
All	72.2	160,000	30.9	95,000	59.4

Source: Munnell, Soto, and Aubrey, *Do People Plan to Tap Their Home Equity in Retirement?*, p. 1, calculated from U.S. Board of Governors of the Federal Reserve System, *Survey of Consumer Finances* (SCF), Washington, DC, 2004.

just like any other asset, although with less rapidity. Rising interest rates press down on the market price of houses by increasing the monthly payment of any potential new homebuyer. So rising interest rates might push our family into the roughly 20% of mortgaged U.S. homeowners who now have negative equity. Finally, inflation running ahead of wage increases erodes our family's living standard. Deflation, by contrast, frees up cash flow for immediate debt payments if – and this is a big if – incomes do not also fall.

Our middle age homeowner household is likely to have a somewhat higher income at around $50,000 or $55,000, and have somewhat higher equity in their house. But they probably also have chosen to extract that equity from their house through a HELOC (U.S. Bureau of Labor Statistics, 2004). HELOCs are effectively a second mortgage secured on the owner's equity. Approximately one-fourth of U.S. homeowners have a HELOC or similar debt, and this is surely more prevalent among our middle age homeowners than the younger ones, who typically have little equity with which to secure a HELOC. Americans extracted about $1.2 trillion in home equity from 2001–04, or about one-fifth of the rise in home prices (Greenspan and Kennedy, 2005). They used one-third of this to retire more expensive nonhousing debt like credit-card balances. By 2004 HELOC debt accounted for one-fifth of all debt secured against primary residences (Federal Reserve Bank). About one-fourth of this group faced housing-related costs in excess of 30% of their income in 2006 (JCHS, 2008, 40).

HELOCs are typically ARMs, making this family vulnerable to interest rate increases, although probably less so than the younger family. Like the younger family, they are also vulnerable to declining home prices if they cashed out substantial amounts of home equity. And they are vulnerable to other owners' defaults in their own local market. Even if they haven't already taken out a HELOC, the widespread use of HELOCs to finance college tuition for children makes owners sensitive to house-price fluctuations. The salience of HELOCs is visible in the steady decline in total aggregate equity for all homeowners with mortgages.

What about our older homeowners? By age 65, about 70% have paid off their mortgage. While their greater dependence on Social Security for cash income – the public old age pension, accounting for 40% of income for people over age 65 – might incline them to prefer higher taxes and larger public incomes, their housing situation also gives them reasons to resist taxes and inflation. The elderly's primary store of wealth is their house; more than 70% of households age 65 and over own their house. As Table 2.5 shows, only the top income decile has substantial non-housing wealth. The elderly increasingly capture that housing equity through reverse mortgages or uses outright sale to finance care in assisted living or a nursing home. By age 75 the percentage of homeowners drops down to about 70%, indicating liquidation of this asset. Politically, this group is likely to be less sensitive to inflation and more sensitive to rising taxes, particularly property taxes, as their incomes are often fixed.

Indeed, the run-up in housing prices has probably made all of our groups hostile to rising taxes (Wilson, 2006). Higher housing prices mean higher property taxes (i.e., "rates"), which squeeze other revenue sources. In the U.S., property taxes are fundamentally a local revenue source that pays for education, policing, and some social services. They provide roughly 70% of local government revenues and 10% of all tax revenue. Their dollar volume increased at twice the rate of all taxes in 2000–05 (OECD, http://www.sourceOECD.org). By 2007, property taxes accounted for 3.4% of total personal income. Visible, lumpy taxes induce economizing preferences in local taxpayers, just as budgetary changes in Denmark in the 1980s and 1990s did (Schwartz, 2001, 131–55). And

Table 2.5 Ownership of home equity and stocks in total financial wealth, 2004

	Decile share of total US net home equity	Net home equity as % of non-financial wealth	Decile share of total US stocks*	Stocks as % of financial wealth	Median total wealth, '000s	Debt as % of income for debtors
Top income decile	36	n/a	75	57.5	924.1	12.7
Decile 9	13	n/a	8	48.9	311.1	18.1
Deciles 7–8	20	n/a	11	41.8	160.0	20.6
Bottom 6 deciles	31	n/a	6	35.4	37.8	18.9
All families	100	32.3	100	51.3	93.1	18.0

Memo item: business equity is 16.7% of total wealth ; vehicles are 3.3% of total wealth

Note: * Direct stock holdings plus defined contribution pension plans and mutual funds.

Source: Calculated from Federal Reserve Bank, *Survey of Consumer Finance*, 2001 and 2004 based on online data at http://www.federalreserve.gov/pubs/oss/oss2/2004/bulletin.tables. int.xls; Federal Reserve Bulletin, 2006, *Recent Changes in US Family Finances*, p. A8.

as rising housing prices feed into higher property taxes through rising assessments, it becomes harder to increase other taxes for national purposes. Falling property taxes present a different problem, as localities find it harder to provide essential services, yet cannot confront cash-strapped homeowners with even higher tax rates.

Homeowners' hostility to inflation reverses the pattern prevailing in the 1960s and 1970s. Then, housing market incumbents benefited tremendously from inflation, which rapidly and effectively reduced the real burden of their fixed mortgages while inflating the nominal value of their home. Homebuyers in the 1960s and 1970s typically used *fixed-rate*, long amortization mortgages and did not have HELOCs. And they typically had reasonably secure jobs with the expectation of some seniority-based increases in their wage. Given these conditions, a fixed-rate mortgage in an inflationary environment was a one-way bet in favor of debtors, particularly since people moved less frequently. These conditions are gone. The massive shift from bank-held fixed loans to securitized, floating-rate loans has transferred inflation risk away from banks and the financial system and on to the buyers of houses and to a lesser extent the buyers of MBS backed by those houses.

One final group encompassing households from all three groups needs to be examined closely to understand the political consequences of the housing market boom. One-third of white households with children have an annual income in excess of $100,000. This group only constitutes about one-fifth of the voting population, but put simply, if you don't win this group, you don't win elections. This group encompasses the people who actually run organizations, form public opinion, and provide the decisive votes arbitrating between parties representing different groups of businesses.

The top decile by income, which encompasses much of this core third of white families, also encompasses two different groups. The top 1% of the population, or top 10% of this decile, controls roughly 20% of wealth (and a bigger share of corporate equities). They are the bourgeoisie, to the extent that this label is useful. The rest of this decile, the other 9%, receives the bulk of their income – five-sixths – from wages (Dumenil and Levy 2004, 107). Their capital income is helpful, particularly in retirement, but does not convey control over capital. But the top 1% cannot control either the economy or the polity without the consent of the rest of the top decile.

This group is sensitive to the value of their housing because they not only have primary residences but often have a secondary residence as well, effectively doubling their bet on housing assets. The median dual homeowner had a 2004 income of $123,000 and total home equity of $376,000, representing 34% of their nonpension wealth (Engelhardt 2005, 54; Federal Reserve Bank 2004). While this later group is not coterminous with the whole upper third of white families, it gives a good sense of this better-off fraction. For the average household in the top decile of the income distribution housing equity amounts to about one-fourth of total wealth. Thus this group is also sensitive to changes in nominal interest rates that might devalue the equity in their houses, even though their financial holdings are substantially larger than their nonfinancial assets.

Finally, it is important to note the substantial difference between the classic processes of wealth and job creation in the era of the "Keynesian welfare state" and the current era. Central banks used high liquidity in both eras to boost employment and growth. What differs is the pathway by which increased aggregate demand is formed. In the Bretton Woods era, lower interest rates mostly flowed through the economy via increased investment in the manufacturing sector that in turn led to higher levels of employment and wages. The broad increase in wages then validated *ex post facto* the original increase in investment. Growth rested on broad and equitable increases in income.

During the 1990s boom, increased consumption flowed not from increased investment percolating through economywide wage increases. Instead, falling interest rates boosted the value of marketable assets, including the newly marketable value of domestic housing. Financial deregulation enabled households to capture and sell that increase in assets, especially housing values, and thus expand consumption. Because housing equity is highly unequally distributed, growth magnified existing inequities by endowing housing market insiders with huge amounts of potential consumption and/or wealth. Meanwhile those without a foot in the housing market at the time prices began rising were shut off from wealth formation. As the other chapters note, this implies widening intergenerational inequities and the kind of financial pressures mentioned above when we considered our typical young family.

The current crisis meanwhile pits the financial sector against households. Households lose from short-run inflation. But the Federal Reserve Bank is abetting the financial sector's desire for an inflationary bailout of their positions in subprime MBS. A little inflation helps sustain the nominal price of the housing that collateralizes those mortgages and thus averts a financial system meltdown. It remains to be seen if this solution is politically and economically stable over the long run. At the time of writing there had been several proposals and programs to bail out defaulting homeowners. None had proven particularly successful. Yet none tried the most obvious solution, which was to have an agency of the federal government take over part of the mortgage using a shared appreciation contract, while relieving the homeowner of payments for a specified period of time. This creates some moral hazard risks, but they cannot be any greater than those created by bailing out financial institutions while leaving their management intact.

Over the longer term, the only solution to the housing finance crisis is to raise people's net incomes to the point where housing payments become less burdensome. This requires massive political changes as well as economic reflation. The contours of each are murky at this point in time. Proposals for reflation via increased federal government spending already hover in the $1 trillion range (about 7% of U.S. GDP). While larger packages are less dangerous than a 1930s-style deflationary spiral, the kinds of income gains needed to validate the entire 20% of mortgages that are in distress are unimaginable.

Finally the crisis has changed the ownership of the mortgage finance industry. The federal agencies – the Frannies and the regional Federal Home Loan Banks – are now the major sources of new capital for housing finance. But this is unlikely to change the core institutional practices away from the liberal model as it represents a return to older patterns. The U.S. will return to its pre-bubble liberal model by abandoning the loose lending standards of the 2000s, and restricting access to dubious mortgage instruments like negative amortization loans (where unpaid interest is simply added to the principal balance). But this will leave intact the essentially liberal combination of long maturity, fixed interest rate loans, and liberal access to refinance.

Conclusion

As Randall Germain argued, all levels of finance are ultimately connected (Germain, 1997). At the lowest level markets are highly competitive and exchange is often anonymous. At the highest levels finance is profoundly political and reflects interventions by central banks and their states. In the middle are national and industrial markets controlled by enterprises of various sizes. But all three markets usually interconnect and the political content of the highest levels inevitably filters down to the lowest levels. The current conjuncture is no different. Asian and oil exporters' central banks abetted U.S. financial arbitrage by recycling U.S. current account deficits. At the local level in the U.S.

and other countries, this arbitrage spread through the housing market system though sales of MBS organized by specialist mortgage brokers, national securitizers of those MBSs, and investment banks.

The housing price boom, low interest rates, and low inflation created compelling reasons for various groups to prefer a continuation of that general environment even as the bust began. Homeowners' consciousness and thus political preferences changed as housing became a tradable asset. The idea that housing (and equities) was the "only game in town" for wealth accumulation and thence for income security in old age became widespread (see Watson in this volume). And indeed, for anyone unwilling to depend on the near poverty line income provided by the U.S. old age pension (the maximum annual payout is currently $24,000), this was certainly true. People's rational (logic of consequences) orientation toward homeownership, low inflation, and low taxes thus inevitably shifted into a more value-rational (logic of appropriateness) attachment to those things.

The decade-plus connection between U.S. global financial arbitrage and domestic housing driven Keynesian demand stimulus also caused similar changes to policy, identity, and preferences in other countries. The connection between rising housing prices and differential growth did not pass unnoticed. Consequently financial regulators in many European countries tried to create regulatory structures that could accommodate a more active and liquid market for MBS, usually based on the Danish system of mortgage-backed bonds. Currently, securitized mortgage debt represents less than 10% of GDP for most European countries, and less than 20% of all mortgage debt for the whole EU (European Mortgage Federation, 1994, 116; 2007, 34).

However, securitization requires standardization, because securities bundle together loans that behave similarly and thus predictably. Securitization rests on common valuation standards, loan contingencies, maturities, prepayment provisions, etc. as well as overcoming differences between Roman and Common Law treatments of assets. Securitization also requires a shift away from short-term loans toward longer loans, since it is pension and insurance funds that are the major domestic buyers of MBS. Securitization thus would further homogenize national markets in Europe and the European market as a whole, because MBS are subject not only to national but also to EU regulation because of their implications for the stability of national financial systems. The EU enabled securitization in a 1988 directive, but the take-up has been slow, and is likely to remain slow while memories of the current crisis linger. But opening the door to securitization and

American-style housing market Keynesianism might create the same constituencies that are politically resistant to inflation and taxes in the U.S. subsequent to its round of housing market Keynesianism.

In the U.S., the disinflation of the 1990s combined with the operation of global capital markets to produce increased aggregate demand because of the U.S. combination of high levels of mortgage debt relative to GDP and easy refinance of those mortgages. In turn, this increased aggregate demand produced a self-fulfilling increase in employment and output that benefited both subaltern groups and politically critical cohorts. These groups in turn now have strong interests in cash income over collective social services and in keeping short-term inflation, and thus nominal interest rates, low. The interests and consciousness created by current housing markets is thus a force for the maintenance of conservative economic policies and politics. Hegemony thus has very local roots, even though those roots are watered by cash flowing down from global financial markets.

Notes

1. Brad Setser (2006) argues that exactly the opposite is true, that the U.S. lends short term to the world and then borrows back long term. But this is not plausible given the rate of return data. His case rests on high levels of U.S. short-term lending to international financial centers in London and the Caribbean. But surely these financial centers are dominated by U.S. banks which then relend long term?
2. Privatization span out the unsubsidized portions of FMNA as FMNA, leaving behind "Ginnie Mae," the Government National Mortgage Agency, to provide subsidized lending for public housing projects.
3. The reverse might also be true: inflation may percolate through housing markets in differentially detrimental ways. Our point here is not that at all places and at all times U.S.-style housing market institutions produce superior employment outcomes. Our analysis only shows that this was true during the 1990s. Lane Kenworthy's (2002) findings are relevant to this point, because he finds that the relative job creation ability of coordinated and liberal market economies inverted around 1990/92. This suggests that *rising* nominal interest rates adversely affected countries with U.S.-style housing markets in the first period.

3
Boom and Crash: The Politics of Individual Subject Creation in the Most Recent British House Price Bubble

Matthew Watson

Introduction

At the time of writing – January 2009 – British banks remained deeply embroiled in the ongoing fallout from the intensification of the credit crunch which occurred in the fall of 2008. On the day in late September 2008 when the U.S. House of Representatives voted down the first attempt to introduce a U.S.$700 billion bailout for American banks, the FTSE 100 index of leading shares fell by more than 5% to 4818, more than 30% down from its peak value. Banking shares led the market slide, posting more than double-digit losses on the day. Just two weeks previously, a spate of short selling against the country's largest mortgage provider, HBOS, prompted the Brown government to suspend its own antimonopoly legislation to allow HBOS to merge with Lloyds TSB, albeit in a move which bore all the hallmarks of a takeover. A moratorium on short selling stocks duly ensued. Yet this was not enough to prevent a similar run on the stock of the Bradford and Bingley bank, the country's most important provider of buy-to-let mortgages. Bradford and Bingley's deposits business was sold off to Santander in a government-engineered acquisition, with its mortgage debt being nationalized. This followed the earlier nationalization of Northern Rock, Britain's fifth-largest mortgage provider and previously its most adept exponent of leveraged mortgage deals.

By the end of January 2009, as the intensification of the credit crunch seemed to confirm fears of a severe global recession, the FTSE 100 index had continued its slide and dipped below 4000 on a number of separate occasions, well over 40% down on its peak value. The hemorrhaging of bank stocks had led to an overall market fall which saw at least one-third of FTSE 100 companies trading at a discount to their book value (*Daily Telegraph*, October 30, 2008). This trajectory in stock prices occurred against a backdrop in which the Brown government had actively been purchasing public stakes in private banks and endorsing a £200 billion state insurance scheme against banks' bad debts. Both of these measure were introduced in the interests of systemic stability and amounted to a largely open-ended financial commitment of taxpayer's money in an effort to prove that the British state would not let banks go bust to the detriment of depositors' savings. Even Lloyds TSB, the supposedly safe half of the proposed superbank partnership with HBOS, the bank most exposed to current price fluctuations on the housing market, was the recipient of state support.

Few things look certain in current circumstances, except perhaps for the fact that the distress of the banking sector and the distress of the housing market are fundamentally intertwined. The government's rush to stabilize the banking sector – first with swaps of essentially worthless mortgage-backed securities (MBS) for pristine government debt, then buying back such securities at their old trading value for cash, followed by various emergency nationalizations and purchases of public stakes in private banks – played out against the backdrop of falling personal wealth as the British housing market stalled. Protecting savings in deposit accounts was made the explicit priority of government spending, as savings accumulated in a previously rapidly rising housing market were increasingly wiped out. The volume of new mortgage business in 2008 fell by more than 60% compared with 2007, and 2007 was itself a year in which house purchases slowed noticeably for the final three months (BBC News, January 6, 2009). Private Cabinet briefing notes made their way into the press, estimating at least a 10% fall in house prices in the twelve months between May 2008 and May 2009 (*Guardian*, May 14, 2008). Industry insiders have forecast that the bottom of the market will not be reached until 2011 at the earliest (*Financial Times*, January 7, 2009), by which time the peak-to-trough fall in prices might be as high as 40% or 50% (*Observer*, September 7, 2008).

The recent British house price bubble was showing all the signs of increasing fragility even before the onset of the credit crunch. The Royal Institution of Chartered Surveyors showed that the generic affordability of private housing stock in Britain – measured as the proportion of take-home pay required to meet mortgage repayments – returned shortly before the credit crunch to the record levels witnessed during the collapse of the 1980s bubble, the only previous time the figure topped 40%. In 2007 it was 42%, up from 25% only four years earlier. In terms of accessibility constraints – measured as the proportion of take-home pay required to meet the up-front costs associated with house purchases – the sense of underlying fragility was even more marked. When New Labour entered office in 1997 this figure was only 20%, but by 2004 it had topped 100% for the first time ever. In the bubble of the 1980s it did not even break the 60% barrier (Royal Institution of Chartered Surveyors, 2007).

It is always easy to be wise after the event, but hindsight does suggest that these figures are indicative of an accident waiting to happen. A decisive trigger appears to have been all that was necessary to begin to unravel the price structure associated with the excesses of the housing market boom. The credit crunch provided such a trigger, because the bubble had survived for as long as it did only because of chronic overlending within the mortgage market. The use of leveraged financial products enabled mortgage lending to take place on ever higher multiples of household income, which brought into reach aspirations for owning homes of ever higher values. This in turn helped to push up house prices. The credit crunch has subsequently activated the reverse price trajectory. The British interbank lending market has dried up on fears of the bad debts which might be lurking unannounced on banks' balance sheets. As banks have struggled to trust one another about the true scale of their difficulties, the LIBOR (the London Interbank Offered Rate) has shot up, making mortgage finance more expensive as a consequence. Most households are now faced simultaneously with the twin pressures of rising mortgage repayment costs and falling house prices. The result for many is that it has become more difficult to maintain repayments at exactly the time that falling prices push the value of the family home below what was paid for it. This creates a personal debt spiral in which it is impractical to sell the house because of the losses that would ensue, but increasingly unaffordable to stay in it while remaining within the expenditure constraints of current income. Britain has consequently witnessed the rebirth of the "debtor occupier," last seen a generation ago during the collapse of the house price bubble in the late 1980s. Such a phenomenon stalls the turnover of transactions on the housing market, leading to further downward pressure on prices.

The current downside phase of British house prices does not invalidate continued study of the politics of the preceding bubble. Indeed, it probably makes it even more important, because the developing politics of the likely crash will be contextualized by the prior politics of the preceding bubble. The recent British bubble was built upon the creation of particular subject positions in the relationship between the individual householder, that person's saving and investment habits, and the expectations which followed that financially responsible behavior would be rewarded by increased wealth occasioned by ever-rising house prices. Cashing out capital gains from the housing market was constituted during the bubble phase in effect as an individual right to be claimed against the Government and manifested in demands for sound macroeconomic management. At the time of writing, the politics of the crash look most likely to be conditioned by reactions to the assumption that this right has now been revoked.

In order to analyze the significance of such an assumption, the chapter proceeds in three stages. In Section 3.1, I develop the framework that helps me to make sense of what makes the most recent house price bubble politically different to its predecessor. The crucial contextual factor in this respect is the change in political priorities regarding the management of the welfare state. The overriding goal of the Thatcher government during the buildup to the 1980s houseprice bubble was simply to restrict the scope of existing entitlements. In this sense, the trajectory of house prices was entirely divorced from attempts to recast the whole manner in which welfare was delivered in Britain. By contrast, the overriding goal of the Blair government in the buildup to the 2000s house price bubble was to catalyze an increasing shift toward a system of asset-based welfare. Sections 3.2 and 3.3 subsequently apply the insights arising from the conceptual discussion to the two bubble experiences. Section 3.2 focuses on the bubble that burst in the late 1980s, as successive failures of macroeconomic policy in Britain led to the interest rate rises which tightened domestic credit conditions. Section 3.3 focuses on the more recent bubble.

The significance of incorporating the housing market into an asset-based system of welfare is that it creates additional incentives for householder subject identification with conservative monetary policies designed to lock in house price growth. The New Labour bubble was self-sustaining for a while, insofar as it contained inbuilt defense mechanisms against deflation. This was achieved politically, through the constitution of more and more people as monetary conservatives. Subject identification of this nature prevented political pressure for expansionary policies that would require interest rate responses that would act punitively against the housing market. The right to have house price growth – if we can indeed call it that – was successfully protected by orthodox macroeconomic management that kept inflation in check and interest rates historically very low. Yet, the credit crunch has subsequently had the same effect on house prices as a significant interest rate rise of the proportions witnessed in the late 1980s. From the perspective of homeowners' new subject positions, it appears as if the right to continuous house price growth has been taken away. Without a direct culprit for the credit crunch to hold accountable for this, blame has subsequently shifted to the government as the ultimate arbiter and guarantor of individual rights. This, I suggest, captures the essence of the current political response to the ongoing housing market crash. The government is partially responsible for its own role as lightning conductor for blame, given the assiduous manner in which it courted through its savings programs the new subject positions that have since come back to haunt it.

3.1   The integration of the housing market into a system of asset-based welfare

The family home is now increasingly likely to be viewed by British households as an investment for the future. The trajectory of house prices is instrumental to such a conception. The average house price in Britain rose more than 50-fold between 1965 and the onset of the credit crunch, from a starting figure of around £3500 to one in excess of £185,000. This works out at an average annual increase of more than 10% (Council of Mortgage Lenders, 2005). Knowledge of such a trajectory makes it much more likely that houses will be desired primarily for the asset accumulation that homeownership makes possible, and that failure to take advantage of the wealth effects arising from buoyant house prices translates into having "missed the boat."

Changes in perception of the family home have also been activated by the dominance of a popular cultural politics of ownership from the 1980s onward. A rather rigid structure of housing classes had developed in Britain by the end of the 1970s (e.g., Rex, 1973; Saunders, 1986). That structure had been built upon cross-subsidization of housing tenure across classes, whereby middle-class owner-occupiers received fiscal support that pegged their mortgage repayments below the true market rate, but were also required to make good some of the monetary value of that support in enhanced tax payments. A proportion of these tax receipts was then recycled as direct subsidization of working-class rents on local authority housing (e.g., Merrett and Gray, 1982). Access to affordable housing was thus constituted as an individual right which operated across classes.

But this has since been overwritten by assumptions that the government will be responsible, not only for ensuring access to affordable housing *per se*, but also for ensuring access to a structure of private homeownership capable of delivering flows of accumulated wealth to homeowners. The ongoing distress of British banks amidst the credit crunch has part of its origins in the lack of oversight of what developed into conspicuous oversupply in the mortgage lending market. While the bubble lasted, overlending was considered legitimate because of the role it played in securing access rights to the structure of private home-ownership. In addition it also helped to feed the house price bubble that hardened popular attitudes that the family home is an investment able to provide free cash flows.

The development of the perception of "home as investment" has had an important impact on the pricing structure of the British housing market. Of all recent British governments, New Labour has been particularly vocal in encouraging individuals to treat the home as a financial asset. It is perhaps unsurprising within this context that house prices have increasingly come to display the characteristics of assets which are susceptible to speculative dynamics. The conceptual framework I will use in an attempt to make sense of the two most recent British house price bubbles will reflect these pricing characteristics. The prices of individual assets tend to fluctuate together in markets where genuinely speculative dynamics take hold. For this reason it is important to be working with an explanatory framework which emphasizes the pricing structure of the housing market as a whole rather than that for individual houses. The intuition underpinning such a framework is that houses are very rarely valued in isolation and on their own merits, so much as in relation to dominant price trends in the market as a whole.

As a result of the social significance which is attached to owning a property in the "right" area and being able to trade up to own more expensive properties, individual houses in Britain have come to form part of an integrated homeowner investment strategy across society. The dominant price trend in every local segment of the housing market reflects dominant price trends elsewhere and, in this way, individual house prices quickly reflect changes in the price of other houses. As a result, the most important indicator of in which way and by how much the price of an individual house is likely to change is the underlying pattern of price changes in the housing market as a whole. This has turned out to be as true for the period in which the credit crunch has undermined confidence in the level at which house prices peaked during the bubble as for the period of the bubble itself. The only real difference is that the earlier period saw individual house prices being driven upward together, while the later period has seen them being driven downward together.

My explanatory framework rests on the assumption that the prices of individual houses, albeit ostensibly determined independently of one another, in practice exhibit a direct and positive correlation. Indeed, such is the influence of overall market conditions on the price of individual houses that it makes sense to think in terms of the serial correlation of all house prices, at least with respect to local housing markets. Donald MacKenzie has recently pointed to a similar effect in relation to the stock market, where a number of individual stocks have been seen to display price changes which directly replicate one another solely because they are known to form part of the same coordinated investment strategy. He describes the ensuing serial correlation in stock prices as the development of a "superportfolio" (MacKenzie, 2006, 225). I intend to use this concept in the remainder of my analysis.

I do so not as a substitute for the notion of a house price bubble but alongside it. A bubble implies a purely speculative price phase in which the psychology of crowds allows individual investors to overvalue systematically a particular asset or group of assets (e.g., Shiller, 2000). While there is clearly a speculative element to many of the house purchases in both of the episodes described in what follows, this is not their only feature. There is also a coordinated element to investments in houses, as individuals seek to "play the market" by trading up their position within it. The speculative element to price formation does not disappear within such attempts, but it is always set within the context in which conditions in one local housing market shape those in all others. Viewed as a whole, the housing market is a social phenomenon to the extent that its underlying price trajectory reflects the coordinated efforts of individuals to issue social signals through their status as homeowners. By using the concept of a housing market superportfolio alongside that of a house price bubble, it is possible to capture such a sense of coordination within the speculative price trend. I use the notion of a bubble to apply to a specific trajectory of house *prices*, whereas I use that of a superportfolio to apply to the broader features of price coordination within the housing *market*.

When treating the housing market conceptually as a superportfolio of serially correlated house prices, a house price bubble can be seen as an asymmetric pricing trend within the superportfolio. For governments eager to appropriate the feel-good factor associated with rising house prices for their own electoral ends, the desired pricing trajectory of the housing market superportfolio is one of continued increases. New Labour has given exactly the same impression as its Conservative predecessor from the 1980s of wanting to claim political credit for presiding over a sustained period of house price rises. Yet, where it has differed has been in its attempts to secure such rises against macroeconomic disturbance by introducing extraeconomic obstacles to the development of self-propelling downward pressure on market valuations. The greater the institutionalization of extraeconomic protection, the more robust house price bubbles are likely to be in the face of disturbances arising from government policy. This is because of the absence of macroeconomic conditions that might otherwise threaten to undermine them.

Of course, the comparable position which the Thatcher and Blair governments placed themselves in by attempting to claim political credit for continued increases in house prices may yet have another dimension to it. The Major government paid a high electoral penalty for presiding over a housing market crash following the Thatcher bubble (e.g., Schoon, 2001, 81). Current opinion poll evidence also suggests a similarly close link between projected house price falls from the peak of the Blair bubble and the growing unpopularity of the Brown government (*Observer*, September 21, 2008). It is as if, having once ridden the wave of the bubble to claim competence in macroeconomic management, governments must then accept that perceptions of their competence will be undermined as soon as confidence in the house price bubble evaporates. From New Labour's perspective, it appears as though it learned rather too well the lessons from the Conservatives' crash. It has sought to avoid replicating the failures of interest rate control which put paid to the previous house price bubble at the end of the 1980s. It has done so by introducing clear elements of extraeconomic support against macroeconomic disturbances originating in domestic policy and leading to significant interest rate rises.

However, this on its own – indeed, *any* degree of extraeconomic support against macroeconomic disturbance on its own – is not necessarily enough to render a house price bubble stable. The speculative dimension inherent in all house price bubbles sees to that. While a faltering macroeconomic position can lead to housing market distress via increased interest rates, the causal relationship between the two can just as easily work in the opposite direction in the absence of any noticeable change in the interest rate stance. If confidence in the housing market temporarily dries up – as with the confidence crisis which is evident at the time of writing due to the fallout from the intensification of the credit crunch – this can have a pronounced negative macroeconomic effect even in the context of interest rate reductions. It is noticeable that the Bank of England's interest rate decisions, ever since the onset of the credit crunch in the summer of 2007, have been markedly more lax than strict adherence to its inflation target would have warranted (Hay, 2008). The economics of the two crash episodes are notably different, even if politically they ultimately prove to usher in the same effect in the form of a change in government.

In other words, there is more than one way for house price bubbles to deflate. They can fall prey to a weakening macroeconomic position when a sudden tightening of domestic credit is used as a corrective for general price inflation. This is the outcome that extraeconomic support for macroeconomic stability is designed to overcome. Irrespective of the success of introducing such support, however, house price bubbles can also fall prey to exogenous shocks which are unrelated to domestic macroeconomic conditions. The ongoing impact on British house prices from the world credit crunch and its associated dynamics of banking sector distress seems to fit this latter scenario.

These, then, are the analytical parameters of the argument that I will employ in the rest of the chapter as a means of comparing the content of the two most recent British house price bubbles. The later bubble appears to stand out from its predecessor insofar as it would seem to enjoy additional sources of extraeconomic protection. This is what lends the later bubble the impression that its continuation has been consciously thought through as a matter of government strategy. New Labour's efforts to enforce agential change in the constitution of people as monetary conservatives help to institutionalize the macroeconomic conditions consistent with the continuation of the bubble. At the same time, though, it has been unable to do anything to protect the bubble from exogenous shocks originating from within the world credit system.

(1) The housing market superportfolio that developed bubble features in the late 1980s experienced very little, if any, extraeconomic protection designed to shelter it from instability in the macroeconomic regime. In the main, the extraeconomic impacts on pricing trends were limited to the way in which the ideological basis of Thatcherism had permeated everyday life. This in itself was a far from inconsequential matter, as it had resulted in the widespread incorporation of individuals into the practices of popular capitalism, as sustained by the ideological imagery

surrounding the notion of "ownership" (e.g., Gamble, 1988; Hall, 1983). However, the principles of popular capitalism, on their own, provided no defense against the adverse price effects on the housing market super-portfolio of the interest rate rises that occurred in the late 1980s. The housing market boom had been activated as a consequence of financial liberalization, but the liberalizing trend itself made house prices more susceptible to the turndown in macroeconomic conditions.

(2) By contrast, the extraeconomic protection for the British housing market bubble of the 2000s appears to be much better developed as a means of creating macroeconomic conditions suited to its continuation. This serves merely to highlight just what a political problem for Gordon Brown and for New Labour falling house prices have become. The housing market superportfolio associated with the later bubble drew sustenance from the ideology of homeownership, just like the earlier one. But this was also augmented by a more coercive mechanism linked to state retreat in the provision of welfare-enhancing resources for facilitating future consumption possibilities. The release of state-sponsored transfer payments to people in old age could once be relied upon to cover the larger proportion of consumption needs at that time of life, with bank-based savings covering the remainder. However, reductions in the value of the state pension, coupled with the increasing demand for the individual to assume responsibility for the costs of care in old age, have increasingly rendered redundant this model of welfare (e.g., Pierson, 1998). In its place, the Labour government has championed the move toward a new asset-based model of welfare (e.g., HM Treasury, 2000; HM Treasury, 2003). The aim of such a move is to encourage individuals to invest in assets at a point in the life cycle when current income is more than enough to sustain current consumption needs. On the proviso that these investments are in strongly performing assets, they can then be cashed out as an expanded pool of savings to meet consumption needs in old age when current income is insufficient to do so. The housing market was used throughout New Labour's first ten years in power as the primary means for securing such assets.

In effect, what has been created is a "two-dimensional superportfolio," in which one dimension relates to the serial correlation of asset-based wealth held in the housing market and the other dimension relates to the serial correlation of house prices themselves. The integration of the housing market into the welfare model links one household's ability to support their own consumption in old age to other households' ability to do likewise, at least insofar as all are attempting to expand their asset-based wealth through homeownership. As such, it should be clear just how much is at stake for the Brown government at the time of writing, as confidence in the prevailing price structure of the British housing market continues to ebb on the back of a record one-year price fall (BBC News, January 6, 2009). The whole of the government's program of welfare reform is now increasingly dependent on reproducing a stable and predictable pricing trajectory on the housing market. If house prices experience the kind of wholesale collapse currently being predicted for 2009–11, then its strategy for incorporating people into an asset-based system of welfare looks unlikely to be successful.

The integration of the housing market into the welfare model acts as an extra line of defense for house prices, but only in certain circumstances. It does nothing to lessen the susceptibility of house prices to exogenous shocks whose origins lie in the world credit system. It offers protection only against the interest rate rises that deflate housing bubbles through the temporary tightening of domestic credit conditions. The increasing entrenchment of the second dimension of the later housing market superportfolio makes it much less likely that social conditions will arise which subsequently lead to a change in domestic monetary policy of this nature. In general, sharp interest rate rises occur after a period of loose monetary policy, and this in turn tends to follow prior popular political mobilization to an expansionary macroeconomic policy. However, the move to a system of asset-based welfare makes this type of political mobilization, other things being equal, much less likely.

Given an appropriate degree of financial education, those people with savings invested in assets will know that the future value of their wealth holdings will be jeopardized by the interest rate response to previous periods of loose monetary policy. As such, it is to be expected that they will resist mobilization to such a policy in the first place. The very act of holding assets as a means of financing future consumption renders individuals increasingly open to political pressures for reconstituting themselves as monetary conservatives. Should they act upon these pressures in any widespread manner then the social conditions which lead to subsequent interest rate rises are unlikely to arise. As such, the macroeconomic conditions which create adverse impacts on the trajectory of house prices are less likely to be forthcoming than in the absence of societal demands for strict anti-inflationary policies.

The extent to which individuals have been reconstituted as monetary conservatives is reflected in the degree to which underlying macroeconomic conditions support the continuation of bubble dynamics in house prices (even in today's context of evident house price falls). In turn, it also reflects the prior extent to which the housing market has been incorporated within the model of welfare. Sections 3.2 and 3.3 seek to shed light on these propositions by examining the two most recent British housing market bubbles and by showing how the first was unrelated to changing norms of welfare provision but the second was integrally embedded in such changes.

3.2 The 1980s bubble: Boom and crash under the conservatives

When the Conservatives came to power in 1979, the structure of housing tenure in Britain was divided pretty much along class lines. Homeownership was concentrated amongst the middle classes and local authority renting amongst the working classes (e.g., Wilding, 1997). As James Cronin argues (2004, 209), there was a noticeable lack of mobility between the two housing classes because both relied to a considerable extent on the state to secure their tenure. The rents on local authority housing were directly subsidized, and the widespread use of mortgage interest tax relief provided a similar degree of subsidization, albeit less directly, for owner-occupiers. The pattern of state expenditures thus entrenched individuals into particular housing classes on the assumption that housing was a merit good associated with social rights of citizenship and should therefore be integrated into state provision of a minimum standard of living (Malpass, 1996, 463). The reforms to housing policy introduced by the Thatcher government were designed specifically to alleviate "entry" constraints affecting owner-occupation and thus to create genuine market conditions for homeownership (Ford and Wilcox, 1998, 625). In effect, they were intended to change the whole concept of housing from a merit good to an individualized investment vehicle capable of generating private wealth (cf. Mortensen and Seabrooke; Broome in this volume).

On their own, though, the reforms do little to explain either the subsequent trajectory of house prices in the mid-1980s or the specific content of the house price bubble that ensued. These came about as the unintended consequence of setting the new policy within the context of extensive changes to the financial system, all of which promoted widespread liberalization (cf. Tranøy in this volume). It was these changes that fundamentally altered conditions on the supply side of the mortgage lending market, relaxing entry constraints for many families who had previously been financially excluded from owner-occupation. It is the creation of more and more potential homeowners as a result of a large increase in available mortgage credit that represents the most important factor in the general upward trajectory in house prices in this period.

The Thatcher government's financial liberalization program had two main goals. The first was to undermine the embedded monopoly interests that had developed within the financial economy by exposing them to the disciplining effects of price competition. The second was to ensure that the free working of the price system allowed sufficient encouragement to financial entrepreneurs to introduce innovative investment products. Both of these impacts were apparent in the restructuring of the supply side of the British mortgage lending market in the 1980s.

(1) The Thatcher government overturned the privileged position of the building societies in providing personal finance for house purchases. In the early 1970s, the Heath government had granted cartel rights in the mortgage lending market to the Building Societies Association in return for the latter pegging the mortgage rate below the prevailing rate of interest (e.g., Grady and Weale, 1986). The cartelized regime created the conditions for relatively cheap mortgages, but such benefits came at the cost of rationing the number of mortgages that could be made available. Thatcherite policy had changed all this by the mid-1980s, most notably by lifting restrictions on the retail banks that had previously prevented them from operating mortgage lending businesses (e.g., Buckle and Thompson, 1995).

Three effects ensued for the housing market. First, the deregulation process vastly increased households' choice of mortgage provider. The entry of banks onto the traditional terrain of the building societies resulted in less rationing of mortgage credit. Second, greater price competition in the mortgage lending market increased the number of people who could afford to buy any particular house that came available on the open market. The heightened level of mortgage credit consequently fed through into a higher general level of house prices. Third, the introduction of genuine price competition into the mortgage lending market increasingly tightened the link between the mortgage rate and the underlying rate of interest. Mortgage providers were able to recycle their capital within world markets, but this tied their business to world interest rates, and the success of their operations thus became dependent on the differential between world and British interest rates. When British interest rates went up relative to the world rate, mortgage lenders were able to defend their business only by passing on the interest rate rises to borrowers in the mortgage market.

(2) At the same time, the scope of feasible mortgage lending strategies widened as a result of the effects of a new process of mortgage securitization. Under such a process, the lender's exposure to a number of borrowers is bundled together into a single asset. The purchase of the mortgage-based asset, usually by a private equity fund created especially for the purpose, is financed by what was always marketed and sold as a relatively low-risk security constructed against the initial borrowers successfully meeting their mortgage repayments. The probability of a mass default on repayments is significantly lower than the probability of a default on any single repayment. During its pre-credit crunch heyday, the process of mortgage securitization consequently allowed mortgage lenders to increase their exposure to the lending market without having to internalize a commensurable increase in risk (e.g., Langley, 2006). The banks cannot avoid credit risk altogether – as the effects of the credit crunch demonstrate with gusto – but the profits they made from transaction fees in the securitization process temporarily offset an element of that risk and enhanced their overall balance sheet position for as long as the good times held.

In Britain, the process of mortgage securitization has historically concentrated on the repayment schedules of "prime loan" borrowers rather than what has now become the famous and often mythologized U.S. subprime borrower (Council of Mortgage Lenders, 2000). Yet the very essence of the securitization technique is to shift the whole basis of what is presumed to be a "marginal" lending case in both the prime and the nonprime sector. Securitization therefore provides entry into all segments of the mortgage lending market for people who would otherwise be treated as unacceptable credit risks for that particular segment. It thus expands the pool of potential homebuyers at a faster rate than additions to the supply of housing stock come onstream (see Schwartz in this volume for the similarities to the U.S. experience). This has the effect of feeding upward price pressures in the housing market as a whole.

The combination of mortgage securitization techniques and the introduction of genuine price competition amongst mortgage providers fundamentally altered prevailing supply side conditions in the mortgage lending market in Britain in the 1980s. While the building societies' previous cartel had led, in effect, to the rationing of new mortgages, the overall effects of financial deregulation created equally clear conditions of oversupply (Taylor and Bradley, 1994, 369). A house price boom ensued as mortgage providers overlent to an increasingly buoyant housing market in the context of constrained supply of new housing stock (Wood and Capie, 1996, 21).

The results were dramatic. Adjusting for the effects of inflation, real house prices almost doubled between 1983 and 1989. From 1985 to 1988, the annual average percentage price rise of all houses was never less than double digits and, for 1988 alone, the figure was 24% (Malpass, 1996, 465). Such rises made house purchases and, by implication, mortgage borrowing increasingly unaffordable as a proportion of income, but this occurred at exactly the moment that ever-greater numbers of people were being enticed to enter the market – ironically, by the allure of those selfsame higher house prices.

This was a house price bubble created specifically as a market phenomenon based on changing conditions of mortgage lending. Serial correlation in house prices emerged from the reform of the supply side of the mortgage lending market, but there was no attempt to forge an increasingly interdependent relationship between the trend in house prices and internal changes to the welfare state. Throughout the British house price bubble of the 1980s, the emergent housing market superportfolio enjoyed almost nothing by way of welfare-related extraeconomic protection against a faltering macroeconomic position. There was only a one-dimensional, not a two-dimensional, housing market superportfolio in this period. The Thatcher government operated its macroeconomic and housing market policies as distinct entities.

Being a purely market-based phenomenon, the 1980s house price bubble was inherently susceptible to changes in market conditions emerging from instability in the macroeconomic regime. These duly arose. The Lawson Boom of the mid-1980s – so-called after the Chancellor of the Exchequer, Nigel Lawson – occurred against the backdrop of convergence between British and world interest rates. In 1985, this pushed mortgage rates below 10% for the first time in more than a decade, consequently providing an extra boost for individuals to enter the mortgage market, either as first-time buyers or in the hope of trading up their position on the housing market.

Yet, as David Smith has argued (1992, 166), British monetary policy was essentially anchorless at this time. The credit-fueled consumption boom of the Lawson years stoked retail price inflation. Having fallen from a high of more than 20% in the early 1980s to below 8% as house prices really began to take off in the mid-1980s, inflation climbed back well into double digits as the decade ended. Lacking an alternative for suppressing inflationary tendencies, the government had little choice but to respond by raising British interest rates above world market levels (e.g., Pollard, 1992, 386–8). The ensuing rise in interest rates triggered accompanying rises in mortgage rates, as the two were now closely tied as a result of the government's concerted attempts to introduce genuine price competition into the mortgage lending market.

Unsurprisingly, the combination of increasing retail price inflation, increasing mortgage rates, and then overall economic recession proved to be a destabilizing cocktail for house prices. They fell increasingly sharply as the recession took hold, propelling the economy into an increasingly vicious cycle of recession and house price falls. Every reduction in house prices increased the real burden of credit repayments as a proportion of income for indebted households. This led to cutbacks in consumption. But every reduction in consumption deepened the recession and, with it, deepened also the falling confidence that was already adversely affecting house prices. Average house prices fell by around one-fourth between 1989 and 1992 (Audas and MacKay, 1997, 869).

The people worst affected were those who had taken out new mortgages most recently in an attempt to improve their homeowner status. As a reflection of the dramatic surge in house prices from 1985 to 1988, in general they held the highest value mortgages as a proportion of current income. When the overall effect of negative equity peaked in the third quarter of 1992, 99% of households so affected had taken out a mortgage between 1988 and 1991. In total, this amounted to more than one in five homebuyers during that period (Gentle et al., 1994, 191). The introduction of genuine price competition into the mortgage lending market saturated it with potential supply and, coupled with the effects of securitization, persuaded many lenders to issue mortgages to support house purchases that were backed by little, or even no, cash down payment. The households most protected from the experience of negative equity were those who had made the largest cash down payments out of accumulated savings on their house purchase. Two-thirds of house purchases with a 100% mortgage advance between 1988 and 1991 led to the experience of negative equity by the third quarter of 1992. This figure fell to around one-third for house purchases backed by a 10% deposit and only one in a thousand for house purchases backed by a 30% deposit (ibid., 192).

The negative equity trap was responsible for further chasing house prices downward and, as confidence in the pricing structure of the market as a whole eroded, serial downside correlation ensued. In both phases of the bubble, the prices of individual houses were affected most obviously by the average price of houses in the market overall. The most important feature of the housing market superportfolio in this period was that its internal characteristics and pricing trajectory were shaped almost solely by institutional changes to the supply side of the mortgage lending market. The fact that there was no clearly visible extraeconomic dimension to the superportfolio made serial downside correlation in house prices just as likely as serial upside correlation. Throughout its life, the bubble remained susceptible to credit shocks arising from domestic macroeconomic conditions and, in particular, to the interest rate rises that tend to accompany domestic macroeconomic disturbances.

3.3   The 2000s bubble: Boom and crash under New Labour

Looking simply at the trajectory of house prices, the most recent British housing market bubble replicates many of the features of its predecessor. Indeed, the price increases for the most extreme year of the earlier bubble, 1988, are almost directly mirrored year-on-year for the three-year period between 2002 and 2004 (Coates, 2005, 171). Since that time a noticeable reduction in the rate of increase has occurred, to the point at which reports at the end of September 2008 revealed an annual fall in excess of 12%, and reports at the end of December 2008 revealed an annual fall of 16% (BBC News, October 2, 2008; January 6, 2009). No industry insider seems to believe at the time of writing that a credible case can be made that the 25% fall in the Major crash will not be exceeded this time.

None of these apparent echoes of the former situation mean, however, that the two bubble experiences are generically the same, despite the fact that both arose from a political context emphasizing housing as a means of accumulating private wealth rather than as a social right. The earlier one was a purely market-based phenomenon, while the continuation of the later one has been tied much more closely to matters of political strategy. The core substantive features of the earlier one were focused on changes in the supply side of the mortgage lending market, while those of the later one were focused on changes in the demand side of the mortgage lending market.

The negative equity of the 1980s was experienced most acutely amongst borrowers who had purchased houses on the basis of very little or even no cash deposit. The bubble was created in the first place on the supply side of the mortgage lending market, but its downside price phase was initiated through a seizure on the demand side of that market, as asset-poor borrowers were exposed by falling house prices. By comparison, New Labour's designs for a system of asset-based welfare have offered a degree of protection for the demand side of the mortgage lending market. The current difficulties have arisen instead as a result of the world credit crunch having undermined the prior strength of the supply side of that market. The government's wish for individuals to become active asset-managers emphasizes the advantages of entering the housing market from the basis of already having accumulated assets. The surest defense against experiencing negative equity when house prices turn down arises from the buffer that comes with having paid a cash deposit on the house. The closer that the mortgage advance comes to 100% of the original purchase price, the smaller is the required decline in price before the household is subjected to negative equity. Savings thus become significant.

Toward the end of its first term the New Labour government set itself the task of facilitating saving in an attempt to encourage people to create an asset base for themselves (e.g., HM Treasury, 2001a; 2001b). This has particularly been the case among the low income families who usually those that lack assets. The policy has been enacted through a combination of moral directive ("do not be responsible for passing on impeded life chances to your children by depriving them of an inherited asset base"), fiscal incentives ("why bother to pay taxes on a proportion of income that can be invested tax-free in special savings accounts?"), and government intervention ("if you can begin to build an asset base for someone previously denied access to one then the government will match your savings out of the public purse"). Alan Finlayson attributes New Labour's savings policy to "a social democratic paternalism" (2008, 98), one whose specific character is aimed at reconstituting the outlooks, values, and economic subjectivities of people who were previously distanced from the savings habit (HM Treasury, 2001b, 7; HM Treasury/Inland Revenue, 2003, 22). The state under New Labour does little to reward the passive recipients of social rights, focusing instead on trying to support active individuals, incentivizing and even coercing that activity if necessary.

Both the Savings Gateway and the Child Trust Fund – in combination the centerpiece of New Labour's savings policy – contain within them coercive mechanisms designed to attack a political culture in which individuals consider themselves to be the passive recipients of welfare rights (Finlayson, 2008, 96). One aspect of this has been the introduction of programs aimed not only at increasing everyday financial literacy but also at using that literacy training as a means specifically of adapting more individualized understandings of the self. The establishment of the Child Trust Fund has been accompanied by placing financial literacy on the National Curriculum in British schools (HM Treasury, 2001a, 19). As part of their formal schooling children are now taught how to manage their own assets, what they should expect to earn as a return on their assets, and how they should proceed to spend their accumulated wealth in a prudent, asset-enhancing fashion. The schoolroom is therefore being used as a means of formally constituting perceptions of the self as a saver, an investor, and an active participant in an asset-owning society. Something very similar is envisioned in the Saving Gateway policy, but this time it is the workplace that provides the opportunity for specially organized seminars that are designed to impart life skills of enhanced financial literacy. Importantly, these are all activities which place people – cognitively if not necessarily physically – in a purely individualized environment. There, they are asked to imagine doing only what is best for themselves and their immediate relations. They are consequently abstracted from cognitive habits which emphasize the collective provision of state welfare and they are encouraged to concentrate instead on accepting personal responsibility for meeting consumption needs in old age.

Learning how to be a responsible saver is envisioned as a family affair (HM Treasury, 2001b, 16). The Treasury pushed for the establishment of the Adult Financial Literacy Advisory Group, which was founded in 2000 to report to the then Department for Education and Skills. It was to be used as a means of ensuring that a culture of saving was integrated into every aspect of the government's active welfare program through enabling lifelong learning of a financial nature (e.g., Froud et al., 2007b). The Treasury also introduced the New Deal reforms, not only to provide a route back into work for parents but also to promote an understanding of how best they might invest the proceeds that arise from undertaking paid work (e.g., Waldfogel, 2004; Sunley et al., 2006).

The image that the government had in mind at the outset of the policy was of intergenerational financial learning in which the whole family joins together to ensure that all generations are able to take care of their own future consumption needs (HM Treasury, 2000, 23; 2001a, 18; HM Treasury/Inland Revenue, 2003, 10). The penalty for failing to do so is to relegate the household to a position in which it has inadequate cover to maintain existing consumption levels throughout the life cycle. The New Labour governments of Blair and Brown have thus been prepared to embrace the qualitative limits imposed on the welfare state by their Thatcherite predecessors and to deepen the disciplinary effects designed to ensure that individuals accommodate themselves to those limits. This is likely to lead to more and more people displaying individualized political values.

Of course, such values have multiple roots, so it is highly unlikely that there will be a simple one-to-one relationship between the degree of asset ownership and political attitudes. But it is also largely unthinkable that no effect on policy preferences will be forthcoming in situations in which individuals have both a greater value of assets to defend and a greater reason to wish to defend them because of the declining real worth of the state pension and the need to make good the ensuing deficit through personal wealth. Put simply, if individuals have more assets then they are likely to want to defend them politically. Pre-credit crunch, homeownership dominated wealth holdings in Britain to such an extent that the defense of asset-based wealth was, to a large degree, the defense of house prices. But the prevailing superportfolio of house prices can only be given protection against the effects of macroeconomic instability on domestic credit conditions, and only then through the institutionalization of a conservative monetary policy. As the Treasury has argued (HM Treasury, 2000, 11): "People need to be able to save without fear that the value of their savings will be eroded by rapidly rising prices [i.e., consumer prices]." It is likely, then, that the incorporation of individuals into a system of asset-based welfare centered on increasing house prices will facilitate the political remaking of individuals as monetary conservatives. It is also likely that, once constituted in this way, individuals will be inclined to punish any government that has been seen to preside over house price falls, no matter what the true source of the price instability. The individual politics of the bubble therefore look as though they will have a direct conditioning effect on the electoral politics of the likely crash.

Responsibility for policing the policy regime that reproduces inflated house prices has therefore been passed on from government to society. This is consistent with the prevailing idea that housing is in any case a means of accumulating private wealth rather than a right drawn against the state. New Labour has continually asked to be judged on its success in creating a low-cost credit environment in which interest rates are held in check by credible anti-inflationary performance (e.g., HM Treasury, 2006). That success has been difficult to question. The interest rate record of New Labour's first ten years in office was a definite spur for activity on the British housing market.

Yet, in delegating responsibility to society for protecting the structure of house prices, New Labour perhaps deserves the blame that opinion polls currently suggest it is getting for the fallout of the credit crunch on British house prices. Many people have willingly bought into the idea of reconstituting themselves politically as monetary conservatives in the interests of defending the value of the assets they have tied up in their home. They believe that they have kept their side of the bargain, but still they are seeing a fall in the price of their home. In their own minds they are entirely free of culpability in the price fall, because they have merely done what New Labour advised them to do in order to keep house price growth rolling along. Perhaps understandably in these circumstances the blame has been passed on to the government for having popularized in the first place a believable but ultimately false promise about constant expansions of housing market wealth. The housing market will almost certainly be a beneficiary of the remaking of political subjectivities in line with monetary conservatism, but only when the sole threat to house prices has its origins in domestic macroeconomic conditions. It can never be enough on its own to protect the housing market superportfolio against all exogenous shocks. When such shocks do arise, the government's reputation is likely to be tarnished because of the selfsame process of reconstituting people as monetary conservatives.

The likely politics of the crash show that the housing market situation under New Labour is rather more complex than a pure price bubble originating solely from the internal dynamics of the supply side of the mortgage lending market. The extraeconomic dimension associated with the integration of the housing market into a system of asset-based welfare is every bit as important for our understanding of the upward price phase as its economic dimension. The current situation could not have arisen in the way it has in the absence of the government's concerted attempts to change the model of welfare provision in Britain to one that emphasizes the personal ownership of assets. The integration of the housing market into the welfare model was the most important facet of the recent British house price bubble, and it is also likely to be the really big story of the politics of the crash as the bubble subsequently unwinds.

Conclusion

I have not tried to second guess the likely bottom of the current downside trend in British house prices. Instead I have sought to compare the two most recent experiences of house price bubbles in Britain in order to isolate their distinctive features as a prelude to discussing the politics of British housing market crashes. The key difference between the two housing market superportfolios lies in the introduction into the latter of a noticeable interdependence between the housing market and welfare reform. The family home is increasingly seen as an investment for the future, and this perception has been appropriated in attempts to turn people from passive recipients of welfare rights into active managers of assets. Within this context, serial downside correlation in house prices is less likely now than in the 1980s as a reaction to monetary policy correctives to macroeconomic instability. However, it is *only* as a reaction to such events that housing market crashes seem less likely. The British housing market remains as vulnerable as it ever has been to exogenous shocks emanating from the world credit system.

The housing market is today caught in a debilitating scissors effect that merely serves to multiply its vulnerability to financial contagion spreading from the banks. The banks are demonstrating very little trust in one another having come clean about the true state of the balance sheet mess they have created through exposure to systematic overlending of mortgage finance. They are acting as if it is rational to assume that there is no integrity at all in the interbank credit market. This has the result of making interbank borrowing much more expensive and, as the mortgage rate today reflects the ease with which interbank borrowing can be undertaken, mortgage repayment costs have been pushed up significantly. The daily costs of maintaining the home have therefore increased at exactly the time that falling confidence in the housing market as a whole has pushed down average house prices by the largest annual fall on record – 15.9% – for 2008 (BBC News, January 6, 2009). Many homeowners have found that it is impractical for them to try to sell a house that is becoming increasingly difficult to pay for because its market value has fallen below the outstanding mortgage debt on the original purchase. In effect this traps them in a spiral of having to find an ever greater proportion of their take-home pay simply to meet the repayment schedule of a house that is destroying their accumulated asset wealth as its price falls.

The nature of this experience can be placed alongside that of the Major crash to be reflected back onto the important debate between Jim Kemeny and Francis Castles which is outlined in Schwartz and Seabrooke's introductory chapter to this volume. Castles' position (1998) that the housing market has been reconfigured politically as "social policy by other means" appears at first glance to be confirmed by my study of the growing interdependence between the housing market and welfare provision in Britain. However, it fails to capture adequately the details of the recent British experience. There is more to the changing relationship between the housing market and the welfare state in Britain than that increasingly they are functional equivalents. The incorporation of the housing market as a *constitutive* feature of both the welfare system *and of the mindset of people operating within that system* suggests that the relationship between the two is more integrally formed than Castles' position allows. Crucially, it involves changing the perceptions and the political preferences of voters. This brings me closer to the work of Kemeny (1980), but my analysis does no more than offer partial confirmation of his thesis. Kemeny believed that the changing subjectivities of homeowning voters restricted the scope of the welfare state via the tax system, but the causality I have in mind operates instead via preferences for increasingly conservative monetary policies.

Yet, this is not to claim that either Castles or Kemeny is wrong on the central premise about private homeownership on which they agree. The recent British experience is clearly cast in the image of their assertion that the money which individuals need to set aside for down payments and mortgage costs impacts adversely on the likely success of trying to sell politically the merits of a fully funded state-sponsored system of welfare. This is the "welfare trade-off" described by Schwartz and Seabrooke in the introductory chapter. Indeed, in the British case, the welfare trade-off was noticeably tightened at each stage at which the most recent bubble ratcheted up both affordability and accessibility constraints. The Royal Institution of Chartered Surveyors (2007) has shown that the generic affordability of private housing stock in Britain at the moment at which the credit crunch struck made private homeownership less accessible than at any time in the country's history. At that point, more money had to be set aside out of take-home pay than ever before simply to service the up-front costs associated with house purchases and to meet mortgage repayments thereafter. With more money than ever before being used in such a way, this led to less money than ever before being available for taxes to pay for public welfare systems.

The New Labour government might not have been responsible in its entirety for deliberately engineering the onset of the most recent British house price bubble. But it certainly staked much on its continuation. New Labour's ability to guide the economy successfully through a period of welfare reform appears to be dependent upon the vitality of the housing market, as does its future political popularity. From the perspective of writing this piece in January 2009, the increasing rate of decline in British house prices spells trouble for the government in both of these respects. By the time that the banking distress occasioned by the world credit crunch finally reaches its nadir, the effect on house prices is likely to be qualitatively more significant than anything previously experienced. The politics of the likely crash therefore have the potential to be of similar proportions unless successfully managed by the government.

4
The Politics of Capital Gains: Building an Asset-Based Society in New Zealand

André Broome

Introduction

Examining changes in varieties of residential capitalism is important for understanding broader changes in financial behavior, which can have a significant impact on individuals' political choices as well as a country's economic performance. In addition, when domestic property bubbles burst this can generate severe consequences for the stability of the international financial system, as became evident when the end of excessive real estate speculation in several East Asian economies contributed to the Asian financial crisis in 1997–8 (Sheng and Kirinpanu, 2000) and as we have seen with the recent subprime crisis (Renaud and Kim, 2007, 9–11). In short, changes in different countries' systems of residential capitalism can engender far-reaching political effects at the national level and the international level, as well as at the more immediate level of people's everyday lives.

This chapter examines the rapid changes to New Zealand's housing finance system during the 1980s and 1990s, and explores the connections between the evolution of residential capitalism in New Zealand and broader changes in the country's domestic political economy. Efforts to build an asset-based society in New Zealand had a significant impact on the country's tradition of state support for the expansion of homeownership among the population as a social right, rather than simply as a means to generate financial wealth through capital gains. While older age groups believe that owning a house rather than renting will help to establish a family's financial security across generations (see Dupois and Thorns, 1996), these changes generated negative social consequences

with respect to intergenerational equity while shifts in everyday financial norms interacted with formal neoliberal policy changes to produce
unintended outcomes. Because New Zealand has often been held up as
a model of reform for other countries around the world, especially small
European economies, studying the unintended consequences of neoliberal reforms in New Zealand is more instructive than simply looking at
what, why, and how specific policy changes were introduced.

The chapter proceeds as follows. In Section 4.1, I briefly examine the
historical context of New Zealand's "homeowning democracy," and
how this was transformed with the wide-ranging financial reforms
undertaken during New Zealand's neoliberal economic policy revolution during the 1980s and 1990s. In Section 4.2, I explore how radical
changes in the country's housing finance system and the emergence of
new financial norms drove changes in homeownership patterns in New
Zealand, which contributed to the worsening of the negative effects of
broader neoliberal policy changes upon low and lower-middle income
groups in society and altered the life chances of younger groups of
New Zealanders seeking access to the property market. In Section 4.3,
I investigate the emergence of what I term a *housing bubble–monetary
policy nexus* in New Zealand during the country's most recent property
boom, which has both constrained the policy flexibility available to
today's policymakers and further worsened the chances for would-be
first-time property buyers to accumulate wealth and gain future financial security through homeownership. In Section 4.4, I discuss the
political and economic impact of the end of New Zealand's property
boom in 2007–08, and briefly explore the country's response to the
global credit crunch. The Conclusion draws together the potential lessons of the New Zealand case for other small economies undergoing
financial liberalization in their distinct systems of residential capitalism. Here I argue that while efforts to build an asset-based society in
New Zealand have enabled greater access to mortgage credit for middle
and higher income earners, the politics of capital gains has also contributed to locking out low and lower-middle income households as well as
younger households from the property market, or has resulted in first-
time home buyers taking on increased levels of debt and financial risk
in pursuit of the "New Zealand dream" of owning one's own home.

4.1 The politics of financial reform in New Zealand

Domestic financial change is not simply a matter of enacting new formal rules that alter a state's policy settings. To be successful, financial

policy changes must also engender a shift in the everyday norms that guide people's financial behavior, which can often lead to unintended outcomes (Broome, 2009). During the past two decades New Zealand's system of residential capitalism has shifted away from the notion of housing as a social right (Ferguson, 1994) toward investment in housing as a means to generate wealth. Combined with full employment policies and universal welfare provision prior to the 1980s, broad access to home ownership in New Zealand that was facilitated by state intervention in the housing market formed the bedrock of the country's implicit social contract and was an important source of household savings and financial security. The ideal of owning one's home has remained a powerful aspiration in New Zealand society. As one observer recently noted in a report for the Centre for Housing Research, "Home ownership remains an integral, and possibly *the* central component of New Zealand culture," with the maintenance of high levels of home ownership in New Zealand an objective that bridges the country's political divide (Morrison, 2007). What has radically changed over the last two decades, however, are the institutional structures that previously helped to transform the ideal of home ownership in New Zealand into a realizable goal for people of almost all income and age groups, with the percentage of households owning their home declining from 73.8% in 1991 to 66.9% in 2006 (Statistics New Zealand, 1998, 2007).

New Zealand is usually categorized as a liberal welfare state with limited social housing policies to protect the least well-off households (Allen, 2006, 258; Doling, 1997, 136). While state support to expand home ownership in New Zealand declined after the 1970s, this had previously contributed to improving housing affordability through maintaining low mortgage interest rates and enlarging the supply of housing (Ferguson, 1992, 233). Rather than focusing primarily on the provision of public housing, New Zealand governments sought instead to expand private home ownership throughout the population by providing cheap credit to new home owners and subsidizing the building industry. For instance, the first Labour government elected in 1935 channeled easy credit to the housing sector through the establishment of the State Advances Corporation in 1936 (Holmes, 2004, 9). State intervention in the housing market under successive center-left Labour and center-right National governments caused a massive expansion in homeownership rates from 50.5% in 1936 to 68% in 1971 (Murphy, 2000, 395). With bureaucratic responsibility for the country's housing finance system consolidated in the Housing Corporation of New Zealand (HCNZ), which was set up in 1974, the government initially continued to be a major player in the provision of mortgage funds, with subsidized loans to low income and lower-middle income households through the HCNZ accounting for 38% of the mortgage market in 1978 (McLeay, 1992). In addition to government support for home ownership, the HCNZ built and managed publicly owned rental housing, which was allocated on the basis of need and comprised approximately 6% of the residential housing stock in the 1980s and 5% during the 1990s (McLeay, 1984, 87; Sheridan et al., 2002, 345).

Homeownership simultaneously endows individuals with a bundle of legal rights, social status, and independence, as well as economic benefits such as a stock of savings and future financial security (Castles, 1998, 16; Conley and Gifford, 2006, 56; Doling, 1997, 152). While it has usually received less attention from political economy scholars than the big ticket changes to the country's macroeconomic policy settings during the 1980s and 1990s, the subsequent evolution of New Zealand's housing finance system stimulated important changes in the distribution of wealth throughout New Zealand society, and especially between different age groups and income groups. It also further advanced and helped to lock in fundamental changes in everyday financial norms, which were spurred by the transformation of the policy mould that had shaped the economic agenda of successive New Zealand governments since the 1930s.

After the election of the fourth Labour government in New Zealand in 1984, the new government rapidly liberalized state controls on foreign exchange, the banking sector, wages, prices, and interest rates. Changes included the removal of restrictions on foreign borrowing by domestic financial institutions, allowing foreign-owned firms unfettered access to domestic capital markets, the elimination of controls on mortgage interest rates, the removal of credit guidelines for commercial banks, and the relaxation of bank reserve ratios. These reforms increased access to mortgage credit, intensified mortgage competition among private lenders, and expanded overseas borrowing to the point where New Zealand banks became more dependent on foreign credit than the commercial banks of any other OECD country (Stuart et al., 2004, 6–7). The key figure driving these reforms was Labour finance minister Roger Douglas, whose agenda for economic transformation became widely known as "Rogernomics."

One particularly important institutional innovation undertaken by the Labour government was the enactment of new legislation in 1989 to govern the objectives and actions of the country's central bank, the Reserve Bank of New Zealand. The key change was the establishment of an explicit inflation target for the Reserve Bank – a world first – which was initially set at 0–2% (later broadened in 1996 to 0–3%, and altered again in 2002 to a 1–3% target). With this significant change from past monetary practice policymakers sought to entrench price stability as the primary goal of monetary policy by raising the credibility costs associated with any future attempt by a government to loosen monetary policy for political gain (Dalziel, 1997; Evans et al., 1996, 1863–4).

To applause from financial markets and international institutions such as the International Monetary Fund (Broome and Seabrooke, 2007, 586–7), the country's political leaders had quickly moved New Zealand from being one of the most "closed" market economies in the world to becoming one of the world's most open liberal market economies, which was often held up as a model of rapid neoliberal economic policy reform for other states to follow. Following the meltdown of the fourth Labour government and Labour's subsequent rout at the 1990 election, the center-right National Party held power through a series of majority and minority administrations until Labour was reelected to government in 1999. In contrast to the National Party's traditional policy conservatism, however, this period of National government initially involved a further intensification of neoliberal economic policy reforms during 1990 to 1992 spearheaded by finance minister Ruth Richardson. Her set of far-reaching labor market, housing, state ownership, and social policy changes, popularly termed "Ruthanasia," prompted widespread public dismay at the breach of the National Party's preelection promises and its uncharacteristically radical approach to state-driven economic change, and served to strengthen public support for major changes to the electoral system to constrain the capacity of future governments to drive through rapid policy changes against popular opposition (James, 1998, 20–1).

4.2   Creating an asset-based society

Every economic revolution has its winners and losers. In New Zealand's case, the neoliberal economic policy revolution of the 1980s and 1990s that radically altered the country's "cradle-to-grave" welfare state, and decreased the allocative role of the state in the economy in general, generated extensive business failures as firms were allowed to "go to the wall." Combined with the prioritization of maintaining a tight monetary policy, this helped to stimulate historically high levels of unemployment, which reached 10.5% in 1991 (Brook Cowen, 1998, 345, 348). While housing in New Zealand was never entirely insulated from market forces, those who were shut out from the housing market had been supported by a universal welfare state (Allen, 2006, 258). However, the policy changes undertaken during the second half of the 1980s and the early 1990s served to intensify the commodification of the property market in New Zealand, at the same time as welfare policy shifted from universal provision to more targeted social support.

Crucial to the process of financial liberalization were efforts to diminish the government's influence over mortgage lending rates. By 1990, the HCNZ share of the mortgage market had dropped from 38% in 1978 to a mere 16.9% and HCNZ mortgages made up only 8.7% of new lending, loans which were increasingly restricted to low income households (McLeay, 1992). With commercial banks taking a much greater role in the provision of mortgage finance, their tighter lending criteria during the 1980s and early 1990s raised obstacles that low income households ineligible for HCNZ loans had to clear in order to purchase their own homes. This contributed to locking low income groups out of the property market and reflected a weakening of the long tradition of state support for expanding home ownership (Murphy, 2000, 396).

For middle and upper income households, however, access to credit expanded following the financial reforms of the mid-1980s and this helped to expand asset-based wealth in New Zealand. During the 1990s, commercial banks' methods for assessing creditworthiness were gradually relaxed, with the amount customers were able to borrow increasing from 75% of a home's value to 95% if the borrower purchased mortgage indemnity insurance (which protected banks if a property had to be sold at a value lower than the amount owing on a mortgage). Creditworthiness assessments also became more personalized, with banks approving higher repayment-to-income ratios for couples on average income without children compared with those with dependents (typically approximately 33% compared with around 25% in the late 1990s). Furthermore, because banks calculate mortgage repayment-to-income ratios in nominal terms without taking into account the rate of inflation, when lower inflation rates during the 1990s enabled decreases in nominal interest rates households were able to borrow much larger mortgages (Coleman, 2007, 5–6).

Following the election of the National Party government in 1990, the state's role in New Zealand's housing finance system shifted farther away from direct housing provision to income support. This was undertaken through the introduction of market-based rents in state-owned houses (with eligible tenants receiving financial assistance to pay higher rentals through an accommodation supplement) as well as the privatization of HCNZ mortgages (Murphy, 1996). The government's policy of shifting from direct provision of housing to providing supplementary payments for market-based rents was intended to create a greater degree of equivalence between state-owned housing and private rental accommodation, in order to widen household choice and end the "dependency" of low income groups on the state rental sector (see Thorns, 2000).

Overall, between November 1991 and January 1999 under the National Party government 27 tranches of mortgages were sold by HCNZ totaling NZ$2.4 billion in revenue, which made the sale of government-backed mortgages the second largest component of the National Party government's policy of privatizing state assets. The transfer of such a large volume of mortgages from the HCNZ to the private sector enabled commercial banks to expand their asset base at the same time as limiting the government's future role in the provision of mortgage finance. In particular, because HCNZ mortgagees had well established credit histories, the purchase of HCNZ mortgages helped to expand the lending portfolios of commercial banks while offering them stable returns from households that (at the time when their mortgages were sold) presented a low risk of default, because the initial risks involved with lending to low income earners had already been largely absorbed by HCNZ (Murphy, 2000, 396–7). Furthermore, while new mortgage lending by HCNZ totaled NZ$746 million in 1990, this had shrunk by 1996 to a paltry NZ$36 million in new loans (Murphy, 2000, 398).

These major policy changes enacted in such a short period of time combined to widen income inequality through the upward redistribution of income to the wealthiest members of New Zealand society. The downsizing of the state's role in the economy worsened the effects on the poor, with particularly negative consequences for employment levels, wages, and rates of home ownership (Rudd, 2005). As a result, average per capita income declined in real terms for the bottom 10% of the population by 8.71% between 1983–4 and 1995–6, while the per capita income of the top 10% increased over the same period by 26.48% (Dalziel, 2002, 44). These changes contributed to building an asset-based society for upper-middle and high income earners while restricting access for new entrants to the property market, both prompting individuals to delay home ownership until later in life and lowering the proportion of home ownership among younger age groups after they began to enter the property market. This produced a negative impact on intergenerational equity, thereby altering the traditional welfare trade-off for a Settler society (see the introductory chapter).

However, evidence compiled from census data also suggests that the trend in New Zealand has been for declining rates of home owner-ship across *all* age groups except for the oldest between 1991 and 2006 (Morrison, 2007, 45–7).

While the removal of financial controls during the 1980s broad-ened the growth of (highly selective) private credit, it also served to increase the cost of mortgages for lower income groups whose after-tax household incomes either remained static or declined in real terms. For instance, financial deregulation enabled interest rates to become posi-tive in real terms, whereas inflation-adjusted interest rates had mostly remained negative during the 1970s and the first half of the 1980s. While this had benefited upper income households with larger mort-gages, negative real interest rates also made it easier for lower income groups to pay off mortgage debt. With higher real interest rates and the need to purchase mortgage indemnity insurance in order to borrow a greater proportion of a property's value, lower income households were either priced out of the mortgage market or faced spending a higher proportion of their income on mortgage payments.

Until the mid-1980s, commercial banks had operated under strict lending criteria and often required would-be borrowers to establish a significant savings track record before they would be eligible to apply for a loan (Coleman, 2007, 4–5). As discussed above, financial deregulation increased access to mortgage credit for middle and higher income house-holds, and especially those who already owned property and were look-ing to trade up or to purchase second and third houses for investment. For low and lower-middle income households and first-time homebuyers, new mortgage products that were offered as inducements by banks (such as lower deposit requirements and revolving credit facilities that allowed borrowers to draw additional funds when needed) were initially com-bined with higher mortgage-repayment-to-income ratio requirements, which served to price many new entrants and especially low income earners out of the property market (Stuart et al., 2004, 7).

High levels of home ownership in a society can potentially function as an alternative form of social insurance (Conley and Gifford, 2006, 57–8, see the introductory chapter for a full discussion). As a result, the changes to New Zealand's housing finance system that led to a decline in rates of owner-occupancy across the board generated highly negative distributional outcomes for lower income groups because they occurred at the same time as the country's system of social protection was cut back. In particular, substantial cuts in welfare benefits during the late 1980s and early 1990s were combined with the tightening of eligibility criteria (Rudd, 2005, 421). For a country with a strong tradition of high rates of home ownership, the social risks involved with changes to the housing market such as those experienced in New Zealand during the 1980s and 1990s are substantial. The confluence of rapid neoliberal policy reforms with declining rates of homeownership – concentrated in particular among younger households – can lead to a regressive housing cycle that perpetuates a greater level of exclusion from the property market for groups who would have previously found it easier to gain access to property. When a property boom – largely fueled in this case by property investors rather than owner-occupiers – is combined with a broader trend towards lower homeownership rates this can result in a higher proportion of younger households living in rental accommodation, as well as prompting them to rent for longer periods of time. Although over the last decade rents have tended to increase at a lower rate than house prices in New Zealand, greater demand for rental accommodation driven by net immigration has placed upward pressure on rents (Hargreaves, 2007, 13, 18). However, it is the potential for future capital gains, rather than rental income *per se*, that has encouraged more investors to enter the rental property market or to expand their property portfolio to gain higher returns, discussed further below. The result has been rapidly increasing house prices that make it more difficult for would-be first-time buyers to save a sufficient mortgage deposit (Morrison, 2007, 57–8). While some households may defer purchasing a home until a later stage in their lives, others may seek to take advantage of new mortgage products based on lower (or zero) deposits, which may lead to higher debt-servicing costs, slower accumulation of equity, and an increased risk of mortgage distress and "negative equity" when the property bubble bursts.

4.3   The politics of capital gains in New Zealand

Following a decade and a half of neoliberal policy activism, the triumph of Helen Clark's Labour Party at the polls in November 1999 came on the back of campaign promises to govern in the interests of social stability, rather than to introduce further radical economic policy changes. Nevertheless, the campaign promised some big ticket corrections to the excesses of the 1980s and 1990s economic reforms under "Rogernomics" and "Ruthanasia." Progressive policy shifts under a Labour-led government from 1999 included a rise in the top rate of income tax by 6% to 39% (from the comparatively low rate of 33%), linking pensions to 65% of the average wage, and removing market-rate rentals for publicly owned housing by linking rents to 25% of tenants' income. In its first term the Labour-led government also abolished interest charges on student loans for the duration of tertiary study and passed industrial relations legislation that in theory reinstated some of the union rights that the National Party had abolished in the early 1990s (Bale, 2003, 205, 207).

Previous property booms in New Zealand in the mid-1980s and mid-1990s ended in financial disaster, with the stock market crash of 1987 and the Asian financial crisis of 1997–8 quickly letting the air out of New Zealand's house price bubbles. The country's most recent property boom began in the last quarter of 2001. Following Labour's return to power in 1999, the downward trend in patterns of homeownership across different social groups that had been stimulated by its own economic reforms in the 1980s continued. Based on census data, a brief sketch of the changes in New Zealand homeownership – which indicate significant changes in everyday financial norms – can be outlined as follows. In addition to a 7% drop in overall rates of homeownership since 1991, homeownership has become concentrated in the middle and upper wealth brackets with 61.2% of households that did not own their houses in 2006 earning less than NZ$50,000 (compared with a median annual income, for those aged 15 years and over, of NZ$24,400). The decline in homeownership is also concentrated among new entrants to the housing market. Between 1986 and 1996 the proportion of adults aged 20–34 who lived in rental accommodation increased from 34.5% to 40.5%, while homeownership among people aged 25–44 declined by 44% from 1991 to 2001 (Thorns, 2006, 24). More recently, the proportion of adults aged below 40 who are owner-occupiers declined from 30.2% in 2001 prior to the property boom to 27% in 2006, indicating the greater difficulties that first-time homebuyers now have in gaining access to the property market in the first place (Statistics New Zealand, 1998; 2007).

These changes are closely related to the increasing tendency of New Zealanders who already own houses to invest in rental property as a means of providing an additional income stream and as a "safe" source of retirement savings. For example, a survey of more than 900 New Zealand property investors conducted in 1999 found that the overwhelming majority of respondents entered into residential rental property investment for the first time during the 1990s (de Bruin and Flint-Hartle, 2003, 277). This represents a shift from individuals seeking to purchase houses for owner-occupancy as a route to a particular lifestyle to a significant increase in the number of individuals purchasing homes in order to acquire a financial asset that may then be rented out (Morrison, 2007, 6–7). Survey and interview data also indicates that while property investors in New Zealand tend not to undertake formal risk analysis of purchasing rental property compared with other forms of investment, most intuitively view residential property as a "low risk" investment over the long term (de Bruin and Flint-Hartle, 2003, 280). As everyday financial norms in New Zealand have altered in response to changing economic incentives and increased insecurity about how individuals will provide for their future income requirements, the number of individuals, trusts, or businesses acting as private landlords in New Zealand has rapidly increased since the start of New Zealand's economic policy revolution in the 1980s. As Figure 4.1 shows, the number of household dwellings owned by private landlords rose by more than one-third from 1986 to 1996, and further increased by more than 50% from 1996 to 2006. Public housing owned by the New Zealand Housing Corporation decreased over the same period from 56,091 houses in 1986, to 52,688 in 1996, and to 49,419 in 2006. Overall, homes owned by private landlords now make up approximately 20% of the country's total housing stock, with NZHC houses accounting for less than 4% (Statistics New Zealand, 1998; 2007).

Survey evidence suggests that most landlords in New Zealand are small-time investors, with 42% of landlords owning one rental property and 20.6% owning two. The expansion of the property investor class in New Zealand during the recent property boom has been concentrated among the upper-middle and higher income groups, based

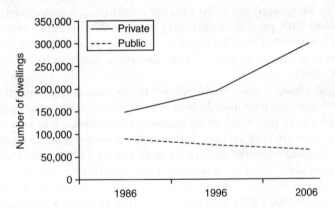

Figure 4.1   Public and private landlords in New Zealand, 1986–2006
Source: Statistics New Zealand (1998, 2007).

on the widespread perception that property is a safe investment and in pursuit of the higher returns that can be gained from investing in housing in New Zealand relative to other forms of investment. From 1988 to 2006, for example, returns on rental housing have been above average returns on financial savings such as shares, bonds, and bank deposits. In part this is because capital gains from housing are not taxed, while investors are able to offset rental property losses from the cost of interest payments, local rates, repairs, and insurance by reducing their tax payments on other income. Therefore, rental income does not need to cover the full costs associated with purchasing property to let because investors are able to reduce their overall income tax liabilities and will accumulate any capital gains untaxed. Most private residential landlords are now couples over age 45, who earn more than NZ$70,000 per year (Burns and Dwyer, 2007, 7–8). A similar phenomenon has occurred across the Tasman (see Mortensen and Seabrooke in this volume).

Similar to the UK (see Watson, this volume), during New Zealand's recent property boom households have taken on greater debt levels and have spent more than they earned in income, with greater consumption fueled by borrowing against higher residential property values helping to generate increased inflation levels despite rises in interest rates to the point where New Zealand had one of the highest official cash rates of OECD member states (Burns and Dwyer, 2007, 3). Freed from the tight regulations that previously governed their lending decisions and the amount of funds they could raise on capital markets, the decline of HCNZ mortgage lending and the rising proportion of commercial bank loans in New Zealand's mortgage market during the 1980s and 1990s is reflected in banks' balance sheets. From 1984 to 1999, commercial bank lending to manufacturers declined from 24.5% of their total loan portfolio to only 4.4%, while lending for residential mortgages increased rapidly over the period from 13.6% of total bank lending to 42.8%. Moreover, with comparatively high interest rates and low inflation in New Zealand relative to many other OECD economies during the last 15 years, commercial banks have found it easy to raise overseas funds to fuel the domestic property market (Badcock, 2004, 60–1). In 2001–02 the Household Savings Survey in New Zealand showed that households collectively owned NZ$444 billion of assets and had NZ$68 billion of liabilities, with owner-occupied homes forming the largest percentage of assets (36%) while rental properties now formed 4% of total household assets. To provide a point of comparison with investment in homes and rental properties, 8% of total assets were held in superannuation and life insurance, 6% in bank deposits, and 4% in shares and funds. With respect to liabilities, 80% of household liabilities were mortgage debt (Burns and Dwyer, 2007, 6–7).

At its peak, New Zealand's recent property boom drove residential property prices in urban centers up rapidly. In Auckland, the country's largest city, the annual rate of house price increases was 19.3% in 2003, compared with 16.2% for the country as a whole (Badcock, 2004, 62). As Badcock (ibid., 67) points out, New Zealand policymakers now face a "monetary 'catch 22'" during a housing bubble. On the one hand, the Reserve Bank may wish to increase interest rates in order to ease house spending and property speculation, while on the other hand such policy actions risk undermining the growth and export competitiveness of the "real" economy.

This problem can be termed a *housing bubble–monetary policy nexus*. When a small open economy such as New Zealand experiences a property boom in a housing finance system that is overwhelmingly characterized by fixed-term interest rates rather than floating rates (around 80% of mortgage interest rates are now for fixed terms), this creates a time lag where households may choose to increase consumption based on nominal increases in house values. This need not involve greater borrowing: homeowners may simply choose to consume more in anticipation of further increases in property values (de Veirman and Dunstan, 2008, 4). Even when interest rates start rising, homeowners may still choose to refinance their mortgage at a new fixed-term rate based on higher house values to protect their spending power against future rate rises. Furthermore, homeowners with revolving credit mortgages may simply choose to draw down more funds – up to their existing credit limit – based on a perception of higher net household wealth.

Greater consumption can place stronger pressure on inflation even if the central bank tightens monetary conditions through a series of interest rate increases, because borrowers are locked in for a set period to mortgages on lower rates of interest. This is especially the case with respect to fixed-term interest rates of five years or more which tend to be funded from offshore capital markets that are "out of reach" for the Reserve Bank (Drew et al., 2008, 10). The problem was deemed sufficiently serious for the Reserve Bank and the Treasury to come up with a "Mortgage Interest Levy" proposal, which would aim to increase the costs of mortgage borrowing to help ease a property boom without increasing the returns to short-term foreign investors, which could serve to push up the exchange rate (Reserve Bank of New Zealand, 2007). In these circumstances, simply raising the official cash rate might result in a higher exchange rate because increases in short-term interest rates generate stronger incentives for speculators in the currency carry trade to exploit interest rate differentials between low-interest and high-interest economies. As an economy that is heavily dependent on commodity exports, and which has experienced a rapidly widening current account deficit in recent years, a stronger exchange rate that makes imports cheaper and exports less competitive risks doing serious damage to New Zealand's economic growth and macroeconomic stability.

With the housing bubble in New Zealand rapidly overheating, the Reserve Bank began raising the official cash rate in 2004, which was increased from 5% at the end of 2003 to 8.25% by the third quarter of 2007 (see Figure 4.2). During this period the exchange rate of the New Zealand dollar against the US dollar reached record highs since it was first floated in 1985, while the average consumer price index was 2.8% from 2004 to 2007, only just within the 1–3% inflation target range mandated for the Reserve Bank (Drew et al., 2008, 1). Overall, compared with the 1990s, when average house prices rose by 50%, house prices in New Zealand doubled on average from 2000 to 2007, rising from four times average household disposable income to six times disposable income. While servicing a standard mortgage on a median-priced house required 40.2% of average after-tax income at the start of 2002, by February 2007 this had increased rapidly to 71.4% (Dalziel, 2007, 3). Commercial bank practices also served to intensify the housing bubble–monetary policy nexus in New Zealand, with banks relaxing lending criteria as the property boom showed signs of slowing in

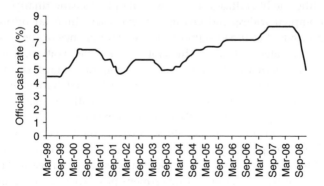

Figure 4.2 Interest rates in New Zealand, 1999–2008
Source: Reserve Bank of New Zealand (2008).

order to remain competitive in a tightening mortgage market (Dalziel, 2007, 13).

While changing everyday financial norms among New Zealanders helped to generate strong support for lower levels of income taxation during the 1990s, and a sharp political divide over income tax cuts versus higher levels of social spending was the central issue in the 2005 election that Labour narrowly won by a margin of 1% over the National Party, the picture here is not as clear cut as it might at first appear. Public support for increased social spending rather than income tax cuts was strong during the 1999 election campaign, which Labour won despite a policy to increase the top rate of income tax from 33 to 39%, and remained strong during the 2002 election (Broome, 2006, 67–9). A brief but sharp surge in support for income tax cuts even if they involved cuts in social spending did occur during 2005, which was framed by the National Party and the news media as a way of providing relief to homeowners servicing increased mortgage payments as interest rates continued to rise (Broome, 2006, 70–3). Nevertheless, recent opinion polling evidence indicates that a majority of voters have returned to the pattern of the past decade in preferring increased spending on health, education, and public infrastructure over having a few extra dollars in their pocketbooks each week (Research New Zealand, 2007a). With 48% of poll respondents in favor of increased spending on social services and public works against 35% in favor of tax cuts, the level of continued support for increasing social spending is striking given that opinion polls also indicate increasing levels of financial insecurity among homeowners with respect to the country's high interest rates (Research New Zealand, 2007b). Although only indicative, this suggests that while the liberalization of New Zealand's housing finance system has prompted widespread changes in everyday financial norms and has contributed to broad support for the maintenance of the country's current low rates and flatter thresholds of income taxation, it has not resulted in a permanent new conservative majority in favor of an ongoing program of reducing income taxation and the state's involvement in the provision of social services like the policy platform that continues to be offered by the National Party at election time.

In all, 82% of poll respondents in 2007 opposed a capital gains tax on profits from property sales in New Zealand. When the question was altered to whether respondents would support a capital gains tax that was levied only on the sale of investment properties rather than family homes, however, support increased to 41% (Research New Zealand, 2007c). Despite evidence of significant public support for government action to differentiate between the tax treatment of investment property and owner-occupied homes, the fifth Labour government focused primarily on providing assistance to households in public housing, with policies such as income-related rents for state housing tenants, and assisting households that were only just below the homeownership threshold, rather than taking on the expense involved with attempting to increase the overall rate of home ownership in New Zealand. In this respect, the National government's policy of privatizing the HCNZ mortgage portfolio during the 1990s removed a large source of capital that could potentially have been used for this purpose, thereby constraining the room for future governments to move back toward directly financing low and lower-middle household mortgages.

4.4   The impact of the credit crunch in New Zealand

With record increases in house prices and strong debt-fueled consumption during the inflation of New Zealand's most recent property bubble, it is hardly surprising that the country has experienced a severe spending hangover in the aftermath of the property boom party. The welfare costs that are associated with a housing crisis are particularly acute in countries such as New Zealand where such a large proportion of domestic savings is tied up in home ownership. In short, by fostering an asset-based society in New Zealand – with a residential property bubble funded by foreign creditors and fueled by households' pursuit of unprecedented capital gains – policymakers also increased the country's vulnerability to both endogenous and exogenous financial shocks. Like the end of previous property bubbles in New Zealand, the decline in residential real estate prices during 2007–08 has generated severe economic and political consequences.

Although New Zealand's financial institutions were not directly involved with the subprime crisis in the US, the country's financial dependence on access to foreign savings and its trade dependence on the export of primary commodities to the US, the European Union, and Asia means that the economic "good times" of the past decade are now over. In 2008, the global credit crunch – combined with higher domestic food and fuel costs and lower agricultural production due to drought – contributed to New Zealand slipping into its first recession in ten years. The New Zealand economy shrank by 0.3% of GDP in the first quarter of the year, followed by a 0.2% decline in the second quarter. The inflation rate as measured by the consumer price index also registered the largest annual increase since 1990, with inflation rising to 5.1% from the third quarter in 2007 to the third quarter in 2008, while the rate of unemployment increased over the year to September 2008 by 0.7% to reach 4.2% (Statistics New Zealand, 2008).

With the housing market already slowing in 2007, the poor economic circumstances during 2008 served to further hasten the decline in New Zealand house sales and house prices. Property prices fell in the year to October 2008 by 6.8% (Bradley, 2008), while the volume of property sales fell by a record 44.3% in the first half of the year compared with the first six months of 2007 – the highest decline since the second half of 1974 (*New Zealand Herald*, 2008). Against a backdrop of a rapidly deteriorating economy during 2008, New Zealand held a general election in November. At its campaign launch in October, the Labour Party announced a new deposit guarantee scheme in response to the international financial crisis in an attempt to sustain confidence in the country's financial system. The new scheme, mirroring a similar scheme in Australia, received bipartisan support after it was announced. It was set up to run for two years and aims to prevent panic withdrawals by guaranteeing savings in banks, credit unions, building societies, and finance companies that take deposits. In addition to protecting retail deposits, the Labour-led government also announced a Wholesale Guarantee Facility that is available to investment-grade financial institutions operating in New Zealand, as a temporary measure designed to facilitate access to international capital markets (New Zealand Treasury, 2008).

The impact of the global credit crunch and the onset of recession in New Zealand spurred the two main political parties to enter into a bidding war by offering competing economic crisis management plans during the 2008 election campaign. In addition to phased tax cuts announced in the budget in May, the first stage of which took effect in October, the Labour Party outlined an economic stimulus package that would be implemented soon after the election if Labour was returned to power. The package was centered on speeding up infrastructure projects, such as school property upgrades and reafforestation as well as road and rail construction developments, in order to increase jobs. In addition, Labour Prime Minister Helen Clark outlined new spending to retrain workers made redundant, while claiming "A curtain is being drawn down on the era of the freewheeling unregulated money traders and financiers whose greed has shaken the international financial system to its core" (Young, 2008). In response, the opposition National Party also announced increased spending on infrastructure projects and tax cuts, as well as a new temporary rescue package for workers made redundant that would provide "transitory assistance" to help the newly unemployed continue to service their mortgage or pay rent (*New Zealand Herald* 2008). Following a sustained period where the Labour Party had ranked well below the National Party in most public opinion polls, the impact of the global credit crunch and the slowing housing market in New Zealand worked against the government, and after nine years in power Labour lost the November election to the National Party, achieving only 34% of the party vote to National's 45%.

Having achieved the highest party vote of any party in the five elections since New Zealand adopted a proportional representation electoral system the National Party is now in a strong position to remain in power over several terms. Yet how well New Zealand weathers the aftershocks of the global credit crunch during this period will depend mostly on events that are beyond the control of the country's policymakers. Because of the timing of the 2008 election, New Zealanders – like Americans – had the opportunity to vote on alternative action plans for responding to the country's dire economic circumstances. Unlike the United States, however, there were few major policy differences in the programs offered by the country's two main political parties, although the new National Party government remains more firmly wedded to market-based solutions to the country's economic problems, at least when they are deemed to be politically palatable.

One future trend that can be predicted with a high degree of confidence is that the new government will continue to foster the growth of an asset-based society in New Zealand, with property wealth likely to remain concentrated in upper-middle and higher income groups. Indeed, this trend is likely to worsen in the short term, following moves by major commercial banks in New Zealand to restrict lending to lower income groups. In a significant change from recent mortgage lending practices, the ANZ and National banking group, which fund more than one-third of the country's home loans, announced in November 2008 that it was changing its credit criteria to restrict loans only to potential borrowers who can provide a minimum 20% deposit. This repricing of risk by commercial lenders in New Zealand, in response to the higher costs the banks face in accessing foreign capital, has further diminished the chances for younger age groups and first-time buyers to gain a footing on the property ladder. Although the impact of higher deposit requirements has been partly mitigated by rapidly decreasing interest rates, with the Reserve Bank lowering the official cash rate from 8.25% in June 2008 to 5% by the end of the year (see Figure 4.2), these financial conditions are likely to further cement the privileged position of existing homeowners and property investors. Those individuals and households who already have significant asset-based wealth have a much stronger buffer against the negative economic consequences of a prolonged recession and will also be able to use their continued access to mortgage credit to pick up bargains in a falling property market.

Homeownership rates in New Zealand are predicted to fall farther over the next decade, with one projection suggesting overall home-ownership will decline to 63.7% by 2011 and 61.8% by 2016 (Thorns, 2006, 24). This trend is likely to be exacerbated by the effects of the global credit crunch. If these projections are realized this will represent a major reduction in the proportion of households owning their home from the 1991 high of 73.8%. Along with falling rates of home owner-ship, many households now also experience greater financial insecu-rity. Among the middle and higher income earners who already own houses, this is partly reflected in their strong preference for investing in rental property as a safe source of savings, which during the past two decades has offered a good rate of return compared with other forms of investment in New Zealand because of the higher (and untaxed) capi-tal gains from rental housing as well the potential to offset losses by reducing tax liabilities on other sources of income. In particular, hous-ing is widely believed to offer New Zealanders a secure form of savings and financial stability to ensure their future security, a concern that has increased with the belief that current state-funded pensions (which remain universally available at age 65) will prove to be insufficient in the long run and that people must make their own provisions to ensure adequate living standards and income in retirement.

Conclusion

This chapter has shown that neoliberal policy changes to New Zealand's system of residential capitalism led to substantial benefits for middle and upper income households that already owned their homes or were able to take advantage of expanded access to mortgage credit to gain a foothold on the housing ladder. For younger and poorer households, however, New Zealand's neoliberal financial reforms have served to pull the ladder up. This has made it increasingly difficult for these house-holds either to gain access to the housing market or to accumulate equity when faced with the higher costs of servicing a mortgage. This is important because homeownership remains the principal source of household savings in New Zealand, as well as providing benefits such as intergenerational equity, social status, and future financial security.

This suggests the need for further research into the social consequences of financial liberalization in small economies and points in particular to the potential benefits of further studies of the relationship between housing finance, monetary, and tax regimes; the link between social norms and financial behavior; and the longer-term impact of neoliberal policy changes on intergenerational equity.

At first blush, contemporary New Zealand has become the asset-based society that was one of the outcomes intended by the designers of the country's neoliberal financial reforms. But as this chapter has shown this has not come without significant social costs. More importantly, changes in New Zealand's housing finance system during the 1980s and 1990s transformed the country's implicit social contract, which had helped to establish the wider social legitimacy of political institutions in New Zealand. In general, this turned existing homeowners into the winners from neoliberal reforms. Many of these housing market insiders were able to expand their investment in property at the expense of outsiders who were shut out of the property market or entered it on much less advantageous terms than their parents had (see also Mortensen and Seabrooke, this volume). Financial liberalization in small economies, as the New Zealand case shows, requires continued government action if it is not to lead to a regressive housing cycle that redistributes wealth upward and the emergence of a housing bubble–monetary policy nexus that inhibits the effectiveness of a country's macroeconomic framework. New Zealand's financial reforms succeeded in enabling more flexible access to credit and greater credit growth, funded by foreign capital inflows. However, the expansion of mortgage finance through access to cheap foreign capital rapidly drove up house prices in response to excess demand, which significantly raised the barriers to homeownership for low and lower-middle income households as well as younger age groups of first-time buyers.

Unlike more newsworthy changes such as the privatization of state assets, fiscal reform, labor market reform, or benefit cuts, many of the formal changes to housing policies in New Zealand largely slipped under the radar, with the general population slow to recognize the negative consequences of the decline of state-subsidized mortgages. Over time, however, the political effects of these changes have become all too visible. By serving to stimulate and reinforce broader changes in people's everyday financial norms, the changes to New Zealand's housing finance system during the 1980s and 1990s generated broader political support for a low taxation and low inflation policy regime. Yet support for *maintaining* the country's new conservative tax and monetary policy settings has not translated into support for further tax cuts funded by additional cuts to social spending. Rather, the opposite has been the case. During the last decade, New Zealanders have strongly supported spending increases on health, education, and social assistance to families – at least while these could be funded from large budget surpluses achieved in a period of sustained economic growth and low inflation, and while the country's property bubble continued to inflate. This suggests that while center-left governments in New Zealand have scope to increase social spending in economic "good times" when homeowners feel they are becoming richer as they see the value of their homes increasing, the political tide will turn more firmly in favor of conservative fiscal policies when a property boom ends. This argument appears to be confirmed by the election of a new center-right National government in November 2008 – albeit one which campaigned on a relatively centrist policy platform by New Zealand standards – by which time the incumbent Labour-led government had found itself out of tune with public opinion and on the wrong side of the politics of capital gains.

5
Recommodification, Residualism, and Risk: The Political Economy of Housing Bubbles in Norway

Bent Sofus Tranøy

Introduction

Over the last 25 years, Norway's social democratic welfare state has experienced two housing market bubbles and one severe bust. Until recently Norwegian boom and bust movements have been even more exaggerated than the corresponding American cycles (see Figure 5.1). After peaking in August 2007, Norway's housing market fell by 18% in real terms through 2008 (E24, 2009). The winter of 2008–09 saw stopgap measures aimed at breaking the fall brought on by the latest round of global and local housing market deflation. The state and Central Bank lowered interest rates to the levels that brought on the last boom, delivered fiscal stimulus, and offered the banks free swaps – MBS against treasury bills.

During the last boom, Norway's growth model grew more and more similar to the American one, in that it was increasingly driven by private consumption based on the creation of new wealth out of the housing–monetary policy nexus (see Schwartz's chapter on the U.S. and the introductory chapter). In turn, the boom made the housing market more speculative and unstable, bringing new distributional issues into Norwegian society, if not its politics. Three major issues, each with its own discourse, then, emerge from the recommodification of Norwegian housing as a more volatile asset market: macroeconomic trajectories, redistribution of wealth and risk, and the politics of macro policy making.

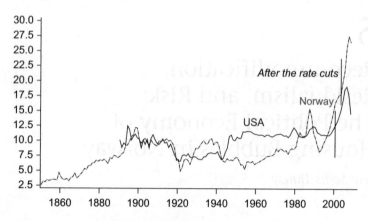

Figure 5.1   House prices – USA vs. Norway

Note: Norway: Cities, NOK per sq. m., 2006 prices; USA: Rebased to Norway in 1900.

Source: Robert Shiller/Norges Bank/First, 2008 estimates; Ecowin, First Securities.

The *macroeconomic governance theme* is concerned with stabilization policy outcomes: The Norwegian experience – which is surely not unique – tells us that housing bubbles destabilize the economy. In the introductory chapter the editors argue that CPE (and IPE) for too long have ignored housing policy. This chapter starts from a similar premise and argues that mainstream CPE should also pay more attention to macroeconomic policy and outcomes. For the last 15 years, mainstream CPE has followed orthodox economics in being too focused on supply side matters, that is the institutions that structure everything from the supply and organization of child care to innovation systems and corporate governance. This comes at the cost of decreased attention to the mechanisms that inject instability into economic performance at the macro level and distribute risk and instability at the level of households and firms.

Therefore this chapter also makes it its business to map and analyze *distributional outcomes* generated by a recommodified market for homes. In the first post war decades Norwegian social democrats pursued the goal of housing as a social right through largely universal programs, complemented by corporatist and residual measures. Even though the markets for housing and credit were heavily regulated, we can still speak of a market: Housing's ability to serve as a vehicle of wealth creation was modified, but not obliterated, by measures that shaped the environment in which property rights were being exercised. Parallel liberalization of

housing and credit markets in the 1980s brought about rapid recommodification (cf. Watson in this volume). Prices increased and debt levels shot
up. Housing policy lost its universalistic flavor. As the state and local
authorities closed pockets of cheap municipal and (public) employer-
owned housing, and as rent-controlled privately owned flats gradually
disappeared, and apartments were turned into condominiums, housing
policy got so narrow in terms of who was targeted that we can now
describe it as mainly residual in character. Indeed as Stamsø (2008) has
recently shown, Norway has fallen from being a world leader in public spending on housing to below the OECD average, while poor relief
for housing related problems has increased. In short, Norway's current
housing policy is market based and marked by a distinct lack of ambi-
tion with respect to both wealth redistribution and risk alleviation.

Norwegian political discourse around the framing of housing and
macro issues can help explain how this can happen in a country whose
social democratic institutions are otherwise largely intact. Although the
specific mechanisms differ slightly from those detailed in other cases
discussed in this volume, the general process is the same: Increased
wealth accumulation in the housing sector has, in the Norwegian case
too, been driving the politics of macropolicy to the right.

Section 5.1 provides a stylized elaboration of the three themes outlined above. In later sections these themes reappear in context, in
specific historical episodes in Norway's housing politics. Section 5.2 outlines the main characteristics of the social democratic housing policy
regime, namely the public provision of lots and infrastructure, cheap
credit targeted toward housing, and generous tax breaks that applied
to all homeowners. Unlike in other social democratic countries, like
Sweden or Austria, owner-occupancy (proper and in its pseudo form of
cooperatives) was totally dominant, and politically encouraged. This
section also discusses how the regime lost support from within. Rather
than passing the right to begin one's housing career on favorable terms
to the next generation, beneficiaries of the cooperative system wanted
to unlock the subsidies they had received and realize the full gains of
the price increases of the 1970s for themselves, thereby turning cooperative tenancy into a functional equivalent of owner-occupancy. In
the early 1980s a newly elected Conservative government granted the
cooperative insiders their wish.

Section 5.3 analyzes the 1980s boom and the early 1990s bust as
cyclical consequences of this recommodification of the markets for
credit and housing in Norway. First, insufficient attention was paid to
the danger of setting off an asset price bubble through mismanaged

sequencing, causing the market to get out of control. Then a similar type of disregard for timing and cyclical concerns, and imperatives flowing from the fixed exchange rate policy, exacerbated the downturn of the early 1990s through too much tightening, too late, leading to a bank and debt crisis.

As rates came down all over Europe after the 1992–3 EMS/ERM debacles, the Norwegian economy picked up. Now, however, the problem of overly low rates in an upturn returned. Thus the foundations for a new round of rapid price increases in the housing market were laid. Section 5.4 tells the story of how, late in the 1990s boom, a new, more inward-looking, macroeconomic policy regime was gradually put in place: a regime based on an autonomous central bank, inflation targeting, and a flexible exchange rate.

This regime did not, however, insulate Norway's monetary policy from the effects of unforeseen external developments. Rather, it made monetary policy susceptible to different kinds of external stimuli. Cheap imports from China into Norway's highly open economy drove inflation down. As in much of the rest of the world, from 2003 this round of disinflation brought on a period of record low interest rates and set the stage for accelerated growth in the housing market, which in turn stimulated the institutional and behavioral changes which we could tentatively label an emerging new growth model. The implications of this model in terms of macroeconomic governance and distributional outcomes is analyzed in the Section 5.5. In Section 5.6, aspects of the financial crisis – in terms of both outcomes and policy responses – as they were emerging in Norway at the time of writing are discussed. The conclusion offers remarks on the politics of monetary policy and its links to the housing market.

5.1   The significance of recommodification

Commodification, in its present usage within the social sciences, dates back to Karl Polanyi's (1944) concept of "commodity fiction," which he used to critique the idea of disembedded and self-regulating markets for money, land, and labor. Commodification reduces or homogenizes the value of something to its market (exchange) value, nothing more and nothing less. Putting a price on something makes it commensurable to anything else with a price and thus strips out all normative and social value. Polanyi presents this as an ideal-typical dichotomy (commodified vs. decommodified), but in empirical analysis it usually more relevant to think in terms of a process along a continuum.

I employ the term recommodification to underline that Norwegian public discourse on housing has swung back and forth on this continuum. Housing was primarily understood in market terms in the first 40 years of the twentieth century. After the Second World War housing was to an increasing degree also seen as a basic need and a right. In line with this Norwegians believed that society had an obligation to regulate the production and exchange of housing. The market was manipulated and regulated on both the demand side (price and credit controls) and the supply side (the allocation of land), but it was still a market. From the 1980s onward housing was recommodified. The view that homes are marketable assets, which in turn increases their potential as an object of speculation, again came to the fore. Significantly, money was also recommodified – in the sense that it became an object of speculation, something bought and sold in its own right – at about the same time. Put simply, the simultaneous recommodification of money and housing produced the property bubble of the early 1980s.

Commodification raises important issues for political economists. I will, as outlined in the introduction, distinguish between three different discourses that I want to engage in the context of the Norwegian housing market.

First, we need to ask to what degree any given macroeconomic policy regime (in the Norwegian case this means institutionalized coordination at the intersection of fiscal, monetary, and incomes policy) is able to deliver macroeconomic stability when faced by more volatile housing prices. In other words, we can investigate how housing prices are translated into inflation and employment performance by the macroeconomic policy regime, and how this feeds back into housing market developments. In the period covered by this chapter, Norway dismantled a highly regulated policy regime based on credit and exchange controls. After a transition phase with no coherent policy regime, Norway tried a hard-currency based regime for ten years. Finally things settled down with a regime based on central bank autonomy and a floating exchange rate. Each period had its own distinct interplay between the overall regime and housing market developments.

Second, we can hypothesize that the ever-increasing weight of housing investments in the average household's financial position changes voters' view of what constitutes appropriate housing, monetary, and fiscal policy. The – in this context – classic contributions of Kemeny and Castles (see the introductory chapter) both argued for a link between the relative weight of owner-occupancy in a society and the strength of "rightist" preferences in economic policy. They both made fairly straightforward arguments based on "objective interests," the crucial mechanisms being linked to *taxation* (young homeowners opposed higher taxes because they need spending power in order to service their debt) and *spending/interest rate levels* (opposition to public borrowing because this can lead to higher interest rates). In addition Castles argued that (older) homeowners are less dependent on (tax financed) public pensions because these can be substituted by imputed income from homeownership. Both Kemeny and Castles took a broad comparative view and tried to explain differences in welfare spending based on homeownership patterns.

At first glance Norway looks like a deviant case in this context, as she – unlike other highly developed welfare states like Germany, Sweden, and Denmark – exhibits owner-occupancy rates among the highest of the OECD member states: 81% if cooperatives are included (Statistics Norway, 2007), see also Figure 1.1 in the introductory chapter) Yet this is combined with a huge tax financed welfare state and a fairly generous system of public pensions. This does not, however, render the underlying logic of Kemeny and Castles useless for analysis of the Norwegian case. Instead we need to do two things. First, we can hold owner-occupancy rates constant and distinguish periods of high and low degrees of commodification. This allows us to hypothesize that an increased degree of commodification increases voters' sensitivity to the mechanisms identified by Kemeny and Castles. At a minimum, it seems reasonable to assume that in a recommodified Norwegian housing market, homeowning voters become more sensitive to changes in taxation that increase the costs associated with homeownership and/ or reduce the value of housing assets. Second, we need to elaborate the spending side of the argument. In an oil rich economy at least, the link does not work through public borrowing. Rather, we need to ask how a preference for low interest rates is mediated through a macroeconomic regime dominated by an independent central bank and a discourse centered on "fiscal responsibility."

The third discourse opened up by recent trends in housing markets is one concerned with the distribution of wealth and risk. Rapidly rising house prices deepen the divide between those who possess houses (primarily old and middleage households) and those who do not (primarily the young). This indicates a development where inherited wealth (or lack of it) becomes more important not only for a household's ability to accumulate wealth (for which housing was always important even in social democratic, egalitarian Norway) but also for its ability to fulfill the basic need of housing.

Speculation, which we may describe as an advanced stage of commodification, reinforces the processes that deepen divide in the housing market. Speculation entails increased detachment from housing's social purpose, and for many players housing is reduced to one of several alternative investment objects. When prices rise dramatically over a period, housing assumes the position of one of the most interesting asset classes in an economy. To an increasing degree it attracts buyers who are not looking for a place to live, as in the Australian and British "buy to let (i.e., rent)" phenomenon. Similarly, "flipping" (buying only for the purpose of refurbishing and selling or buying into new projects as they start up and reselling when they are finished) becomes a profitable activity. This type of speculation we can term offensive, to signify that it is a gain-oriented act, actively pursued by people seeking profitable opportunities. Offensive speculation drives up prices farther, making life even more difficult for first-time buyers. This in turn stimulates what we can call defensive speculation. Defensive speculation is about avoiding further losses. It occurs when first-time buyers pay what they themselves consider to be over the odds and at the limits of their budget, in order to "get in" before prices increase even farther.

In the short term all speculation contributes to price growth; over the medium to long term speculative behavior also increases volatility. Volatile prices for what is a basic need, and simultaneously also an average person's most important store of value, introduces an element of involuntary gambling to many households. At what time you enter and/or exit the housing market – a decision that is normally more influenced by where you are in your private life – can have decisive consequences for your finances for decades to come. Political scientists often conceptualize the welfare state in terms of spending and/or redistribution of resources. A supplementary perspective is to view the welfare state as an insurance system (Barth et al., 2003; Hacker, 2004). This directs our attention to how well it protects its citizens from unwanted risk. Commodified housing markets increasingly expose citizens to an undesired level of risk.

5.2   The social democratic project: Decommodification and internal pressure 1945–81

In order to appreciate properly the extent and significance of recommodification of housing in Norway, it is necessary to outline the social democratic housing regime built up in the first three postwar decades. This section also discusses why this regime was liberalized, providing our first example of how increased wealth accumulation in the housing sector really can drive politics to the right.

For reasons like late urbanization and the severity of the interwar crisis, Norway did not have an adequate number of dwellings of acceptable quality going into the postwar era. The social democratic governments that ruled from 1945 to 1965 devoted a lot of resources toward improving this situation. The analysis was that housing represented a more fundamental need than most other goods sought by people. Secure and adequate tenure was perceived as a right and housing became embedded in a discourse of social purpose.

Norwegian social democracy also worked from the premise that private ownership and cooperative ownership are more dignified forms of tenure than privately rented dwellings. This position was a reaction to the meager rights tenants enjoyed in the prewar landlord-tenant relationship. For these ends a strong organization for housing cooperatives and a state bank for housing were both established in 1946.[1] This established a three-tier model for the cooperative sector.

At the lowest tier were individual estates. They owned the dwellings into which members bought a right to rent "their flat." For most practical purposes – with the major exception of reselling – this right resembled ordinary ownership. The individual cooperative estates were separate juridical entities. Some were members of regional organizations, while others were independent, that is stand-alone cooperatives consisting of one or few buildings located next to each other. The second tier consisted of the regional organizations. They performed services (such as accounting) for the individual estates, but more importantly, they were the main vehicles for developing new projects. To this end they enjoyed privileges with regard to gaining access to municipally developed sites and "Husbank" financing. The third tier consisted of a national organization, the "NBBL." This organization performed services for the regional organizations and devoted itself to housing policy at the national political level.

It is worth noting that ambitious housing policies based on a quick buildup of housing capital through owner-occupancy and cooperatives stood in a fundamentally harmonious relationship to the social democratic macroeconomic governance regime. The policy routines of the two spheres were highly compatible. Seen from the vantage point of housing policy, the ability to secure cheap credit was an important part of the macroregime. The authorities defined maximum nominal rates charged by banks and even as these slid upward, real interest rates were kept low through very liberal deductibility rules: all interest paid could be deducted from taxable income. In a system of progressive taxation, such rules have a regressive effect. Unable to manage the volume of credit using real interest rates, the Central Bank and the Ministry of Finance sought to manage credit volume using an arsenal of credit controls that grew more complex and far reaching over time.

It is also worth noting that the use of credit and tax policy to achieve these goals gave housing policy a universalistic as opposed to a selective flavor. Cheap finance was a right granted to people willing to accept the quality norms for subsidized credit. Customers to the Norwegian "Husbank" were not means tested. Even those who wanted homes above the standard deemed eligible for direct government support were subsidized. Generous (and regressive) tax breaks and a low capital tax on houseownership were universally available.

Because cooperative housing was even more subsidized than noncooperatives, the state needed to regulate those cooperativess in order to assure that subsidies were passed on to new generations of homemakers, rather than being realized in the market by the individuals who initially enjoyed them. Three separate types of regulation repressed prices in the secondary market for cooperative dwellings. First, authorities set the maximum price level for cooperatives. Second, price levels were contained by rules of first refusal. These rules meant that the cooperative as such had to organize a hierarchy according to the duration of the estate/regional cooperative membership of the individuals in question. In the independent cooperative sector such rules normally did not apply. In reality, being free of rules of first refusal brought prices closer to the market level. As long as owners of independent cooperative flats had the right to chose to whom they were selling, this choice could and often was, determined by the buying party's willingness to pay hidden fees directly to the seller. The third type of regulation that had an effect on secondary prices was more indirect. In order to defend maximum prices and rules of first refusal it was important to enact legislation that more or less blocked cooperatives from turning themselves into owner-occupied estates (condominiums) for whom such rules did not apply.

The distributional struggle over the equity locked in by cooperative regulation is also a story about how interests related to housing capital can swing voters toward the right. It followed a typical "game pattern" also known from the credit market: First, market players – stimulated by inflation – try to circumvent price regulations through evasive actions in the market. Second, the authorities try to counteract this through tighter regulation. In turn this stimulates outright political action on the part of those who stand to gain from liberalization.

In 1977 the Stortinget (Parliament) amended the law on cooperatives to make first refusal rules mandatory for all of them. This was an effort to overcome the problem of hidden fees, which were particularly important in the independent part of the cooperative sector. The potential to "privatize" and realize the historically accumulated subsidies and reap windfall profits were, however, present for most cooperative owners, so long as the maximum price lay below the price one could achieve in a free market. This was true in all the biggest cities. Against this background, the 1977 tightening of regulations provoked a populist backlash against detailed regulation of the cooperative sector in general, and an ad hoc organization against mandatory first refusal emerged (Annaniassen, 1996, 24–5).

The Conservative Party soon sensed the political rewards of catering to this interest. The promise of reform along these lines, which Labor initially opposed, was most likely a vote winner for the Conservatives in their highly successful 1981 election. Bay (1985) shows that support for the Conservatives grew more among owners of cooperative flats than in any other segment in the big cities before the 1981 election. In fact, Bay's results show that while cooperative tenants left the Labor Party in droves to vote Conservative, support for Labor was stable among owner-occupiers. Bay (1985, 124–5) interprets this as saying that cooperative owners had a special affinity for the Conservative's promise of windfall profits.

Bay argues that Labor's belief that tenure forms were stable and thus constituted a permanent divide led to their electoral failure. We could take this argument one step further and say that Labor presupposed a society where people were more or less born into cooperative tenancy and owners of cooperative flats were solidaristic toward the institution and thus to future generations. These cooperative owners would remain uninterested in their own potential windfall profits because they had no intention of realizing such gains in a market anyway. Rather they would wait for their turn before they moved up in the price-regulated cooperative hierarchy. The Conservatives, on the other hand, had by the late 1970s understood that there was more mobility in the housing market than Labor realized: Cooperative flats were simply used as one station in a longer tenure career whose ultimate goal was outright owner-occupancy. In other words, Bay's analysis points us toward deeper structural forces that explain why cooperative tenants showed an increased interest in being able to bring their assets to the market. This interest triumphed very soon after the Conservatives came to power in 1981.

Liberalization of prices in the secondary cooperative market immediately led to rising prices on those flats, which then led to all-round price increases in the real estate market (Norges Offentlige utredninger, hereafter NOU 1992, 30, 33). Many households used windfall profits to boost their purchasing power. This meant that many who had formerly been restricted to housing careers within the cooperative sector could now compete for dwellings in the owner-occupied market. While the exact impact of the cooperative reform is impossible to estimate, in hindsight it is beyond doubt that Norway experienced a housing bubble in the mid-1980s. In the three years from the end of 1984 to the end of 1987 second-hand housing prices (per square meter) rose by 40% in real terms.

5.3   The 1980s boom and early 1990s bust: Cyclical consequences of structural reform

Recommodification in the housing market interacted with aggregate demand to severely destabilize the macroeconomy by gradually shifting the housing market into a speculative mode. Rather than compensating for the shock produced by a rapid increase in the price of an important asset class, other sequential reforms of structural policies and the macroeconomic regime itself fanned the flames of asset price inflation. Instead of considering the cyclical consequences of the ordering of structural reforms, reform followed a political logic where decisions that catered to concentrated interests – cooperative and share market liberalization – were driven through in 1981–2. This created the basis for an asset boom if credit flows were to be liberalized, which they duly were when credit controls were all but lifted in 1984 (Tranøy, 2000, 106–11). In contrast, an effort to use real interest rates to dampen demand for credit did not get underway until interest rate controls were abolished and the value of tax breaks was reduced several years later. This section deals with the politics of taxing and interest rate policy that eventually led to a real interest rate shock. First, however, the bubble itself must be considered.

The policy described above sounds like the recipe for creating a bubble, and indeed it was. Norway got her "Yuppie period" with flash consumption and unsustainable credit-driven growth in culturally potent new businesses like cappuccino-serving cafés, video rental, and tanning salons, as well as office buildings and fish farms. By the mid-1980s, new attitudes had taken hold on both sides of the credit market. The majority of Norwegian banks abandoned traditional cautiousness, while on the demand side attitudes to debt changed. Crudely put, the lesson learned by the postwar generation of baby boomers, as they gradually replaced the interwar generation in the credit and housing markets, seemed to be that inflation and tax breaks in combination would take care of such a large part of the debt burden that the best individual strategy was to borrow to the hilt and then some.

These developments are borne out by key statistics for the period. The household savings rate fell dramatically from +5.2% in 1984 to –5% in 1986 and 1987. Correspondingly, the balance sheet of each of Norway's two biggest banks grew 100% during 1985–6 (Tranøy, 2000, 110–11).

The Norwegian housing bubble of the 1980s was not so much pricked, as it was burst and then trampled on for several years. Once more the interplay between housing market developments and regime change dynamics at the level of macroeconomic policy matters.

The essence of the Norwegian story at the turn of the decade was a downward spiral dynamic, kicked off and boosted by policy. Again developments got out of control and again the fundamental reason was that politicians pursued structural reform without sufficient (or any) attention being paid to its cyclical consequences. After several years of overheating and bubble conditions, policymakers – at the behest of Central Bank and Ministry of Finance officials – gradually came to realize that the real after-tax rate of interest had to be raised in order to make a credit market without credit controls function properly. The reasoning behind this was elementary: The old regime based on credit controls had low interest rates as one of its central goals but now that credit was being allocated on more market conforming terms, the price mechanism had to be utilized in order to control credit volumes.

The task then was to get inflation down, increase nominal interest rates, and most importantly to reform the tax system so that unlimited deductibility could be abolished. This was difficult to achieve in the middle of a boom. First, tax policy is inherently problematic. It is complex and includes many privileges that give many players reason to oppose reform. Second, the Conservative Party – the champion of high income, high marginal tax groups in particular and homeowners in general – held the Prime Ministerial post until April 1986.

In hindsight one can identify the spring of 1986 as a turning point. The background was the reverse oil price shock of that winter. When oil prices plummeted the country's current account went from a surplus of around 6% of GDP to an equally large deficit. The oil sector's contribution to GDP fell from 19.1% in 1985 to 8.6% in 1988 and tax revenues from the sector fell by four-fifths. The Conservative-led cabinet found it difficult to administer cuts and fell in late April 1986. The Labor Party took over ten days later and during the interregnum the exchange rate came under massive pressure. As soon as they took office the incoming government devalued the Norwegian Krone (NOK) by around 10%. Exchange rate policy became the centerpiece of a new macroeconomic strategy geared toward disinflation. Because of Norway's devaluation history, and the current account deficit, defending the currency entailed keeping interest rates much higher than the European average. In 1987 and 1988 Norwegian rates were about 6% points above a trade weighted European average (NOU, 1989, 1; Tables 5.6 and 5.7). Thus the Central Bank finally secured interest rate levels that would soon have a dramatic effect on *credit demand*. Quite simply, a 40-year-old political tradition of regulating the nominal rate of interest downward was abandoned. Because Norwegian banks have never offered U.S.-style "caps" on variable rates loans, interest rates were now free to rise to whatever level the banks dared charge.

The theory informing this change of exchange rate regime is known as vicious cycles theory. The central proposition here is that a devaluation to improve competitiveness works only in the (very) short run. In the long run it is counterproductive, as inflationary pressures will soon worsen rather than improve the competitive position of the economy that devalued. The policy prescription that follows from the vicious cycles analysis is to defend the exchange rate at all costs, and gradually reap the rewards in the form of lower inflation, increased investor confidence, lower interest rates, and improved competitiveness.

The Gordian knot of tax reform was also gradually untied in this period. In the budget for 1987, Labor succeeded in shifting some of the tax burden over from net to gross income. This allowed for a decrease in marginal rates on net income, which translated into the state subsidizing proportionally less of people's interest rate expenses. In 1987 inflation was increasing so rapidly that this did not have a significant effect on after-tax real interest rate costs in the economy. By 1988 things were about to change, however. Real after-tax interest rates started a steep climb. Inflation and the value of tax breaks both fell, thereby bringing real rates upward year by year until 1992.

The reason that the value of tax breaks could fall every year until 1992 (when a new tax system was introduced), was that when the current account crisis hit home during the spring of 1987, Parliament managed to produce a broad-based compromise on tax policy. The tax compromise of 1987 and the eventual full scale structural reform of

1992 was long overdue, but therein laid the problem: The way it was phased in during an ever-deepening recession and falling inflation levels gave a dramatic and negative effect. The Norwegian economy was on the receiving end of a real interest rate shock. Loans taken up during the boom in a context of rising prices became much harder to service while the value of properties (and therefore debtors' collateral) fell. In 1986 the real rate of interest for high income/high marginal tax groups was still negative. In 1992, when the full reform was implemented, marginal tax on net income was standardized across income levels at 28% and the real rate of interest jumped to +7%! Norway's economy was seriously destabilized and went into a banking and eventually a currency crisis.

The effects of the real interest rate shock are easy to read off from the traditional indicators of macroeconomic performance. GDP fell and unemployment figures rose sharply from 1988 and onward. The price for business property fell by 50% from 1987 to 1991, and household property prices fell fast, too. The boom dynamics of asset price inflation were driven in reverse. In a falling market, people (or banks if people defaulted) could not cover the cost of the loan even when collateral was sold. This depressed the property market farther. Norway's indebted household sector reacted by increasing its propensity to save, as people tried to get out of trouble. The savings rate went from around –6% to around +7%, but these figures mask a significant number of hardship stories. The link between commodification and exposure to unwanted risk was demonstrated as people had to leave their homes with negative equity and live on carrying old debts. As the propensity to save shot up, credit growth was negative in the years from 1991 to 1993, in a phenomenon unheard of until then in the postwar era.

By mid-1990 it was thus clear that Norwegian banks and many households and businesses were in deep trouble. Reduced interest rates and a more expansive economic climate would have been most helpful, but were not forthcoming. Instead the gradual reductions in tax deductibility continued while the hard-currency approach was pursued with great conviction and rigidity. Vicious cycles thinking had taken a strong hold, and it seemed that leading decisionmakers truly believed they had no other choice than to hold out and wait for better times. Perversely, better times arrived in the shape of currency turmoil. During the fall of 1992 one currency after another of the noncore EMS countries fell: Finland, Italy, Britain and then in November Sweden, Norway's close neighbor and important competitor in several export markets. Finally, on December 10, the NOK was released from its ecu-peg.

5.4 Late 1990s: Stumbling toward a new macroeconomic regime

In the shadow of the chaotic and confusing situation Norwegian decisionmakers suffered during the fall and early winter of 1992, a new
national macroeconomic governance strategy – the so-called *solidarity
alternative* – was worked out. This entailed a division of labor between the
three key policy areas. Fiscal policy was to be used to control aggregate
demand. Incomes policy was given the task of improving competitiveness by aiming for wage inflation below that of Norway's competitors.
Finally, monetary policy was geared toward stabilizing the NOK against
European currencies in order to secure a stable monetary framework for
incomes policy.

By the mid-1990s, however, it became clear that the solidarity alternative was too much a product of the business cycle circumstance ruling
at its inception: It was best suited for a rainy day. Countercyclical fiscal
policy was more easily achieved so long as it implied spending increases
rather than cuts, and wage moderation was more easily achieved while
unemployment was high. To make matters worse for the "Solidarity
alternative," the NOK got stronger during the upturn, while the continental economies were still in a slump. This meant that interest rates
had to be cut in line with German interest rates in order to fend off
upward pressure on the exchange rate even though employment, GDP,
wages, and housing prices started another steep climb. By 1997 real
housing prices in Norway's biggest regional market (the greater Oslo
area) were back to their historic peak from 1988, albeit in a situation
where real incomes were much higher, which indicated room for further growth.

So, the problem where exchange rate considerations forced a procyclical monetary policy upon the Norwegian Central Bank returned, albeit
this time in the form of lower rates in an upturn. At the heart of this
problem were – simply put – oil revenues. These grew phenomenally
during 1996 and 1997 and this strengthened the position of the NOK
vis-à-vis the core EMS currencies.

The booming oil sector also contributed to an increased output gap
differential between Norway and Europe. This gap illustrates well that
Norway and the big economies of continental Europe had divergent
monetary policy needs in this period. The Central Bank realized that
Norway's departure from the path of the continental European economies was systematic and probably structurally determined, but felt
hamstrung by the exchange rate regulation.

The new Central Bank Governor as of 1999, former top Ministry of Finance official Svein Gjedrem, took this into account when he decided to expand his technocratic power in a way that had been unimaginable to his immediate predecessors. He reinterpreted the exchange rate regulation that had so seriously narrowed the previous Central Bank Governor's room to maneuver. By deciding to take a more long-term view of events in the currency market, and claiming that long-term trends were driven by relative inflation rates, he in effect defined an inflation target (by implication the European Central Bank's target of 2%), rather than an exchange rate target for Norwegian monetary policy.

In the spring of 2001 Parliament formalized the new system, giving the Central Bank a symmetrical inflation target of 2.5%.[2] Thus instead of the "solidarity alternative's" principle of division of labor, with one policy area responsible for one target each, the Central Bank Governor established a *policy hierarchy* with the instrument he controlled – monetary policy – on top. This interpretation rests on the – in the CPE literature – well established notion that the societal interests that ultimately shape fiscal and incomes policy (democratically elected politicians and trades and employer union leaders respectively) might be responsive to financial discipline imposed by empowered technocrats in the Central Bank. If they decide on budgets or wage settlements respectively that the Central Bank deems to be inflationary, they will be punished through unpopular and costly interest rate hikes (Hall and Franzese, 1998; Iversen, 1998).

5.5   The emerging growth model and its consequences

In the introduction to this chapter and Section 5.1, three discourses related to recommodified and therefore more volatile housing markets were outlined. The link between macropolicy and housing market developments on the one hand and the relationship between housing market developments and the distribution of risk and welfare will be dealt with in this section. The Conclusion offers some reflections on the new politics of economic policy. In between, Section 5.6 offers a brief report on the financial crisis as it appears in Norway at the time of writing.

The new macroeconomic policy regime with an independent Central Bank at its core seemed to have the potential to deliver all-round macrostability, since it promised to bring renewed coherence to Norwegian macroeconomic policy and most importantly, bring an almost 20-year practice of procyclical monetary policy to an end. As a function of this, and in line with the historical argument pursued in the sections above, it also seemed reasonable to expect a less volatile housing market. The impact of inflation targeting on house prices would have to be indirect, though, through general macro conditions, because asset values in the property market are not well represented in the inflation measure used by the Central Bank. The bank is not geared toward reacting to house price inflation. This is because the proxy used for property prices is rents. But as is evident from the Price/Earnings(P/E) ratios given in Figure 5.2 below, rents have not kept up with house prices.

In 2003, asset prices and prices as measured by the index used by the Central Bank departed from each other in a dramatic way. Developments from that year onward show that the new macroeconomic policy regime did not, after all, insulate Norway's monetary policy from the effects of unforeseen external developments. Rather, it made monetary policy susceptible to a richer mix of external stimuli. In a small, open economy the exchange rate still matters even if the Central Bank has turned to inflation targeting, but the exchange rate-interest rate link's role as a transmission belt between Norway's housing market and the world economy was much less pronounced with the new regime. Still, interdependence remained a fact. During the 1990s the lack of cyclical synchronicity with the core continental states had persistently resulted in inappropriate interest rate levels. In 2003, the deflationary impact of cheap imports after China entered the World Trade Organization (WTO) added to America's extremely loose post

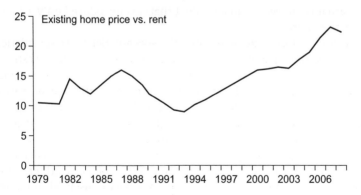

Figure 5.2 Housing P/E ratio
Source: Norges Bank/SSB/First.

Information and Communication Technology (ICT)-bubble monetary policy. Even mediated by the new institutional setup, these forces generated another round of extreme price growth in the property market.

This happened because the Central Bank's Governor took his inflation mandate literally and reduced his key signal rate in close to monthly installments until it reached a historically low level of 1.75% in 2004. The impact on the housing market was strong. Through the three years from 2003 until 2006, housing prices rose by more than 50% in real terms (around 60% nominally), which was an even steeper climb than in the most heated three-year period in the mid-1980s. Reflecting this, household debts grew at more than 10% per year.

What we could see emerging was a growth model with a functional similarity to the U.S. model depicted by Schwartz in his contributions to this volume. Two key traits that provide a strong feedback mechanism between the macroeconomic regime and the housing market can be identified: First, the predominance of floating rate mortgages (95%) means that lower interest rates are quickly translated into reduced costs for the household sector. Second, Norway's banking sector aggressively sold a new type of flexible loan to established homeowners. This type in effect allows homeowners to manage their own credit line as long as they stay within a certain limit. As in the U.S., the key attribute of this type of loan is that it is an ideal instrument for "unlocking" (the rapidly increasing) wealth bound up in residential property, thus strengthening the link between property prices, private consumption, and – ultimately – aggregate demand. It is therefore highly significant that this type of loan represented 70% of all new credit extended from the banks to households in 2007, up from 50% the year before. A strong performance indeed, from a product that was introduced only a couple of years earlier.

The long boom stimulated both offensive and defensive speculation. Older, wealthier people were attracted to property as an investment object. P/E ratios (measured by rents, see Figure 5.2) in the housing market rose until 2007, but the yield was deemed more than satisfactory as long as prices continued to rise. When ever-larger sections of the populace view property as an investment object and not as a necessary good, a further turn on the spiral of recommodification is made. For young people entering the market, a climate of fear which leads to defensive speculation contributes to the price spiral. While older wealthier households speculate in order to make a gain, younger households often feel forced to speculate and assume large risks in order to avoid further losses. This happens because the impression is created that one has to get in before the market rises even further. The dynamics of defensive speculation can read off from the numbers. In the under 35 age group, property purchases with more than 80% debt financing reached close to 80% of all new loans for purchasing property in 2006, and 37% of those loans were for more than 100% of the home's value.

This moves us toward the discourse centered on the distribution of risk and welfare. A significant, and now well known and much talked about trend at the housing-credit nexus of U.S. markets is the growth in subprime lending from 2003 to 2006. Seen from the supply side this development is essentially about increasing demand for homes and credit. This was achieved by drawing in groups that under older, more sober criteria would not have been deemed creditworthy. Only innovative securitization-based risk-management techniques created the impression that it made good business sense to give loans to these groups.

The financial regulatory authority has not allowed the securitization of mortgage risk in Norway to go this far. Still, we can see the same underlying dynamic of using product innovation in order to draw in groups that would otherwise have been ever more marginalized by asset price inflation. In Norway this innovation process is the result of direct collaboration between developers and financiers. The new product is projects based on large amounts of collective debt with long time horizons. The traditional Norwegian owner-occupier mortgage with a bank involved repayment over something between 15–25 years. The new contracts offered young people short on capital loans with up to a 50-year term and with a 30-year interest only period. If rates remain low (these deals are normally based on floating rates) and property prices continue to rise, this arrangement can work well for the takers. They do, however, expose vulnerable groups to a new risk situation. Homeowners have always, and will always, assume a risk linked to the value of the asset they buy. Under older financing models however, the debtor's ability to handle this risk would improve rapidly as the principal was being paid down. Now, with new financing models, the period of high vulnerability to asset price risk is prolonged. The same goes for the risk of falling into payment problems. This is so because the new financing model also prolongs the period where one carries a high interest rate risk, a problem that is exacerbated by banks willing to dole out credit in large measures to low income families.[3]

Who are the winners and losers in this process? Newcomers to the property market with parents and grandparents from the greater Oslo are to an increasing degree entering it with the help of their parents (who can take new flexible loans on their own paid up property). In 2005 a survey commissioned by the Norwegian Savings Banks Association, reported that 35% of all housebuyers between the ages of 25 and 32 received financial assistance from their parents (*Dagbladet,* 2007). This trend, which it seems reasonable to assume grew in strength during 2006, is bolstered by inheritance laws that encourage a direct transfer of wealth from deceased grandparents to the third generation, bypassing the intermediate generation.

The losers are typically entrants from outside "metropolitan areas," with parents of mediocre means, and immigrants. We are not quite there yet, but Norway, one of the most egalitarian societies in the world, is taking steps along the road to the British situation where people who are needed for low paid jobs cannot afford to live in the capital.

Norway has traditionally – among other things because of its free schooling and educational system – had one of the highest rates of social mobility in the world. What we are seeing now is a situation where the recommodification of housing could contribute to reducing this trend.

5.6   Crisis Norwegian style

There are many lines of transmission running between a small, open economy and a global financial crisis. Among the most important are demand for exported goods and services, in particular as expressed through the price of oil and other commodities. International capital flows constitute another such line. The first real visible sign of the international crisis hitting home in Norway was when Norway's biggest bank, the state dominated, DnB NOR (the state controls 34% of the stock) ran into an acute liquidity crisis as international money markets seized up in the aftermath of the Lehman Brothers' bankruptcy in mid-September 2008. This also exposed a trend and a new kind of vulnerability that had been growing more or less unnoticed in the previous years (by this author, too): Norwegian banks had to an increasing degree funded their growth internationally, so when the markets froze, and they could no longer roll over their loans, they were in trouble.

As if to underline the urgency of the situation, Norwegian authorities chose to present their response on a Sunday. On October 12, they presented a 350 billion NOK facility where the banks could swap their own mortgage-backed bonds against treasury bills. In effect the state was letting the banks live off the creditworthiness of one of the richest states (in per capita terms at least) in the world. At the same time new fixed interest rates loans, particularly suitable for smaller banks were made available in the Central Bank which also eased the demands placed on bank's collateral when borrowing from the Central Bank.

The property market had peaked well before this, however, falling roughly 9% on average in 2008, and a cumulative 18% in real terms since the peak in the summer of 2007. The building industry also ground to a halt and began to see its first layoffs during the fall of 2008. There was also a series of foreclosures in the real estate business. In one particularly hot location in Oslo – "Grünerløkka" – just four out of ten offices survived 2008, while in the city as a whole around 20% of the real estate business (measured in operative licenses from the regulator) was wiped out in one year (*Aftenposten*, 2008).

All the bad news from home and abroad notwithstanding, the mood within the governing red-green coalition was quite optimistic. A widely shared analysis was that Norway was in better shape to deal with whatever the crisis threw compared to how she fared in the early 1990s and compared to most other countries.

Compared to the U.S. for instance, Norway has the advantage of a highly developed welfare state. It is commonplace to speak of automatic stabilizers in the macroeconomic sense. In a crisis, aggregate demand is defended by unemployment benefits and the like. This line of argument, linking welfare benefits to economic stability can, however, also be made at the micro level, as insurance against personal risk. Since unemployment and serious illness does not have the same immediate and severe impact on personal finances as it has for large groups in for example the U.S., unemployment does not as quickly (and frequently) translate into payment problems on mortgages. It can also boost the public's confidence in its own future repayment capacity, and can thus moderate the impulse to engage in the kind of collective problem inducing behavior that characterizes a liquidity trap.

A further ground for – relative – optimism is that Norway, due in no small part to her oil wealth, has very solid public finances.[4] The "somebody has to pay for all this one day debate" that has occurred in other countries as they have been preparing their respective bailouts and stimulus packages – although relevant in Norway as well – simply doesn't resonate with the electorate.

Apart from in the housing market, the specter of deflation has not risen in Norway compared to for example the U.S. One reason for this is the plight of the NOK. The crisis, falling oil prices (from $145 to around $40 per barrel during the fall of 2008), and the return home of dollar-based investment funds, all contributed to a fall of about 20% in the value of the NOK against the dollar and the euro.

If we move from spatial to temporal comparisons and look to the late 1980s/early 1990s crisis, the most striking difference is that Norway now had a floating exchange rate. This means that the Central Bank was now free to cut rates, instead of increasing them in order to defend the currency as in the last crisis. And so it did. In December its key rate was cut by 1.75% down to 3%. It was too early to tell at the time of writing whether this would be sufficient to get the property market going again or if deflationary expectations would take hold and stimulate a widespread "wait and see" sentiment. The housing market also had to absorb the onset of risk aversion in banking circles. Several commentators claimed that the banks – in spite of swaps and interest rate cuts – had more or less overnight switched to being too tightfisted. This was hard to document beyond anecdotal evidence that emerged during the fall of 2008. Still, a general argument for why this was not an unreasonable diagnosis would run as follows: As the banks were bracing themselves for new losses in the New Year, the well known procyclical effects of capital adequacy standards and "mark to market" (and "mark to model") accounting rules, should produce exactly this kind of effect.

Conclusion: Recommodified housing and the politics of economic policy

By way of conclusion I will return to the issue of how and to what degree the recommodification of Norwegian housing has affected the politics of economic policy and ultimately the future of the Norwegian welfare state.

As we have seen recommodification has involved several significant trends. First of all, despite of all the efforts by the economic policymaking elite to create a stable and stabilizing framework for macroeconomic policymaking, housing prices have not found a smooth and moderate growth trajectory. A bubble was followed by a bust phase that created a debt crisis in significant portions of the populace in the early 1990s. In turn, a long boom, disturbed only by the 1997 Asian crisis, inflated into a bubble when the China effect started in 2003. In 2008 this bubble burst. Until 1999 it was tempting to interpret volatile housing market developments as a subset of the volatility produced by a procyclical monetary policy. If this had been true, as the present author was inclined to believe at the time (Tranøy, 2000), we could have expected less volatility in the housing market when the Central Bank switched to inflation targeting. The reason that this was so manifestly not the result is easier to understand in hindsight. What happens when a central bank is given an inflation mandate in a welfare state full of owner-occupiers with a tradition for variable rate loans is that in effect the housing market becomes the safety valve for pressure in the economy. Irresponsible wage settlements or overly enthusiastic investment plans in the oil sector? Increase interest rates! Imported disinflation? Reduce them! And so on and so forth. As a mature welfare state Norway has policies and institutions directed toward stabilizing any number of individual and societal level outcomes. Employment, income, inflation, growth, health, and education – all of these measures are targeted. Not so with housing prices.

Instead a rollercoasterlike trajectory has distributed risk in a close to random ways. At what time you enter or exit the market – a decision that is normally more influenced by where you are in your personal life cycle (marriage, divorce, child rearing, and change of jobs are probably the most important reasons) – can be decisive for your finances for decades to come. The housing market is producing winners and losers in more pronounced ways than before, by making age and inheritance even more significant determinants for wealth levels. It is also worth noting that this 25-year period of instability has produced no political reaction of substance apart from at the level of the macroeconomic regime. Market instability, with its associated redistribution of wealth and risk, has been passively accepted by the policymaking elites. No new housing policy initiatives have been made, the deducibility rules have remained untouched since 1992, and there has been no attempt to give a better representation of asset prices in the inflation measure (variants of the consumer price index) used by the Central Bank. When the crisis emerged and the banks were given help, no demands were placed on them with regard to credit distribution or bonus schemes. Calls have been made by the NBBL for "Husbanken" to make a "comeback" and again assume a greater role in financing Norwegian housing, but with no response from the authorities so far.

So even if the crisis has not had the effect of moving Norway (back) toward less residual and more universalistic housing policies, there is still scant reason to speak of a turn to British style asset-based welfare (see Watson, this volume). Apart from housing, there has been no "downsizing" of the welfare state. Norwegians are neither under ideological nor practical pressure to become crucially dependent on their own wealth in order to sustain good quality schooling, higher education, health, or even income maintenance. In Polanyian terms, Norway has experienced a recommodification of her markets for money and housing, but not, yet, of her labor market.

Instead, we can ask, will the developments described here undermine the welfare state and the decommodified status of labor over time? Do Kemeny and Castles' arguments yield insights in terms of the Norwegian case? In short, has a recommodified housing market driven politics to the right? As noted in Section 5.1, here we need to investigate both the taxing and the spending side of the equation.

The taxing argument is simple. When the real price of housing increases over time and housing costs weigh ever more heavily in the average household's finances, one can expect homeowning voters to become more sensitive to changes in taxation that increase the costs associated with homeownership and/or reduce the value of housing assets. At the height of the bubble in the summer of 2006, voices within the ruling center-left suggested limiting the effect of tax breaks by introducing a 5 million NOK ceiling for couples on loans that are eligible for tax deductions. The idea was to shave a bit off the top end of the market without hurting average families. This idea was instantly killed by the center-left government's top brass (the Prime Minister and the Minister of Finance), reflecting a worry about the political consequences of hurting owner-occupiers. In the same vein, continued (and in the economics of globalization terms fashionable) suggestions to increase taxes on immobile objects, for example property, toward the levels seen elsewhere in Europe have never moved beyond the expert committees that keep bringing this suggestion up.

The spending side of the argument is more complex. The premise is that one can expect homeowning voters to become more one-sidedly interested in policies that are perceived as contributing to keeping interest rates down. And if this is the case, we need to ask how these preferences are mediated by a regime dominated by an independent central bank mandated with an inflation target. More crudely put: if growth becomes dependent on private consumption fueled by rising housing prices, which in turn is partly dependent on low interest rates, this can "crowd out" part of the public spending upon which welfare state development depends. This is so, because welfare spending, unless it is fully tax financed, stimulates aggregate demand and will thus lead the central bank – other things being equal – to increase interest rates. This ordering of preferences and the world view that sustains it is fully built into both the political discourse and how the media covers macroeconomic policy (Øvald, 2007). In political exchange over macropolicy political opponents routinely accuse and blame each other's policy for contributing to increased interest rates. The media reinforces this framing by asking leading private sector economists about the impact of the budget on interest rates.

Over time, if the year-on-year effects of this institutionally mediated conservative bias are allowed to accumulate, the effect might well be a slow erosion of the welfare state that currently still protects Norwegian citizens from the kind of grave risks that regimes of asset-based welfare expose for example Australian and British citizens to (see Watson; Mortensen and Seabrooke in this volume).

If this analysis is anything to go by, and given the state's unique fiscal strength, a solid, but not too dramatic, crisis is just what the Norwegian social democratic welfare state needed. This is so for at least two reasons. First, because a decline in private consumption creates room for the kind of government investment in the infrastructure of the welfare state that has so far been held back by the privileged position of interest rates in the macro discourse. The fiscal stimulus package presented in January 2009 included accelerated spending on everything from school buildings to railroads. Second, the short-term electoral effect of the crisis seems to be that it has engendered support for the ruling, broadly speaking, social democratic coalition. In short the crisis has both moved politics to the left by filling a hitherto administratively oriented cabinet with a stronger sense of purpose and at the same time strengthened the political basis for such policies.

Notes

1. *Norske Boligbyggelags Landsforbund* (The Norwegian Federation of Cooperative Housing Associations, hereafter "NBBL") and *Den Norske Stats Husbank* (The Norwegian State Housing Bank, hereafter "Husbanken").
2. The extra 0.5%, compared to the ECB rate, provided room to phase in oil income and thus accept a moderate appreciation of the real exchange rate.
3. Some new Cooperatives based on this financing model, have indeed run into serious problems. The Consumer Council has branded many of the developers as ruthless, with one additional problem being that costs related to cooperative fees or homeowners association dues have been systematically underestimated in order to ease the initial marketing of the projects. http://forbrukerportalen.no/Artikler/2008/Ungdomsbolge%20og%20boligpolitikk
4. The Government Pension Fund – Global – in spite of heavy losses incurred during 2008, was still worth close to $400 bn at the end of 2008, that is, a bit less than Norway's annual GDP.

6
Egalitarian Politics in Property Booms and Busts: Housing as Social Right or Means to Wealth in Australia and Denmark

Jens Ladefoged Mortensen and Leonard Seabrooke

Introduction

Do property booms and busts change a population's views about whether housing should be considered as a social right or a means to wealth? This chapter investigates this question by comparing changes to taxation and housing finance regimes in what is defined in the editors' introductory chapter to this volume as corporatist and liberal residential property market types. While the types of residential capitalism differ in Australia and Denmark, the cases discussed here share some important similarities. The first is that political discourse is saturated with egalitarian ideals in both societies, be it the "fair go" of Australian society or "equal opportunities" (*"lige muligheder"*) in Danish society.[1] How egalitarianism is constructed through political framing, and how it is expressed as a broadly shared normative goal in society, informs attitudes and behavior toward housing markets. The second similarity is that both states have liberal mortgage finance (LMF) systems that provide securitization or covered bond options, and within both states changes to taxation and housing finance systems facilitated residential property booms. These reforms, particularly those following financial deregulation, introduced new mortgage instruments and changed economic incentives for selecting residential property as an investment vehicle. From these changes, the largely transnational process of financial liberalization rubs up against national taxation systems and their treatment of residential property in ways that privilege certain groups over others (such as owner-occupier, renters, or landlords). Such struggles have not disappeared since the housing boom went bust, but continue in political and everyday life.

To help to understand how these struggles play out, we separate the normative framing of residential property markets into two ideal-types: "Housing as Social Right" and "Housing as Means to Wealth." These two types are not mutually exclusive but we suggest that the framing of residential property markets, including conflict over normative goals that are tied to discourses of egalitarianism, will tend to favor one or the other of these ideals. These frames will also be expressed in the institutional design present within the national system, and will influence political debates on what changes are possible (Blyth, 2002; Campbell, 2004). Frames of egalitarianism are particularly important with respect to understanding the intergenerational consequences of housing politics, including the potential perception that the "old are feeding on their young," or that the property booms have increased stratification and market exposure for economically vulnerable groups. The Australian and Danish cases highlight differences in this regard.

The chapter is organized as follows. In Section 6.1, we briefly describe differences in the Australian and Danish cases. In Section 6.2, we trace the evolution of the Danish property boom in the decade prior to the property market collapse, highlighting institutional incentives related to taxation and housing finance. We also consider how debates over residential property markets were framed. In Section 6.3, we do the same for the Australian case. In Section 6.4, we contrast the Danish and Australian experiences since the housing boom went bust. In the conclusion and speculations, we consider the question of whether there is a changing conception of housing as a social right or a means to wealth in these cases. We stress that the construction of how the economy should work is critical in how homeowners and would-be homeowners are politically motivated to call for change.

6.1 Egalitarian politics in two different homes

As the editors' introductory chapter to this volume clarifies, within the comparative and international political economy (CPE and IPE) there is not much of a role for residential property markets, even if there has been a surge of interest in everyday aspects of financial socialization (Langley, 2008; Seabrooke, 2006). In general, analyses of residential property markets lend themselves to approaches in CPE and IPE that seek to explain institutional stability through institutional complementarities within a national system. The work associated with studying varieties of capitalism (VOC) or worlds of welfare provides powerful ways to map different systems. Such typologies should be embraced to integrate the study of residential property markets into CPE and IPE but, as the editors' introductory chapter to this volume makes clear, these typologies need to be heavily modified to understand change in residential property markets.

In particular, we suggest that they are not powerful in helping to understand reasonably quick changes in ideas about how the economy should work. To access information on change, we argue that the work on discourse, ideas, and framing among economic and political elites is important (Blyth, 2002; Hay and Rosamond, 2002; Schmidt, 2003), including work that concentrates more on the influence of everyday actors on policy change (Hobson and Seabrooke, 2007; Seabrooke, 2007). For example, for most of the period discussed Australians and Danes exhibited stable behavior and attitudes toward housing that constitute distinctive norms. Australian homeowners typically have most of their lifelong wealth in their home and they gamble with that wealth. If there is a "big trade-off" between having welfare and owner-occupation within an economy (Castles, 1998; Kemeny, 1980, 2005), then Australians' behavior demonstrates a clear preference for seeking economic security via high owner-occupation rates (~70%) and the potential for big economic gains in residential property markets rather than through state-based welfare. Part of the Australian egalitarian "fair go" is that everyone should have access to owner-occupied property, with which they can to build assets and wealth that they can call upon during the life cycle and use to ease retirement. As Fred Argy has argued, "Australia's high level of home ownership (by international standards) and ease of access to low-cost accommodation has been traditionally viewed as part of the social wage" (Argy, 2003, 32). Egalitarian politics on housing are therefore tied more to the use of housing as a means to wealth rather than as a state-provided social right.

Danes do the opposite. In their big "welfare trade-off" Danes have traditionally preferred high welfare and comparatively low owner-occupation (~50%), with those who do have mortgages carrying enormous amounts of debt underpinned by an extremely stable housing finance regime. Despite their wealth, Danes do not rely on owner-occupation to build assets over the life cycle and, instead, pay high taxes for social services and welfare that will see them through working life and retirement. Egalitarian politics on housing has been traditionally tied to viewing it as a communal or state-provided social right rather than as a way for an individual to generate wealth.

Through a comparative lens, Australians tend to see housing as a means to wealth while Danes tend to see housing as a social right. However, as we detail below, the recent property boom and bust in both states has unsettled these verities. Housing booms and busts can create powerful political forces that inhibit support for a traditional welfare state, and they can also embolden groups to call for state intervention to ease housing affordability. This is why it is important to understand how political debates over residential property markets are framed by economic and political elites, as well as the potential for ideas to change general societal attitudes about the legitimacy and appropriateness of policy change.

Both Australia and Denmark have a shared experience in that they both went through a property boom during the last decade which has now tapered off. In 2006 OECD economists estimated that the Australian residential property market was overvalued by 51.8% in 2004 and that the Danish residential property market was overvalued by 13.1% (Girouard et al., 2006, 25). In 2008 the IMF estimated that the "housing price gap" (the difference between housing prices and economic growth explained by "fundamentals") was 22% in Australia and 17% in Denmark (in the U.S. it was a mere 11%, see International Monetary Fund, 2008, 11). Both Australia and Denmark experienced exceptionally high economic growth after 2000, which was based, in part, on the capacity of residential property markets to fuel consumption and demand (see also Schwartz; Watson in this volume).

To provide a brief comparative profile, Australians paid nearly double what their British and American cousins spent on interest payments as a percentage of disposable income in 2003 (7.9% in Australia compared to 3% in the U.K. and 4.5% in the U.S., see OECD, 2005b, 203). Australia also increased its residential mortgage debt in percentage of GDP from 24.2% in 1992 to 50.8% in 2002 (OECD, 2004b, 135), with the boom continuing into 2003–05 and then falling slightly before the current financial crisis. Given the increased financial stress, it is particularly important to note that Australians prefer to have flexible loans (73% in 2002, compared to 33% in the U.S. and 20% in New Zealand, OECD, 2005b, 203; Broome, this volume). In general, Australians prefer flexible rates on home loans that are normally for 30 years – leaving them especially vulnerable to shocks that increase interest rates and households' debt burdens. This vulnerability is even more apparent if we consider that 66% of most Australians' lifetime wealth is in the family home, compared to 44% in the UK and 32% in the US (Reserve Bank of Australia, 2005). Accordingly, Australia had four distinct episodes of housing price collapses between 1974 and 1993, three of which were strongly associated with recessions, and with an average housing price decline of 16.5% (Berry and Dalton, 2004, 87). The Australian memory of housing price crashes may be more salient in motivating Australians to vote for governments with a track record of low interest rates as a way of mitigating their mortgage gambles (Easton and Gerlach, 2005). This is clearly related to the perception that housing price collapses in the Australian context are from external market conditions, which can be prevented by governments with a greater capacity to manage "economic fundamentals."

As for the Danes, their "hybrid" market economy distinguishes it from its Nordic cousins (Campbell and Pedersen, 2007). They are liberal in housing finance but otherwise corporatist, permitting high mortgage indebtedness for those who own property in a state where just over half own property as a result of the high proportion of social housing. Denmark has experienced growth in housing prices that outstrips its Nordic and western neighbors and they now beat the Dutch as European champions for their overall mortgage debt per capita (Catte et al., 2004, 7; see Aalbers in this volume). They also paid more than double what the Swedes paid in interest payments as a percentage of disposable income in 2003 (8.3% in Denmark compared to 3.3% in Sweden, OECD, 2005b, 203). Denmark increased its residential mortgages as a percentage of GDP from 63.9% in 1992 to 74.3% in 2002 (OECD, 2004b, 135), not a particularly stunning rise but a reflection of the stability of the Danish housing finance system. Accordingly, the percentage of loans at adjustable rates for the Danes, at least up to 2003 (more on this below) was 15% and housing loans were typically for 25 years (OECD, 2005b, 203). The historical memory of the most recent significant housing collapse in 1987 had a strong effect on attitudes toward the Danish housing boom until around 2003, and then again when the boom went bust. This may be in part because the late 1980s Danish housing collapse was engendered by a government policy choice more so than an external economic constraint. We may then speculate that in liberal economies, with majoritarian political systems, governments rely on external economic shocks to pop a housing bubble, while in corporatist economies with consensus-based political systems governments are crucial in popping bubbles through policy change.

In assessing institutional incentives and the frames for debates, we place attention on how these systems changed since the 1980s, and what kinds of new politics these changes dragged up. In discussing taxation we focus in particular on two politically sensitive groups, landlords and private investors, and first-time homeowners. In discussing housing finance, our aim is to locate trends in the marketplace.

6.2 Institutional incentives and frames in the Danish property boom

Institutional incentives

Taxation

The Danish tax system strongly favors existing homeowners, especially the older generation of homeowners, who brought their property before 1998 (see Green-Pedersen, 2002, 127). In 1998, the social democratic government decided to cool the economy by, among other things, limiting the value of tax deductibles on property. The effect was a minor market crash. Since the current liberal conservative government came to power in 2001 the Danish property tax has been subject to a tax freeze. This spurred a property boom that hurt first-time buyers and tenants.

To understand the relationship between property politics and tax policy in Denmark, it is necessary to go back to the two major property crashes, those in 1979 and 1987. The first crash is less interesting for our purposes. It occurred in the wake of the general macroeconomic instability of the Danish economy after the second oil crisis. The crisis displaced the social democrats from government in favor of a decade of liberal-conservative coalition 1982–92 (Schwartz, 1994). The second crash was caused by the tax reform of 1987, known in Denmark as the "potato diet" or *"kartoffelkuren"* in which society should return to basic living rather than engage in excess. The 1987 tax reform lowered the amount homeowners could deduct in mortgage interest rate payments to 50% from a possible 70%. The 1987 reform package also included a tax surcharge of 20% on consumer borrowing and extensive use of regulations in the mortgage market. The market suffered a prolonged depression thereafter, with a 70% drop in market transactions for owner-occupied properties by 1989 while forced home sales tripled (Boelhouwer et al., 2004, 424–5). From 1990 to 1994, both social democratic and liberal governments sought to revive the housing market. They removed rent controls for new private rental properties and permitted increases to cover owners' maintenance costs. Further tax reforms also reduced the tax value of deductible interest payments (down from 46% in 1998 to 33% in 2002) to increase private savings in the Danish economy as well as to reduce the marginal tax burden. As such, tax policy reduced the share of income tax in government revenue from 48.5% in 1994 to 39.1% in 2005, while the tax base had been widened to include mandatory labor market contributions and green taxes. The housing boom was thought by government agencies to be an extension of sound economic fundamentals rather than extraordinary growth for a particular class of assets (Wagner, 2005).

Landlords and property investors.   The institutional setup of the Danish welfare state discourages potential private landlords. Denmark is an example of a corporalist market economy with a pro-tenant housing policy where their rights are very strong. Nonresidential landlords who rent out property on the private market are directly taxed on their income; profits from private rental are taxed as personal income at 28% while rental surplus from properties owned by pension funds is taxed at 15% (OECD, 2006, 19).[2] The Danish tax system is premised upon the existence of a social norm of housing rights rather than wealth creation. Consequently, there is an insignificant proportion of investor-led property purchases and greater reliance on the state and corporations for access to housing (for example, tenants typically access "cheap" rentals by joining a list through their pension fund or insurance company, with preference determined by tenure). Tax policy has also contributed to the decline of private rental properties on the market over time.

First-time buyers.   The full effect of the reduction of the deductible interest payments negatively affected first-time homeowners. Until 2005, the effect of this increase was easily offset by the low interest rate level and the provision of new financial instruments in the mortgage market. After 2005, however, the full scale of this barrier was evident in the rapidly declining number of first-time buyers on the market. In general, the combined effect of the property boom, tax freeze, and tax incentives to residential homeowners favored existing homeowners, creating a razor thin intergenerational fault line in Danish politics. Many first-time homeowners had to rely on their parents' equity to buy an apartment and then rent it from the parent (*"forældrekøb,"* or "parent-buy"). No official statistics exist on the scale of the parent-buy property market in Denmark. Anecdotal evidence suggests that it was one of the key drivers behind the boom. Easy credit access, low interest rates, and booming markets suddenly made it look like a good investment, despite the tax disincentives. As Danish tax law prevents a transfer of the property, children must rent the property and the parents are taxed at full market rent. The parent-buy market collapsed with the end of the property boom. While it is fair to state that there is no serious intergenerational equity problem in Denmark with regard to income or welfare access, the levels of indebtedness over generations are quite different, with the young much more heavily indebted than their parents' generation (Lunde, 2007; Realkreditrådet, 2008). This capacity for indebtedness is largely a consequence of innovations in housing markets that are consistent with transnational trends, as can be seen in many of the cases in this volume.

Housing finance

In December 2008, the Association of Danish Mortgage Banks (*Realkreditrådet*) ran TV commercials to reassure homeowners that the Danish mortgage system was – probably – "the best in the world." One analyst found that "Danish mortgage banks have in practice structured their mortgage lending business in such a way that they do not assume significant financial risks with respect to lending and the underlying funding activities" (European Mortgage Federation, 2008, 23). Indeed, by late 2008 both Danish economists and international market leaders, such as George Soros (*Wall Street Journal*, 2008), advocated the Danish model of securitization (which is based on a "balance principle" where institutions carry the risk and do not remove the loans from their balance sheet) as a way to reform the American financial system.

The trumpeting of the Danish model as solution to the financial crisis is based, in part, on the long-term stability of the system. But is not to suggest nothing has changed, as the Danish mortgage market has been extensively liberalized since the 1990s. Financial institutions with the capacity to issue mortgage bonds provide the main point of entry alongside the key banks in Denmark (such as Danske and Nordea). During the period of liberalization, the government introduced new types of loans. These offered new choices of fixed-rate mortgages with adjustable rate mortgage debt, as well as interest-only repayment. This is arguably one of the most remarkable features of Danish property politics during the boom period and an aspect that quickly fell away when boom turned to bust. When Danes were given the choice of new repayment options, an increasing number of

homeowners opted for more risky, flexible rate and repayment profiles during the boom. Until 2000, mortgages were fixed-rate loans.
By 2004, fixed-rate loans accounted for about 40% of total outstanding mortgage debt. By contrast, the share of flexible loans grew to the
same level by late 2005, with additional growth in the new market
for fixed interest-only loans (for 10–15 years) soaking up approximately 8% of the market (OECD, 2006, 136). The growth of interest-
only loans in Denmark was "exceptionally quick" from a European
perspective (Lunde, 2007, 12). The new flexibility for homeowners
drove up housing prices and also paved the way for a restructuring
of mortgage debt, and conversion of property value into private consumption, which then fueled the economy. The use of the flexible
loans peaked by the end of 2005, dropping from 50.8% to 46% in
2006. Reforms in 2007, for EU compliance, introduced new financial
instruments that permitted delayed amortization beyond ten years
for those with loans with less than 70% of the value of the property – suggesting a new system of financial benefits for those with
extraordinary incomes that could afford hefty deposits (Danmarks
Nationalbank, 2007, 15).[3] In short, this new mortgage market ignited
an unprecedented property boom in Denmark and had the effect of
redistributing wealth geographically and intergenerationally. Once
the boom went bust financial institutions ran to safe instruments
and proclaimed that Denmark was risk free by world standards, while
also carrying extremely high levels of personal debt for those who
own property.

Frames during the Danish boom

In Denmark, the regulatory traditions of the welfare state and a social
rights discourse shaped property politics prior to the 1990s. However,
in the Danish context, there has been a change from viewing housing
as a social right within a pro-tenant discourse to a gradual transformation of viewing residential property as a means to wealth. This was particularly prominent in the boom period and is now being reevaluated
during the bust. On some aspects of housing, however, there may be no
turning back to the former more egalitarian principles. Here we focus
on property tax debate, as well as the "liquidation" of housing cooperative associations (*andelsboligforening*).

In response to signs of overheating in the Danish economy, the
Danish Economic Council (*Økonomisk Råd*) in 2006 warned the government of counterproductive tax policies that were generating distortions

within the economy, especially the "tax freeze." Their recommendation may have constituted "good economics" but not "good politics." The Council subsequently changed its advice to: (1) revenues from property tax must follow market prices, reinstating the automatic stabilizer of public assessments; and (2) that the low tax rate on real estate purchased before July 1, 1998 must be cancelled (Danish Economic Council, 2006, 374). The OECD voiced similar criticisms. Yet, the expert consensus favoring increased property taxes and a shift from taxing labor to property met with hostility from the government and opposition. For instance, Minister of Taxation, Kristian Jensen, dismissed it completely: "We think it is beneficial for society if people own their homes. And we want to assure homeowners that today's tax system will remain in place under the current government" (*DR Nyheder*, 2005).

In 2005 the two socialist parties (*Socialistisk Folkeparti* – SF – and *Enhedslisten*) gave support to the idea of increasing the property tax, as well as a reduction of on the costs of property sales. The most radical idea was the establishment of a public mortgage fund that would reduce rent for tenants. This would be financed by revenue collected from increased property taxes. But in the 2007 election SF made a political U-turn concerning its policies on property taxes a fortnight before the election, fearing that the continuance of their policy stance would seriously diminish their electoral hopes and mark their party as unfit for governing (Børsen, 2007). The election result gave more power to SF, was a disaster for the far left, and, most importantly, confirmed the conservative leadership of the more free market *Venstre* party. SF's U-turn signaled that any suggestion of moving tax burdens from work to property is now rejected across the political spectrum. There are important knock-on effects here: tax reforms, public investments in housing, rent reduction for tenants, and extensive urban renewal programs are constrained by the fear of disturbing market forces, not only during boom periods but also now during downturns.

The extent of institutional change within the Danish system may also be seen in the rapid "liquidation" of housing cooperative associations (*andelsboligforening*). The system of housing cooperatives permitted entry for those on moderate incomes to purchase the right to reside within an apartment complex owned by a mutual association, and was typically associated as a community-based rights form rather than a wealth creation form of property for public service employees, such as nurses and police officers. After 1993, at the same time as changes to housing finance for EU compliance, the pricing mechanism of housing cooperatives evolved from the "original sale price" through "state defined evaluation" (with incremental increases) to "market-based evaluation." Within this sector the change in evaluation permitted price increases of 69% between 1996 and 2000 and 110% between 2000 and 2005 (Danish Ministry of Taxation, 2006). Nearly 40% of housing cooperative associations which decided to change to the last method experienced price increases of more than 50% (Erhvervs-og Byggestyrelsen, 2006), with some associations reaping a tenfold increase in extreme cases. As this form of property represents nearly one-third of residences in big Danish cities, this transformation is particularly significant. It is, at base, an intergenerational shift and the destruction of a housing system based on social principles, where associations would deliberately hold down prices, to one where many in housing cooperatives have moved to market-based evaluations in order for them to enter the freehold property market later on. In doing so, they have closed the door once open to them and contributed to the move from housing seen as a social right to, instead, a means to wealth.

6.3   Institutional incentives and frames in the Australian property boom

Institutional incentives

Taxation

Australia's taxation structure for residential property markets is something of an oddity within the OECD. Where most OECD member states give tax preference to owner-occupiers' mortgage interest payments, the Australian system instead provides landlords with clear incentives to invest in rental properties (see Gruis and Nieboer, 2007). This is particularly so, given that landlords can "negatively gear" the difference between rent paid by tenant per week and the mortgage interest payment made per week.[4] Landlords' losses are deductible against their taxable income, including expenditure on interest, housing improvements, taxes, and administrative services. Changes during the last decade on capital gains tax reforms also greatly benefited those engaged in the resale of residential property for personal profit. In support of this system, or perhaps as a consequence, within the OECD Australian personal investors have stood out for their aversion towards foreign investment and their preference for domestic investment in investment properties to make money from house price appreciations and, effectively, receive tax breaks through their tenants (Mishra and Daly, 2006).

Changes during the late 1980s and the 1990s encouraged this behavior, particularly for investor landlords. Along with the drop in the marginal rate on average incomes from 38% in 1992 to 30% in 2001, in 2005 and 2006 there were further tax cuts for high income individuals, with the wealthiest 1% receiving 9% of tax cuts and the richest 10% receiving 43% of all tax cuts (Leigh, 2006, 5). Another important change in the Australian taxation system was to capital gains taxation. Prior to 1985 capital gains in Australia were untaxed, and after 1985 (during the reign of the Australian Labor Party, hereafter ALP) capital gains above a certain level were counted within the normal personal income tax assessment and then taxed at the appropriate marginal rate. Importantly, for owner-occupiers the sale of principal residence did not accrue capital gains tax (Yates, 2003, 2), making Australia one of the lowest transaction cost OECD member states in which to buy and sell residential property. In 1999, under the Howard conservative Liberal government (in power from 1996–2007), pro-investor reforms to capital gains tax halved the amount of tax payable on net capital gains on assets held by individuals for more than a year, reducing the maximum rate to 24.25%, while superannuation funds received a concessional rate of 10% (Costello, 1999). Furthermore, the Howard government also cut personal income taxes on numerous occasions while in office (and during election campaigns). Most significant here was the introduction of "A New Tax System" (ANTS) in 2000, including the highly controversial Goods and Services Tax (GST, a consumption tax) that excluded rent as a GST item (Eccleston, 2004). These tax conditions encouraged the property boom and generated questions about whether the system was in favor of homeownership or existing homeowners. In May 2008 the new ALP government, elected in late 2007, announced "Australia's Future Tax System Review," including a review of the taxation of housing and, in particular, negative gearing (Australian Senate, 2008, 64–9).

Landlords and private investors.   The Australian taxation system for residential property markets is heavily biased toward landlords, especially through negative gearing.[5] In 2005–06, landlords received AUS$19 billion in rental income and claimed $14 billon in interest payment deductions on the rental property mortgages, and AUS$10 billion in deductions (such as real estate agent fees and council taxes), of which AUS$1 billion was in capital works improvements. Their "loss" of AUS$5 billion was then offset against their taxable income (Australian Senate, 2008, 64). Furthermore, of those claiming deductions, half had a taxable income of between AUS$21,601 and $63,000 (2006 median household income in Australia was AUS$53,404), suggesting that Australian landlordism is a widespread social phenomenon among what would normally be considered the working to middle classes (Australian Taxation Office, [ATO], 2007, 12).[6]

In addition to negative gearing, changes to superannuation systems under the Howard government's "Transition-to-Retirement" (TTR) scheme (introduced in 2005) also permitted a "more flexible and adaptable retirement income system" for those over 55 who are still working, permitting them to access pension income, as well as "salary sacrifice" in order to reduce their taxable personal income (Australian Treasury, 2004). From July 2007 the scheme was extended to all over age 60, permitting those with TTR pension schemes to reduce "sacrificed" personal taxable income to zero while also drawing on tax-free pension payments to supplement income, and many over age 50 effectively to reduce their taxable income to 15%, as opposed to the highest marginal rate of 45% (The Australian, 2007). Clearly the tax system was distorted in favor of baby boomers.

Between 1992 and 2003 the proportion of investor-led residential property purchases increased from 15% to 30% (OECD, 2005b, 140). In 2003 45% of new mortgage lending went to investors, while the share of the market for first-time homeowners shrank to 14%, down from 25% in 2001 (Murphy and Harley, 2003, 8). There was also an absence of "social landlords," those who invest in the provision of social housing (only 6% of the Australian rental market). This intensified pressure on those who are not only noncreditworthy for home loans but considered unsuitable as tenants by landlords (Wulff and Maher, 1998; see also Broome, this volume).

First-time buyers. While the Australian government temporarily experimented with a mortgage interest payment tax deductibility scheme for young homeowners (with a cap on claimed rebates) in 1982 (Yates, 2003, 26), there was no significant federal support for first-time homeowners until the boom was framed as a political problem for Australian egalitarianism (see below). During the introduction of the ANTS system, the federal government introduced first-time homeowner grants, which were administered by state governments. Some state governments have chosen to provide a First Home Owners Grant to offset the costs of government stamp duty on purchases. The decrease in Australia's level of owner-occupation, from 72% in 1990 to 69% in 2006, points to increasing stress on first-time buyers (Australian Senate, 2008, 17;

OECD, 2004b), with serious social effects in a society where access to private property is viewed as the most important way of storing wealth. The general relationship between the late 1980s and 2008 was that average incomes doubled while housing prices increased fivefold. By 2006 a household needed seven times its after-tax disposable income to afford a home, compared with five times in 1996 (NATSEM, 2008, 7, 12). In cities with big property booms such as Sydney, Melbourne, and Perth, it became common for Generation X families to rely on parents for financial assistance to purchase an ordinary home (Australian Senate, 2008, 33).

Housing finance

In the words of the former Australian Treasurer, Peter Costello, interest rates during the 1990s were the lowest "since men walked on the moon" (Berry and Dalton, 2004, 74–5). During this period there were significant innovations, mainly from financial deregulation, that spurred competition for housing finance in Australia, cut margins on mortgages and permitted Australians to take on even riskier forms of engagement with the residential property market. Within Australia the "Big Four" large banks (Commonwealth, Westpac, National, and ANZ) traditionally dominated mortgage lending. During the property boom new mortgage brokers aggressively entered the market (such as Aussie Home Loans) and accounted for some 30% of new loans (Ellis, 2006; Reserve Bank of Australia [RBA], 2005).

The securitization of home loans contributed to the growth of mortgages within the Australian economy, given the capacity of securitization more generally to provide a means to recycle capital through a domestic system (cf. Seabrooke, 2006; Schwartz, 2009). In Australia in 2005 securitized mortgages accounted for AUS$170 billon, or 7% of total system financial assets in Australia (compared to the U.S. at around 20%). The growth in this market has been remarkable given that in the 1990s securitized assets accounted for less than 1% of system financial assets (Reserve Bank of Australia, 2006a). Australian residential MBS have also been able to attract significant foreign investment. In 2005 losses on these securities were AUS$8 in every AUS$1 million (Reserve Bank of Australia, 2006a, 65). More generally defaults on mortgages are extremely low (0.2% in 2004 and even only 0.4% in 2007, see Reserve Bank of Australia, 2005; Reserve Bank of Australia, 2008a), which is especially important given that residential mortgages account for nearly half of all bank credit in Australia.

As stated above, most loans have flexible rates, and fixed rates are typically readjusted every five years. During the housing boom fixed rates on new home loan approvals dropped to as little as 5% (in 2002, see Reserve Bank of Australia, 2008a, 52), placing Australia in stark contrast to most other OECD economies and especially their cousins in New Zealand (see Broome this volume). In addition to the overwhelming preference for flexible loans, the growth of interest-only loans in Australia has been even more aggressive than in Denmark. In 2005 60% of new investor loans and 15% of new owner-occupier loans were interest-only, typically with the borrower paying off only part of the principal after 10 to 15 years (Reserve Bank of Australia, 2006b, 42). This particular financial innovation was popular because of confidence that property prices would continue to rise. The transition from boom to bust thus placed a lot of financial pressure on investors seeking to exploit the housing finance system and generous tax breaks.

Frames during the Australian boom

Within Australia there is little doubt that housing is seen as a means to wealth, even to the extent that it has created a range of intergenerational equity problems. Ian McFarlane, the Reserve Bank of Australia Governor from 1996 to 2006, commented in 1995 that it "is not too much of an exaggeration to suggest that a significant rise in the real price of housing, in effect, makes some people better off at the expense of their children" (*The Age*, 2003a; *Sydney Morning Herald*, 2002), and continued to criticize the boom as driven by speculative demand. This view was not shared by Prime Minister, John Howard, who, on national public radio in 2003, responded to a question about the possible deleterious effects of the property boom on intergenerational equity, with: "I don't get people stopping me in the street and saying John, you're outrageous, under your government the value of my house has increased ..."[7] The contrast here may be understood as independent economic advice for sustainability versus short-term political expediency.

Within the Australian political debate the property boom raised issues of fairness centered on the question of whether housing should be automatically seen as a means to wealth or as a social right. On social justice grounds the younger and poorer have a lot to complain about. For example, given the taxation incentives for landlords and private investors, those in the eighth to tenth income deciles own 65% of investment properties, and landlords in general are typically people in the late forties up to age 65 (Kohler and Roster, 2005, 18–19; Reserve Bank of Australia, 2005, 20). In the year John Howard became Prime Minister, 1996, Australians in low income households spent 30% of their disposable income on mortgage repayments. In the year he lost his own electoral seat and position as Prime Minister, low income households had to spend 47% of their disposable income on their mortgage repayments to maintain the same standard of living as eleven years earlier (Australian Senate, 2008, 38). More generally, homeownership for young households (25–39 year olds) dropped from 65% in 1986 to 58% in 2006, and the capacity for these households to access all transacted dwellings had decreased from 45% to 33% (Richards, 2008). In the context of Australia's "wage earner's welfare" system (Castles, 1985), the capacity to access residential property markets is key. The 2008 Senate Committee on Housing Affordability asserted, "home ownership is a universal dream in Australia, regardless of economic circumstances" (Australian Senate, 2008, 15). So while there is no pervasive attitude about the need for the state to provide housing, egalitarian politics comes into play when discussing how ordinary families can enter the market and begin to accrue wealth. In the Australian debate such concerns were automatically linked to access to property over generations, with prominent Australian economists suggesting that an intergenerational fallout from the property boom was a consequence of the taxation system (Yates, 2003, 26). The problem, so to speak, is that the tax system encourages the old to eat the young.

The political sensitivity of housing markets was clearly apparent through behavior during election campaigns. The Howard coalition government (1996–2007) used interest rates fears in the last four election campaigns, during the last week of campaigning, to polarize Australians, who mostly have flexible rate loans, against the key opposition party, the ALP. These last-week blanket campaigns played on the idea of the ALP as a bad economic manager who would increase welfare spending and push up interest rates (Easton and Gerlach, 2005). The Howard government also relied on tax cuts to gain popularity. However, attitudes can change. For example, when asked about their preference between increasing welfare spending or tax cuts, surveys suggest that in 1990 58% of Australians wanted tax cuts while only 11% preferred more social spending (with the remainder choosing "depends"), while in 2004 38% called for more welfare and 35% called for tax cuts (Leigh, 2006, 2). This shift in attitudes may help to explain the Howard government's defeat in 2007 and the ALP's landslide victory.

During the 2007 election campaign, the ALP made the "crisis" in housing affordability a central part of their policy platform. There were good economic grounds for raising the alarm. Some 62% of households who bought their first home between 2003 and 2005 were spending more than 30% of their disposable income on housing (and were defined as under "housing stress," see NATSEM, 2008, 2). Overall, about 10% of low and middle income families were under "housing stress" by 2007 (Australian Senate, 2008, 37). In 2008 the ALP introduced First Home Saver Accounts to provide a 17% government funded top-up to any marked savings on the first AUS$5000 from individuals per year, with a cap up to $75,000, and tax-free withdrawals for owner-occupied first-home purchases. In a twist on the TTR discussed above, it would also provide investors with a tax of 15% on funds invested into the scheme.[8] In addition the ALP promised the introduction of a modest Housing Affordability Fund to subsidize housing infrastructure costs, as well as a new National Rental Affordability Scheme. The ALP's victory cannot be solely attributed to their stance on property politics, but the framing of affordability as a crisis for "working families" was important in a debate in which prominent economists feared rental "ghettos that will lock the have-nots out of housing, and spell the end of Australia as an egalitarian society" (*Sydney Morning Herald*, 2007; *The Age*, 2007).

6.4   Responses to property busts and the global credit crunch

The Danish bust

When the global credit crunch hit, the Danish residential property market was believed to be one of the most overvalued in Europe as property prices grew by 169% from 1993 to 2007 (Lunde, 2008). The combination of a low interest rate regime, higher homeowner indebtedness, and supply side innovations in the financial market, fueled the Danish crisis. In this regard Denmark appears to be a textbook example of new social attitudes coupled with an oversupply of credit producing volatility and a subsequent market crash. During the boom journalists worried whether Denmark was the next *geyser* economy to go bankrupt after Iceland. Yet Denmark is not a case of carry-trade crash and the persistence of egalitarian politics can explain why, along with the government's good fiscal position and low unemployment in the economy.

On the face of it, the Danish case is very much a globalization poster child. The share of foreign investors in the Danish mortgage market nearly doubled during the boom period, while the Danish mortgage bond market became the largest in the world relative to GDP, with foreign investors holding approximately 20% of the total volume of Danish mortgage bonds (Nykredit, 2008, 20).[9] However, while the politics of the residential housing market are now much more global than earlier, the economics remain local. This chapter has identified many of the drivers behind the property market crash, including the tax freeze regime that, from 2001, fueled a buoyant property market, and the credit expansion following the introduction of more flexible mortgage products. These factors, combined with historic low interest rates and a record low unemployment rate, produced a boom that outpaced most other European markets.

In Denmark the reaction to the end of the boom was an immediate contraction in economic activity. Ambitious new building projects slowed down or showed signs of becoming white elephants. The total number of initiated private residential constructions fell from a high of 30,564 in 2006 to 17,631 in 2007, with widespread expectations that there would be a further decline in 2009 (Danmarks Statistik; *Erhvervsbladet*, 2008). Changes to the housing cooperatives also fueled concerns about moral hazard problems. Because the liquidation policy of housing cooperatives is incomplete, it unintentionally promotes irresponsible financial behavior. Financial market innovations allowed individuals to take out mortgages on what technically is a share of a communal property and a permit to use one of its apartments. By allowing individuals to take out a mortgage on a shared property, the reform unintentionally transferred individual choices of risk into the collective risk of a housing cooperative. Not surprisingly, calls for a complete liquidation of housing cooperatives are increasingly voiced.

Another unique feature of the Danish case is the depth of the mortgage market. Denmark is, by some commentators, believed to be near a property meltdown of British and U.S. proportions. Jens Lunde (2008) found that the high proportion of "risky" interest-only and adjustable-interest mortgages were, in effect, equivalent to American subprime lending practices. Indeed, he argued that most European countries, including Denmark, had inflated the credit volume to same extent as the US. Furthermore, interest-rate only mortgages were quickly associated with irresponsible subprime loans. While the Association of Danish Mortgage Banks advertised the mortgage bond system as the best in the world, the Danish Trade Council felt obliged to explain that "... *there is essentially no subprime sector in Denmark*" (Trade Council of the Danish Ministry of Foreign Affairs). The essential nature of subprime is the topic for ongoing debate and intimately linked to welfare trade-offs rather than a category in isolation. Danish indebtedness outstrips U.S. indebtedness by quite a way and the difference between the two systems is really the role of the welfare state in permitting such risk tolerance. Still, the collapse of Roskilde Bank in October 2008 was not linked to a Danish subprime crisis but to irresponsible corporate property lending practices. Most Danish banks had little problem weathering the liquidity crisis due to high capitalization (Jonung, 2008, 576), but did reduce lending.

Egalitarian policy frames matter in the Danish debate and arguments for a return to a "potato diet" similar to the late 1980s have resurfaced. The Danish mortgage bond market reflects Danish society and vice versa. The crisis signaled to many Danes that their variety of residential capitalism was becoming too speculative and new homeowners ran from mortgages with flexible rates to fixed rates. The issuance of fixed-rate mortgages grew from 43% to 48% between 2006 and 2007 and by late 2008 only about 28% of total new mortgages were flexible (while interest-only mortgages continued to be popular with the very young and the very old). In general lending declined by 13.4% in 2007 compared to 2006 (European Mortgate Fund 2008, 7–8, 10, 12). Banks tightened their lending by increasing interest rates. In early 2009 the official Danish lending rate was 3%, while a private bank loan for an ordinary property started at around 8% and upward. In late January 2009 the Danish government provided U.S.$18 billion to banks to stimulate new lending to "the sound projects of businesses and citizens," but also with the expectation that the government would receive a 10% return on its investments! (Reuters Online, 2009). In general, the crisis has reversed the policy framing back to its traditional emphasis on stability of the market and less innovative lending policies, while some aspects of the housing market, such as the cooperative sector, were irreversibly changed.

The Australian bust

During the Australian housing boom the younger generation were under heightened financial stress to meet a commonly accepted social norm of homeownership, while the older generation received tax breaks and financial incentives that exacerbated the young's problems. The end of the property boom and the entry of a new ALP government, which had campaigned on the crisis of housing affordability, provided a desire to reevaluate the taxation and financing systems. The Australian system was relatively unaffected by the U.S. subprime crisis, with only a handful of hedge funds and institutional investors burnt. However, once the global credit crunch worsened the politics of who can access credit for property was raised, including what institutions should be providing it.

In 2008 the new government initiated a range of inquiries into housing affordability and also competition within the financial sector, with the aim of thinking about potential reforms. The issues addressed above, taxation and finance, were up for public scrutiny. For example, the heavy bias within the tax system toward landlords and investors was questioned. The Senate Select Committee on Housing Affordability in Australia found that the sum of tax exemptions on capital gains (where investors pay a half rate on property sales for profit), land tax exemptions, and negative gearing was approximately AUS$50 billion per annum. This was compared to the AUS$250 million per annum to be spent on the planned National Rental Affordability Scheme and the Housing Affordability Fund over a four-year period (Australian Senate, 2008, 59–60). Capital gain exemptions for investor properties in 2005–06 were estimated to be AUS$5 billion (Australian Senate, 2008, 61; Australian Taxation Office, 2007, 77, 80). Combined with the exemptions given to owner-occupiers, including on capital gains, the fairness of the tax system was questioned. For example, Julian Disney, the Chair of the 2006 National Affordable Housing Summit, told the Australian Senate that tax breaks had fueled the boom and were in the "favor of current homeowners but they are not in favour of homeownership" (Australian Senate, 2008, 59–60). Proposals followed to change the tax system, especially proposals to reform negative gearing to include means testing, such as restricting it to the bottom three income quintiles, or differentiating tax breaks from newly built rental as opposed to existing properties (Australian Senate, 2008, 65, 68). The debates are to continue in the "Australia's Future Tax System Review."

For the financial system the effect of the credit crunch was to concentrate more power in the hands of the Big Four banks at the expense of the smaller more aggressive mortgage lenders, including those heavily engaged in securitization. To provide confidence to the system the Australian Government announced in October 2008 that it would guarantee all bank deposits (some AUS$700 billion) for three years for those with less than AUS$1 million in their accounts, as well as support wholesale funding to banks. It also announced that it would use AUS$8 billion to purchase MBS to support ongoing lending in a plan that, according to Prime Minister Rudd, is part of "international measures designed to unclog the arteries of the global financial system" (*Sydney Morning Herald*, 2008a). Of the AUS$8 billion, half was dedicated to purchasing MBS from nonbanks (Sherry, 2008). The government view was that the competition introduced into the financial sector during the boom period was in principle positive for increasing access to homeownership and relying less on the Big Four. Indeed, the increased market share going to Big Four raised alarm bells in Australia and led to discussions on how the market could be more competitive yet underpinned by a sturdier institutional form. In the Australian Parliament the idea of creating an "AussieMac" based on a mix of the U.S. Frannies (see Schwartz's chapters in this volume) and the Canada Housing Trust was put forward and a Parliamentary Standing Committee was formed to investigate the idea (it turned it down) (House of Representatives, Standing Committee on Economics, 2008). The committee stressed the importance of improving financial literacy (cf. Watson, this volume), as well as regulating to increase the transparency of fee structures for mortgage products. The stress placed on ensuring that the Australian residential MBS market had strong support is noteworthy in that the market was not suffering from bad loans, but from a lack of capital as investors fled from property. The Australian nonconforming "subprime" market represented less than 1% of the market (see Debelle, 2008). The risky market for home loans in Australia is the low documentation ("low-doc") market, which was 6% of the market in 2006. Arrears for these loans were up to 3.6% in June 2008, while prime loans were at 1.2%, or 0.9% if only those from the Big Four are included (*Sydney Morning Herald*, 2008b). For MBS supported by these loan types, in June 2008 the arrears rate for prime loans was 0.5%, "low-doc" loans was 1.2% and nonconforming loans 8.5% (Reserve Bank of Australia, 2008b, 45). In general, the Australian MBS market was in good shape, even if investors had become shy.

The emphasis in the Australian response to the crisis has been to support new lending to those who were hard hit or excluded by the property boom. In this regard there was some good news as the financial institutions moved away from lending for property investment and also from "reverse mortgages" (*The Australian*, 2009). Both investments were increasingly risky now that the boom had gone bust. Rather, first-time owners increased their share of new loans from 19.5% to 23%, the highest level since 2002. The Rudd government's introduction of a temporary 'First Home Boost' in October 2008 of AUS$7,000 for established properties and AUS$14,000 for newly built houses also assisted. There was also a rapid increase in first-time owners who stated that the government was providing them with sufficient support to acquire property.[10] The property bust therefore permitted a reevaluation of the excesses that created the boom, as well as a desire to increase competition in the market via securitization to permit greater access to credit among the broader population.

Conclusions and speculations

Did the Australian and Danish housing booms and busts change their conceptions of housing as a social right or a means to wealth? We have identified changes in both directions in both cases, as well as intergenerational equity problems and, in different ways, the use of egalitarianism to justify policy changes or construct a crisis. The Danish case demonstrates a gradual shift from seeing housing as a social right toward viewing it, for some, as a means to wealth. Property politics encouraged a new generation of more market-minded homeowners who are risk tolerant because of the generous welfare state. In this environment first-time buyers had no other alternative during the property boom but to accept higher risks, such as adjustable-rate, interest-only loans in order to afford higher property prices, while the older generation benefited from the freezing of property taxes. In this system there is still considerable redistribution through tax mechanisms and safe finance for homeowners, as long as they are willing to enter the market at a higher price. The cashing-out or "liquidation" of housing cooperatives signals the abandonment of a view of housing as primarily a social concern for many. The freezing of property taxes by the Venstre-led government and, perhaps, more importantly, political U-turns on the issue of property taxes by espoused socialist parties (like SF) during the 2007 election demonstrates the new anxiety over any threat to owner-occupiers in a country in which just over half the population own their residences. We expect that egalitarian politics in Denmark, where all should be treated equal and where access to housing is a social right, will face some tests in the future (see also Blyth, 2008, 398). While the crisis has led to calls for stability and prudent financial behavior, the political effects of who has access to private or cooperative housing, and who should pay fair taxes on property, will reemerge when the economic slowdown presents some hard constraints on who can borrow and at what price.

In the Australian case an extreme form of housing as a means to wealth during the boom fueled a countermovement where access to credit for housing for the younger and poorer was presented as a social right via egalitarian principles. During the Australian housing boom there was considerable redistribution through tax mechanisms to landlords in a high-risk environment, leading the residential property market to be crowded out by investors, specifically those in upper generational brackets. Younger and poorer Australians found it increasingly difficult to access owner-occupied housing or, if they did, to maintain mortgage payments as they dramatically increased as a proportion of their pay packets. The ALP's success in calling attention to a crisis of affordability in the 2007 election reflects this sensitivity and vulnerability, especially when compared with the success of previous coalition governments in using interest-rate scares as an effective tool (see Beer et al., 2007). While it is fair to state that egalitarianism in Australia continues to take a beating from heightened income inequality, egalitarian politics are not only about relative income among a population but the normative goals shared by the population. The ALP's attempts to create policy directly targeted at supporting first-time homeowners, as well as seeking to draw investors into these schemes rather than the atomized private rental market, indicates recognition that Australia faces a significant intergenerational problem with its type of residential capitalism. In the Australian case the crisis has led to the government attempting to save securitization to maintain competition in the financial sector and to evaluate taxation policies such as negative gearing. We expect that these measures cannot compensate for the damage to intergenerational equity created during the boom, and the current slowdown will lead the old to fight the young as the former try to protect their wealth while the latter seek ways to accumulate it.

By comparing the politics of property booms and busts we can better understand how the everyday politics of accessing a residence creates general attitudes about whether housing should be seen as a social right or a means to wealth, and the knock-on effects of these attitudes upon domestic welfare systems.

Notes

1. Both countries foster a collective sense of identity based around egalitarian principles (for example, *"Janteloven"* in Denmark and the "Tall Poppy Syndrome" in Australia provide examples of antielitist discourses), while clearly differing in how these ideals are supported through the state welfare apparatus. Egalitarianism does not automatically suggest that a society has less income inequality. Nor does it suggest that all groups in society are considered to be equal – for example, we need only look at the socioeconomic status of indigenous peoples in the Australian case. Homeownership for indigenous households is 36% compared to 69% for the Australia in general. While the indigenous population is less than 1% of the total Australian population, 8.5% of Australia's homeless are indigenous peoples and discrimination on access to private rental accommodation is an ongoing problem (Australian Senate, 2008, 26–7).

2. However, deductions on maintenance costs, association fees, etc, are possible: http://skat.dk/SKAT.aspx?oId=86007&vId=201188&i=2#i86007. The Danish government also enforces price ceilings on rent in the private market. In general, private landlord rentals have declined while state-supported rentals have increased. See Danmarks Statistik and "Huset" March 2008, http://www.ejendomsforeningen.dk/index.dsp?area=289

3. It should be noted that key financial institutions, including *Realkreditrådet*, found financial innovations unnecessary for the Danish financial system and suggested that they were linked to European economic integration rather than a domestic desire for reforms. Leonard Seabrooke interviewed two senior staff from *Realkreditrådet*, October 23, 2008.

4. Variations of this system are present in many countries, including Britain, Canada, Germany, Sweden, and New Zealand (see Broome in this volume).

5. Welfare groups, such as the Brotherhood of St. Laurence have long opposed negative gearing as highly regressive (see Brotherhood of St Laurence, 2003).

6. According to the ATO, 72.5% of landlord investors own only one property (Australian Taxation Office, 2007, 13). Median income data from Australian Bureau of Statistics (2007).

7. Australian Broadcasting Corporation, Radio National, "AM Programme," August 4, 2003. A month later Ken Henry, Secretary to the Australian Treasury, acknowledged that there was indeed a property "bubble" that had to burst sometime soon. (See *The Age*, 2003.)

8. Information about First Home Saver accounts can be found at http://www.homesaver.treasury.gov.au/

9. In comparison, the share of foreign investors' holdings of Danish government bonds was 27.8% of the total volume. Mortgage bonds are primarily held by primarily Danish financial institutions and Danish insurance companies and pension funds (respectively 44% and 26% of the total volume of mortgage bonds).

10. Approval of government policies for first-time home owners increased from 14% in April 2008 to 38.8% in November 2008 (Broker News, 2009).

7
Residential Capitalism in Italy and the Netherlands

Manuel B. Aalbers

Introduction

In the 1990s it became fashionable to argue that economic globalization in combination with deregulation would lead to a deterritorialization of economic activities and the prevalence of the global scale over the local, regional, and national scales (e.g. Levine, 1997; Ohmae, 1990; Wachtel, 1986). Some authors even proclaimed *The End of Geography* (O'Brien, 1992). This position remains dominant in mainstream, neoclassical, and orthodox economics, but has been challenged by many others, most notably by international political economists and human geographers, who claim that deterritorialization and convergence claims are not only theoretically simplistic, but also empirically inaccurate (e.g. Corbridge et al., 1994; Cox, 1997; Hirst and Thompson, 1996; Hollingsworth and Boyer, 1997; Porter, 1990; Scott, 1998; Storper, 1997; Whitley, 1998). Against mainstream economic theory, political economists and geographers have argued that globalization does not diminish the significance of economic organization. The increasing internationalization of economic activities has not replaced existing forms of capitalism and nationally constructed business systems; globalization processes are path dependent and reflect (national) historical legacies (Whitley, 1998; see also Hudson, 2003).

There is now work mapping the "varieties of capitalism" (e.g. Hall and Soskice, 2001), but most of this works ignores a very important form of capitalism: residential capitalism (see the introductory chapter to this volume). Political economy and housing are usually not discussed together. Political economists may write about political systems and international finance, but not about the political and financial systems that underpin housing markets. Housing is often seen as either a residual or a not very significant economic sector. Academics who work on housing, on the other hand, are often preoccupied with housing policy, and although linkages to social and urban policies are common in this body of work, housing is hardly ever linked to the wider political economy. Like the other chapters in this book, this chapter brings housing and political economy together. I do this through a comparative analysis of residential capitalism in two European countries, the Netherlands and Italy. In discussing both of these cases, my main focus is not so much on the respective countries' national housing policies, but on the regulation (widely defined) of their respective mortgage markets. Of course, to understand changing regulation in both countries it is important to focus on the wider housing policies in both countries.

One problem with the varieties of capitalism literature is that it only specifies two models of capitalism, an American-style liberal capitalism and a German-style (or Japanese-style) coordinated capitalism.[1] Although such an approach is more sophisticated than a one-size-fits-all model, it is still limiting in its understanding of "variegated capitalism" (Peck and Theodore, 2007). There is not a simple dichotomy of models of capitalism or a continuum with the U.S. and Germany at the two poles – there is a whole range of indicators in which capitalisms can differ from one another, as Schwartz and Seabrooke also propose in the introductory chapter. A model of capitalism may look very coordinated according to one indicator, but not according to another. A country may, for instance, have a high redistribution of income (which suggests coordination), but also a very financialized economy (which suggests liberalism) – this is the case in countries like the Netherlands and Denmark. Alternatively, a country may have a relatively low degree of redistribution while also being less financialized, like Italy or Greece. In addition, the varieties of capitalism approach, ironically, shares one element with neoclassical economics, which is that it has a hard time explaining change, being "able to explain stability but not rupture" (Howell, 2003, 122; but see Hall and Thelen, 2008). In this chapter, therefore, we will not limit ourselves to a coordinated and a liberal model of capitalism. We will also take a dynamic view of institutions that enables both stability and rupture within mortgage markets.

At the end of 2004, there was €4.7 trillion of outstanding mortgage loans in the European Union and €11.3 trillion worldwide (European Mortgage Federation, 2005). Mortgage markets are not just important as a result of their sheer volume, but also because most homeowners depend on them, because they fuel the economy both directly and indirectly (through equity withdrawal) and because they serve an ideological purpose in the neoliberal age. Mortgage markets – and credit markets more generally – have been "liberalized" in order to widen access to mortgage markets and thus to fuel economic growth and increase homeownership rates. That is, the "liberalization" of mortgage markets is not just a goal in itself, but also a means to further the neoliberal agenda of private property, firms, and growing profits. It comes as no surprise, then, that this neoliberalization of the mortgage market took place earlier in the U.S. than in Britain, and earlier in Britain than in most of continental Europe. In this process, households have become more dependent on financial markets. Old arrangements of social rights have been replaced and continue to be replaced by new arrangements in which social rights and guarantees are transferred from the state to financial markets. Indeed, the restructuring of welfare states has resulted in a "great risk shift" in which households are increasingly dependent on financial markets for their long-term security (Hacker, 2006). As a result of the commodification and financialization of housing, housing risks are increasingly financial market risks these days (Aalbers, 2008). The current mortgage crisis or credit crunch makes this more evident than any theoretical argument can.

I focus on the Netherlands and Italy because these countries' mortgage markets in many respects offer opposite trajectories within Europe: "Italy is the world's most affluent large country that has such a low level of mortgage activity" (Ball, 2005, 95), while the Netherlands has the largest mortgage market in the world relative to population size or gross domestic product (GDP). In terms of the use of mortgage credit the countries could not be much more different. We see convergence and continued divergence at the same time. To some degree, these two markets are becoming more like one another as a result of processes partly located at the European and partly at the global level. Different mortgage market trajectories are not necessarily a barrier for the implementation of similar formal and informal credit regimes. That does not imply we will see only convergence: different national trajectories are still significant and we can see continued divergence between Italy and the Netherlands.

7.1   European mortgage markets

Europe's mortgage markets are fragmented. Each national mortgage market is conditioned by national rules and regulations as well as by a set of common ideas about the mortgage market demonstrated by players' shared rules of thumb and shared analyses of market conditions.

The rules and regulations structure the shared ideas, but are also structured by them; this is the internal dynamic. For example, a national rule that does not allow loans exceeding four times annual income, as in Italy until recently, structures the rules of thumb used by mortgage market players, but a shared idea that a loan of four times annual income is not that high and that it is possible to supply mortgage loans up to five times annual income without necessarily exceeding acceptable risk levels, as in the Netherlands, may – over time – lead to a change in national regulation. There is also an external dynamic that is formed by both state and nonstate regulation, as well as by international market developments. Examples of regulation include EU initiatives to open up markets, and the global spread of risk management policies such as credit scoring (Aalbers, 2005) made possible by ICT devices and applications. Examples of international market developments are cross-border joint ventures, and mergers and acquisitions. Foreign players may push national players to redefine their shared ideas. Of course, developments in other markets, both financial and nonfinancial, also play a part. For example, Dutch mortgage companies are less willing to take up high-risk loans today than they were five to eight years ago because the global financial crisis casts a shadow on the mortgage market.

Some typical statistics illustrate but do not explain the differences between European mortgage markets.[2] Firstly, typical and maximum loan-to-value-ratios (LTV-ratios) differ greatly between countries; out of the eight European countries shown in Table 7.1, the Netherlands has the highest average and maximum LTV-ratios and Italy the lowest.

Table 7.1 LTV ratio, average loan term and default rate in eight EU countries, ordered by LTV ratio

Country	Typical LTV ratio	Maximum LTV ratio	Average loan term in years	Default rate
Netherlands	90	115	30	0.6
Portugal	83	90	27	1.8
Denmark	80	80	30	1.3
Spain	70	100	20	6.0
Britain	69	110	25	1.0
France	67	100	17	2.8
Germany	67	80	23	n/a
Italy	55	80	15	5.2

Source: EMF, 2001; Low et al., 2003; ECHP, 2004.

There is a strong correlation between LTV-ratio and loan-to-income-ratio (LTI-ratio). The Netherlands and Denmark have the highest LTI-ratios and Italy and Belgium the lowest out of nine European countries (Table 7.2). As a result, the average mortgage debt tends to be higher in countries with high LTV- and LTI-ratios; again the Netherlands is on top of the list and Italy at the bottom (Table 7.2). Maximum LTV and LTI are strongly related to the average loan term: higher LTVs take longer to repay. The average loan term in Italy is half that of the Netherlands and Denmark. One would expect default rates to be high in countries with high LTV- and LTI-ratios, but in a comparison of 12 European countries between 1994 and 2001, default rates were the lowest in the Netherlands, followed by Austria, Britain, Luxembourg, and Denmark; and the highest in Finland, followed by Spain, Ireland, Italy, and Belgium. The differences between the countries are remarkably large, as Table 7.1 shows.

Distribution of mortgages in all eight countries examined by Low et al. (2003) is dominated by bank branches: in Italy almost 90% of mortgages are distributed through bank branches, in Germany and France this is 80%, in Portugal and Denmark just over 60%, and in the Netherlands, Britain, and Spain around 50%. Mortgage intermediaries (brokers and independent agents) play a more significant part in the latter countries, which are characterized by a greater variety in and complexity of mortgage products. Indeed, product differentiation and the emergence of niche markets are facilitated by mortgage intermediaries,

Table 7.2 LTI ratio and mortgage debt in nine European countries, ordered by LTI ratio

Country	Typical LTI ratio	Typical loan term in years	Average mortgage debt per recent buyer in €
Netherlands	3.4	30	103,204
Denmark	3.2	30	89,156
Spain	2.7	15–20	47,589
Britain	2.2	20–30	71,950
Ireland	2.1	20–30	76,512
France	1.4	15–20	35,830
Austria	1.3	20–25	32,466
Belgium	0.9	15–20	40,532
Italy	0.9	10–15	11,019

Source: Neuteboom, 2003, 2004.

and the growth in the number of mortgage intermediaries is enabled by product differentiation. In all eight abovementioned countries, mortgage intermediaries are gaining market share. Changes in the Italian mortgage market, for example, have resulted in the increasing importance of intermediaries in recent years. In addition, Italian and French real estate agents play a significant role in steering homebuyers to certain lenders. Other differences exist in the level of transaction costs, the average time taken to register a mortgage, and average repossession times. The last two are indicators of process efficiency, which is the highest in Denmark and the Netherlands, and the lowest in Italy followed by Portugal.

Market concentration also differs: in general, in smaller countries the largest five mortgage lenders together tend to have a bigger market share than in bigger countries. Denmark shows the highest concentration because the five largest lenders control 80%–95% of the market, depending on the source (European Central Bank, 2004; European Mortgage Federation, 2003; Low et al., 2003). Italy is the only big country with a high degree of concentration: 65%–75%, the same as for the Netherlands. Concentrations in other large countries are between 45% and 60%. A large degree of concentration is not necessarily related to a small number of mortgage lenders: because of the wide variety of minor players in the Dutch market, there are about as many lenders active as in the British market.[3]

Strikingly, the size of the mortgage market is relatively small in many countries with a large owner-occupied sector (Figure 7.1). In many southern European countries, homeownership is the norm and renting the exception. Castles and Ferrera (1996) even argue there is a distinctive Mediterranean culture that explains the significance of homeownership in Southern Europe. Here, most homeowners have either paid off their mortgage or even bought a house without a mortgage. This is made possible by intergenerational transfers of both property and equity (Aalbers, 2007; Allen et al., 2004), as well as by self-promotion and self-provision of housing (Allen et al., 2004; Arbaci, 2002). Throughout the EU15, 24% of households held a mortgage in 1996, compared with 13% in the southern EU member states (Allen et al., 2004, 25). Northern European countries, in general, have a younger homeownership tradition and intergenerational transfers are less significant. Therefore, the share of the owner-occupied market in most Northern European countries is significantly smaller (with the exception of Norway, see Tranøy this volume), yet most homeowners have taken out a mortgage loan to buy a house.

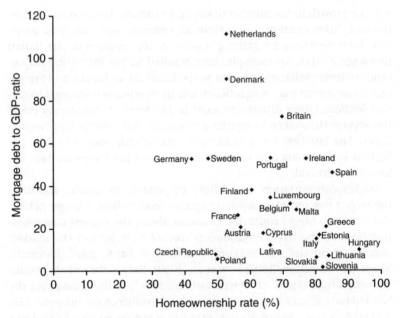

Figure 7.1   Size of the mortgage market related to homeownership rates

7.2   The globalization of mortgage markets?

Regulation

In both the Netherlands and Italy, but also in most other European countries, national mortgage lenders continue to dominate the national mortgage market. Are the effects of globalization on mortgage markets really so insignificant? Starting with regulation, it is important to realize the difference between harmonization and globalization: "Countries can adapt the same regulatory standards or principles and yet construct different rule-based systems of regulation" (Drahos and Braithwaite, 2001, 104). The implementation of many EU and EMU rules and regulations displays this phenomenon. EU rules are supposed to harmonize the different European mortgage markets and thus enable "a market without borders," but in their implementation they often take a different turn because EU and EMU rules and regulations are filled in differently in the legal and economic framework of each country. In addition, wide differences exist in contractual rules (see Forum Group on Mortgage Credit, 2004) as well as in tax and subsidy schemes (Scanlon and Whitehead, 2004). Important differences are related to the level of national regulation of mortgage companies and markets, and to direct government intervention. Government intervention is substantial in Germany, France, and Portugal, but limited in Spain, Britain, and Italy. The Netherlands has introduced guarantees through a private not-for-profit institution backed up by the government. This has the same effect as private mortgage insurance, namely the externalization of payment risk and thus a greater willingness among lenders to grant loans on relatively cheap houses.

In addition to EU, EMU, and national regulation, global regulations also play a part. The most important of these are the regulations and requirements established by the Basel Committee on Banking Supervision. The Basel II Accord specifies the "internal rating based" method as the new system for measuring solvency as of 2007. This means that providers who apply credit risk management will attain higher solvency scores from the national or European Central Bank than providers who do not, and they will therefore require less equity. This will create both internal and external incentives for banks to apply credit risk management.

Firms

At first sight the globalization and Europeanization of firms seems to be very limited: international corporate ownership is low (Wójcik, 2002) and foreign market shares in different national mortgage markets tend to be low. In most Northern European countries the market shares of foreign credit institutions are rather small and together they are well below 20%, and in some cases even below 10%. If we look only at mortgage products, market shares of foreign mortgage lenders drop even further. In the Netherlands, the market share of all foreign players together is around 5%, most of which is taken up by the Belgian bank Argenta, the Bank of Scotland, and the American mortgage company GMAC RFC.[4] In Italy the situation seems quite similar, in the sense that foreign mortgage companies have only small market shares. In addition, in Italy acquisitions by foreign banks have been blocked for years.

Dutch bank ABN-AMRO was the first to gain access to the Italian market in 2005, because it was allowed to buy a large amount of shares of Banca Antonveneta. But this only happened after a protracted battle for the bank in which the Governor of the Bank of Italy had initially blocked ABN-AMRO's attempts, and had favored a small financially unsound Italian bank, Banca Popolare di Lodi, in its attempt to take over Antonveneta. Banca Popolare di Lodi's bid for Antonveneta failed when Consob (the Italian market regulatory agency) and magistrates accused it of market manipulation, insider dealing, and illegal pacts. As a result of the battle, the Governor of the Bank of Italy resigned and now faces prosecution, while BPL's chief executive is charged with a number of violations and is in prison. Not much later French bank BNP Paribas was able to take over the Italian Banca Nazionale del Lavoro. The merger and acquisition wave set in motion by ABN-AMRO may soon increase foreign market shares above the current 10%. Currently, the British companies Abbey National and Woolwich are the most important foreign players in the Italian mortgage market, but Deutsche Bank and Dutch bank ING are also gaining market share. In the meantime, and after a failed merger with Barclays (UK), ABN-AMRO was bought by a consortium of three European banks: Bank of Scotland (UK) and Banco Santander (Spain) took over ABN-AMRO's foreign operations in 62 countries, including those in Italy (Santander), while the Belgian-Dutch bank Fortis took over most of its operations in the Netherlands. Santander, however, resold part of Antonveneta to the Italian bank Monte di Paschi di Siena.

Yet, aside from Central and Eastern Europe, the Netherlands and Italy, together with Britain, have seen the largest number of foreign entries in their mortgage markets. In general, while banks and other financial institutions have become international and are present not only in the EU but also in the rest of the world, their mortgage companies remain national: "the internationalization of finance has comparatively little impact on mortgage systems" (Stephens, 2003, 1018). Wójcik's conclusion on the low level of credit market integration in Europe is also valid in one of its submarkets, the mortgage market, but Wójcik's claim that what we see is Americanization rather than Europeanization (Wójcik, 2002, 486), does not hold in European mortgage markets as U.S. (-owned) mortgage companies have only very small markets shares.

Primary and secondary markets

Since most national mortgage markets in Northern and Southern Europe are dominated by national mortgage companies, one could easily assume that mortgage markets are also not very globalized. This would be jumping to conclusions. Many mortgage companies get part of their equity from countries other than their home countries. Take the example of Dutch pension funds: they are small players in the Dutch mortgage market but large players in global investment and have important stakes in some American financial institutions (see also Engelen, 2003). ABP, the largest Dutch pension fund, and the world's second or third largest, has a global investment portfolio of over €215 billion that includes significant shares in U.S. mortgage lenders and securitizers.

In addition, the importance of the secondary mortgage market has increased over the last ten years. In the secondary market, so-called residential mortgage-backed securities (RMBS) are sold to investors. This process, called securitization, requires not only a vastly expanding market, but also the deregulation and internationalization of domestic financial markets (Sassen, 2001, 72) leading to a rapid growth in trade of securities, of which RMBS are only one element. Securitization of mortgage loans takes different dimensions in different countries. In the U.S., secondary mortgage markets have grown tremendously and now represent up to two-thirds of the mortgage market. Close to the peak in 2003, RMBS had been issued for a value of over U.S.$3000 billion. In 2004–07, issuance in the U.S. was down to U.S.$2000 a year (half of it handled by Fannie Mae, Freddie Mac and Ginnie Mae. In Europe, RMBS were introduced much later, but are also growing in number and volume; the volume tripled in less than four years (i.e. by 2005) to €326 billion. Recently, secondary market securitization has become more established in several countries, including the Netherlands and Italy (Table 7.3) (Forum Group on Mortgage Credit, 2004; International Financial Services, 2006). In 2005, 15% of the value of outstanding mortgage loans was securitized in the Netherlands; RMBS issuance in that year valued €36 billion (26% of newly issued loans). At the end of 2007, 21% of outstanding mortgages was securitized. In Britain, RMBS were issued for a value of €145 billion in 2005; in Spain issuance valued €42 billion and in Italy €33 billion (European Securitisation Forum,

Table 7.3 Securitization in Europe, total issuance per country, 2000–2005

Country	Billion euros	% share
Britain	428.6	40.0
Italy	154.8	14.4
Spain	137.8	12.8
Netherlands	101.3	9.4
Germany	52.3	4.9
France	38.8	3.6
Pan-Europe	69.6	6.5
Other countries	89.2	8.3
Total	**1,072.4**	**100**

Source: ESF, 2006; IFS, 2006.

2006). RMBS are sold to both national and foreign investors, and as a result of securitization mortgage markets indirectly become more globalized. While most primary mortgage markets remain firmly national, the secondary market becomes globalized.

The current financial crisis demonstrates that many RMBS are not as transparent in reality as they are in theory. As a result, the reduced liquidity of mortgages in the secondary market will make it harder for lenders to securitize loans. And considering that two-thirds of the U.S. mortgage market is securitized, the impact can only be massive. This is why major bank lenders are hit hard and have lost billions of dollars in the crisis, but the ones going bankrupt (e.g. New Century Financial Corporation) or closing down (e.g. American Home Mortgage) are the nonbank lenders that rely fully on the secondary mortgage market to sell their portfolios. In addition, many investors in RMBS, both inside and outside the financial sector, are announcing losses of billions of dollars. Although securitization was designed to limit risk by spreading it over a wider area and to increase efficiency as a result of economies of scale, it now turns out that the spread of risk gives the crisis wider latitude, affecting not only subprime loans, but also prime loans; affecting not only mortgage markets, but also other credit markets; and affecting not only the U.S., but also other places around the globe including Italy and the Netherlands (Aalbers, 2008).

7.3   Housing in the Netherlands

The Netherlands is famous for its social rented sector. There are about 500 housing associations managing more than two million units of social housing. The share as well as the quality of social housing is considered to be high. Because of these characteristics, many households with middle incomes like to live in social housing as well. This especially holds for the (larger) cities where the share of social housing is even larger (Table 7.4). Private rented housing has become relatively unimportant, while the owner-occupied sector increased (Table 7.5). Table 7.5 may suggest that private rented housing has been converted to owner-occupied housing, but this has happened only to a limited degree. More importantly, private rented housing has been converted to social housing, while construction of new private rented housing has been limited. The conversion of social rented housing to owner-occupied housing started to take shape only after 2000. New construction has focused mostly on owner-occupied housing and to some extent social rented housing.

Table 7.4 Housing stock in the Netherlands and three largest cities by tenure (%), 2005

	Owner-occupied	Private rented	Social rented	Total number
The Netherlands	55	10	35	6,800,000
Amsterdam	20	25	55	375,000
Rotterdam	30	13	57	285,000
The Hague	37	25	38	220,000

Source: Ministry of VROM, 2007.

Table 7.5 Housing stock in the Netherlands by tenure (%), 1986–2005

Tenure/sector	1986	1990	1995	2000	2005
Owner-occupied	43	45	48	52	55
Private rented	28	23	17	11	10
Social rented	29	32	35	37	35
Total number	5,400,000	5,800,000	6,200,000	6,600,000	6,800,000

Source: Ministry of VROM, 2007.

After the Second World War, there was a severe shortage of housing in the Netherlands. Hundreds of thousands of homes had been destroyed or damaged and very few new homes had been built. Out of necessity many families had to move in with others. A baby boom aggravated the shortage of housing. This led to a new phase in the history of social housing. After the Second World War, the Dutch central government took the lead in public policies, including housing. Although the most important social landlords, the housing associations, were privately regulated institutions, they became increasingly subject to public regulation (Salet, 1999). In reality, the housing associations became branch offices of government in that (1) central government determined rents and set very detailed building requirements through subsidies and loans and (2) local government determined the choice of architect, the manner in which contracts were tendered, and handled supervision during construction. Local government also took charge of housing allocation. During this period solving the quantitative housing shortage was a number one priority and object subsidies (supply side, bricks, and mortar) were a natural ingredient of this policy (Aalbers, 2003). In order to reduce building costs, attention was given to increasing efficiency, normally achieved by mass prefab production which resulted in a great deal of mid-rise construction.

The government's role changed in the 1980s. The belief that a society could be governed down to the smallest detail by regulation was dropped. Growing central government deficits led to cutback after cutback. Because of a slowly declining housing shortage, social housing received a lower priority. With the policy document/white paper *Housing in the Nineties* (1989), government took some steps to withdraw from the housing market. The housing associations were cut loose from central government in several steps in the 1990s. The most important change was made by the *brutering* or *operatie balansverkorting* (1995) by which the operating subsidies for years to come were canceled out against government loans. Although after the *brutering*, only a few financial ties between the government and the housing associations remained, there are still a lot of hidden subsidies involved.

While subject subsidies (demand side, housing allowances for both the social rented and the private rented sector, and recently also for some owner-occupiers) should solve the affordability problem for low and moderate income people, both suppliers of housing and housing consumers got more freedom: freedom of contract and negotiation, but also freedom of choice. Solving the *quantitative* housing shortage was no longer a major issue, while solving the *qualitative* housing shortage (the gap between the demand for and supply of housing amenities) was. The basics of this policy were strengthened in the 1990s and will be carried on in the years to come, as the next major policy document/white paper on housing (2000) had the following major purposes: (1) deregulation of the housing market, (2) more resident control and more choice for housing consumers, and (3) the promotion of homeownership and the selling of parts of the social housing stock.

Compared to other European countries the private rented sector in the Netherlands is rather small. One reason for this is that many housing associations, and in particular those in the cities, buy property from small landlords. The associations either renovate these buildings to rent them out as social housing or they replace them with new buildings in urban renewal schemes.[5] Another reason is that some units are sold when a vacancy occurs or sold to the sitting tenant. Next to the small private landlords, private investors such as pension funds and insurance companies own a large number of dwellings, mostly fairly new high-rise complexes with relatively high rents (cf. Mortensen and Seabrooke in this volume).

To summarize, we see two main shifts in the Dutch housing market: from a suppliers' market to a consumers' market and from a renters' market to a buyers' market (Aalbers, 2003). This is further enhanced by the liberalization of the social housing regime and the selling off of social housing. Until the early 1990s, the idea of selling social housing was virtually unspeakable in Dutch politics. But since the 1990s, white papers on housing all note that the promotion of homeownership is needed because (1) the Dutch rate of home ownership is relatively low, (2) citizens should have more control over their home and housing environment, (3) home ownership fits better in the government's philosophy of deregulation and privatization, and (4) home ownership can contribute to social goals such as the formation of property and equity. This will not cause complete marginalization of the social housing sector because only one-fourth of social housing is to be sold off and new social housing (albeit in smaller amounts) continues to be built.

7.4 The Dutch mortgage market

Just like in Denmark (Mortensen and Seabrooke, this volume), the Dutch market can be characterized by relatively liberal housing finance system within an equalitarian welfare state, a relatively low homeownership rate, very high mortgage indebtedness and a rapid growth in house prices. This is unlike another egalitarian welfare state like Norway, which is more homeownership focused and has a less expanded mortgage market (Tranøy, this volume). As in many northwest European countries, financial deregulation was also an issue in the Netherlands in the 1980s and 1990s. For example, the legal separation of banking and insurance services was abolished in 1990. Consequently, financial conglomerates developed through a wave of mergers and acquisitions. Van Leuvensteijn (2003) characterizes the Dutch mortgage market as a noncompetitive market in which lenders possess some monopolistic market power derived from imperfect information. Perhaps a more accurate description of the market, however, is that of a system of a few relatively big players, who have oligopolistic powers and a relatively low degree of market differentiation. In other words, although banking products are heterogeneous, there is little heterogeneity among banks, all of which offer similar levels of heterogeneity in their products.

In comparison with other European countries fewer people in the Netherlands own their homes. However, homeownership increased from 42% in 1981 to around 55% in 2005 (Table 7.5). A number of factors have encouraged this trend. First, structurally low interest rates have made mortgage loans not only cheaper but also more secure. Second, landlords are encouraged to sell their rental stock and a small subsidy is available to give tenants an incentive to buy if the opportunity arises.

Third, the government has actively supported homeownership by offering tax incentives to buyers, the most important one being an income tax break known as the *hypotheekrenteaftrek*, which allows owner-occupiers to deduct all interest paid on a mortgage loan from their income. This tax break is referred to as "the H-word"; because of the electoral consequences it is considered political suicide to suggest limiting the current tax breaks. Fourth, bank policies of accepting higher risks for home mortgages have made it easier to purchase a home. Since the early 1990s, the acceptance policies of banks have become increasingly lenient, and credit limits (i.e., the maximum amount that can be borrowed through a mortgage) have expanded. In the second half of the 1990s, all banks that provided mortgages widened their average credit limits by similar margins. For example, in the past, a second income within a single household was not taken into consideration when calculating credit limits; today, however, all banks include such income in their calculations. In addition, banks have begun using a higher housing-expense limit (*woonquote*), which is the part of the household income spent on accommodation. The Dutch National Bank (*De Nederlandse Bank* [DNB]) estimates that the average *woonquote* used by banks increased from 31% to 33% of income between 1995 and 1999. Until 1990, the use of *woonquotes* over 30% was considered highly unusual. (Fannie Mae's debt-to-income ratio was 28% for total housing expenses (PITI) and 36% for all debt payments.) DNB calculated that credit limits widened by 86% within five years for households with one income of €30,000 and one income of €12,000 (i.e., the "average 1.5-income household"). This can be attributed largely to an average increase in income of more than 10% and a low rate of interest; the second income and the increase of the *woonquote* are important factors as well (DNB, 2000).

The percentage of the "execution value" used to calculate the size of a mortgage has also increased. The execution value is the value that a house would have if it had to be sold immediately, and is lower than the market value. When financing a house, mortgage providers do not consider the purchase price of a house, but rather its execution value. The number of new mortgages that exceed 75% of the execution value tripled between 1995 and 1999, which has increased the amount of risk faced by banks. Higher loan-to-value loans were necessary in order to enable people to buy homes, because the average household income was not increasing as quickly as average house prices were. In return, however, larger loans contributed to higher house prices as well. Thus, the structural shift in the housing system helped to stimulate the long market boom. Prices in the owner-occupier market rose by 81% between

1990 and 1998, which was the second highest jump within the EU.[6] The boom in the housing market provided fuel for the boom in the mortgage market, and vice versa. Growth that is not based on production but on growth itself of course brings along some risks.

Other factors that increased risk during this period, and which paralleled processes in the U.S., included (DNB, 2000):

1. The quality of the administrative organization came under pressure
2. Few reports were written by mortgage agents (or intermediaries) to mortgage providers (i.e., banks)
3. Many mortgage brokers failed to abide by certain internal guidelines for acceptance; for example, a test was omitted at BKR, the national credit registration
4. Housing mortgages were unlawfully used for purposes of credit repair or the repayment of consumer credit

Lenders also developed many alternative forms of mortgages that while financially beneficial, entailed high levels of risk, in some cases for the applicant as well as the provider. The high-risk "investment mortgage," which bet on increasing equity prices to fund the principal, overtook the traditional "annuity mortgage," with steady monthly payments composed of increasing principal payments and decreasing interest payments, as the most popular mortgage at the end of the 1990s. In addition, financial intermediaries and mortgage agents had an incentive to impede the push toward transparency; the lack of transparency was what made it possible for them to exist. In addition, all mortgage providers make use of the expanded acceptance policy, but not to the same extent. The acceptance policies of various providers differ, and not all providers are equally eager to extend high-risk mortgages. Some providers target a share of the market that is left aside by others. The mortgage portfolios of these providers consequently have higher risk profiles (Van Dusseldorp, 2003).

7.5 Housing in Italy

Italy is a country of homeownership, but traditionally it did not have a very developed mortgage market. Owner-occupation increased from 40% in 1950 to around 80% today (Table 7.6), but is somewhat lower in the north than in the south, and lower in cities than in villages (Table 7.7). Homeownership rates are increasing for both higher income groups and blue-collar workers (Tosi and Cremaschi, 2001). The rental

Table 7.6   Housing stock in Italy by tenure (%), 1986–2005

Tenure/sector	1951	1971	1991	2001
Owner-occupied	40	51	68	75
Rented	49	44	25	19
Other*	11	5	7	6

Note: * For example, freehold or occupancy in exchange for services.
Source: Ave, 1996; Mezzetti et al., 2003.

Table 7.7   Housing stock in Italy by city size and tenure (%), 1998

	Owner-occupied	Rented	Other
Metropolitan cores	59	33	8
Metropolitan belts	69	23	8
More than 50,000 inhabitants	68	25	7
10,000 50,000 inhabitants	70	20	10
2000–10,000 inhabitants	74	14	12
Fewer than 2000 inhabitants	77	12	11
Italy	69	22	9

Source: Tosi and Cremaschi, 2001.

market takes up most of the other 20% of the Italian housing stock, one-fifth of which is public housing, that is 4%–5% of the total housing stock (Andreotti et al., 2000). Actually, the lack of alternatives in the rental sector is mentioned as one of the reasons for the high proportion of homeowners in Italy (Del Boca and Lusardi, 2003), because the market structure is quite rigid and the decrease in the rental sector has made the overall market less flexible, while demand for housing itself has become more flexible (Tosi and Cremaschi, 2001). Moreover, several rounds of liberalisation[7] made private rented housing much more expensive while the small stock that remained rent controlled became frozen and virtually inaccessible as tenants refused to move out (Bernardi and Poggio, 2004; Tosi, 1990). Meanwhile, the social rented housing stock has received little investment, and is aimed at satisfying the need of only poor households (Indovina, 2005).

In addition, fiscal treatment of homeownership is rather favorable: "until the early 1980s, owning real estate properties in Italy was basically tax free" (Ave, 1996, 77); imputed rents are taxed on the basis of administrative values that are below real market values; tax rebates do exist for mortgage interests; and intergenerational transfer are taxed in a favorable way (sometimes almost tax free) (Bernardi and Poggio, 2004). Other reasons for the high homeownership rate are the low cost of higher education (which enables people to save or invest in housing), the relative stability of the Italian family, the sale of (social) rental housing, the very low geographical mobility, the existence of homeownership programs, and the slow rate of population growth (Aalbers, 2007; Ave, 1996; Del Boca and Lusardi, 2003; Indovina, 2005).

Historically, the Italian credit market offered few feasible methods to finance homeownership. Compared to most other European countries, the Italian mortgage market was characterized by very restricted lending policies. Until 1980, mortgage LTV levels were legally limited to 50% of the estimated property value. Even when the LTV cap was increased to 75% in 1980, and to 80% in 1993, many financial institutions, as well as many households, preferred smaller and thus less risky loans. An important reason for financial institutions to ration credit is that Italy has a complicated system for repossessing property on defaulting loans: it takes five-and-one-half years on average to repossess collateral. Also, the information system in the mortgage market, and credit market in general, was up till some years ago not very well developed, which also resulted in higher risk (Bernardi and Poggio, 2004; Chiuri and Jappelli, 2002; Del Boca and Lusardi, 2003; Generale and Giorgio, 1996; Sironi and Zazzara, 2003; Villosio, 1995).

Other important features of the Italian credit market, in particular in the late 1970s and early 1980s, are the unusually high inflation and real interest rates. Even though inflation and interest rates decreased in the mid-1980s, until the beginning of this century they stayed remarkably high compared to other European countries. The most striking change is undoubtedly the inflation rate, which declined from 12.1% in 1980 to 3.9% in 1994, and below 3% in recent years. High and often changing interest rates in the credit market at large, coupled with high inflation, also made mortgage loans less attractive for both banks and households compared with many other (European) countries. Finally, mortgage loans used to be the responsibility of specialized credit institutions; banks were excluded from operating in the mortgage market because their role was limited to short-term credit. But after the deregulation operation of the 1980s, banks also entered the mortgage market, and the number of mortgage loans rapidly increased. In 1995, the average mortgage LTV in the largest 13 cities was 42 (Ave, 1996), and mortgage credit comprised less than 6% of GDP. During the late 1990s, however, economic growth and the fall in interest rates have led to a boom in mortgage loans, resulting in annual increases of more than 15%.

Once banks were allowed to offer mortgages, it took some time before a well developed mortgage market arose and today Italy's capital market is considerably less developed than that of the Netherlands or most other northern European countries. Up to the mid-1990s, "mortgage conditions supplied to Italian households were among the worst ones within Europe, in terms of both typical loan-to-value, real interests and maturity applied" (Bernardi and Poggio, 2004). For a long time, ten years was the maximum maturity, while in many other European countries and in the U.S., 25–30 year maturities were common. In addition, and in line with Italian clichés, loan applications were processed in a slow and very bureaucratic manner.

In Italy, there is a coevolution of the institutions of family and home-ownership, by which the first enables the second, and the second increases the importance of the first. While the traditional family may be stronger in the south of the country, the high prices of real estate in the north compel especially first-time homebuyers to rely on their families. Indeed, the family is an important source for the down payment, for monthly payments, and also for inheritance (Bernardi and Poggio, 2004; Guiso and Jappelli, 2002; Tosi, 1987). In the early 1990s, it was estimated that intergenerational transfers supported about 30% of Italian homeowners, and about 20% of homeowners even received their houses as gifts or inheritance (Guiso and Jappelli, 2002). The incidence of becoming a homeowner in this way has only increased, leading to what Nuvolati has called a sort of "treasurisation" of the dwellings (Mingione and Nuvolati, 2003; Nuvolati and Zajczyk, 1990).

7.6　The Italian Mortgage Market

Since the early 1990s, but especially in the late 1990s and early 2000s, there have been some important changes in the Italian mortgage market. First, there is no longer a law on the LTV cap. Consequently, it has become possible for banks to grant higher loans. Second, information on the supply side has improved, which makes it less risky for banks to grant loans because they can better estimate their risks. Third, the organization of the mortgage market has changed dramatically. Not only has the external regulation changed in order to adapt to a more "European" banking system, but the internal regulation of the banks has also changed. Additionally, the *Amato Act* (1990) allowed banks to provide mortgage loans, which in the past was possible only for specialized credit institutions (Casini, 1995). Financial deregulation is coupled to a major and ongoing restructuring of banks leading to bigger banks and to cooperation- and information-sharing between banks, resulting in an increased transparency on the supply side of the market. Fourth, competition in the mortgage market has increased as a result of the abovementioned factors as well as through the entry of foreign players into the Italian credit market. These new entrants see providing mortgages to Italians as an attractive growth market, particularly when their home markets offer few opportunities for expansion. For example, Abbey National, a British bank specializing in mortgages, was one of the first banks to open foreign branches in Italy (Del Boca and Lusardi, 2003), but many other banks such as ING (the Netherlands), Paribas (France) and Woolwich (Britain) are also active in the Italian mortgage market. Italian banks consequently feared losing their market share and so increased the availability of mortgage loans.

Four changes on the demand side of the Italian mortgage market parallel these four supply side changes. First, there seems to be a higher consumer acceptance of the risk of mortgage loans in general, and of higher LTV- and higher LTI-ratios in particular. Second, the much faster rise in housing prices than in income, which means that people need to borrow more to buy a house, reinforces demand for bigger loans. Third, since the rental market continues to offer fewer alternatives, there is a higher demand for mortgage loans, even among groups that traditionally favored renting or were forced to rent because of market constraints. Fourth and last, real estate is seen as a good investment, and it is increasingly understood that ownership of real estate holds a key to future income generation, and (as was traditionally well realized in Italy) to security. While there is a general sense of economic depression, real estate is seen as a safe haven (Nomisma, 2002).

Even though the Italian economy in the last eight years has witnessed a more serious crisis than most other European countries, the mortgage market has expanded rapidly and house prices have increased significantly. Some of these changes have been encouraged by the EU, and in particular by the EMU, which demanded changes in national banking regulation, not just to shrink the differences in financial systems between countries, but also within each country (such as short-term versus long-term financial institutions in Italy).

Altogether, there has been a steady increase in the supply of and demand for home mortgage finance as well as a number of new, often large, suppliers. The changes in the mortgage market resulted in lower interest rates, higher possible LTV-ratios, higher possible LTI-ratios, and longer maturities. Lower interest rates made mortgage loans more affordable, but also caused rising house prices. In particular, higher LTV-ratios are important as they mean that the down payment required to buy a house is lower. This has a potentially strong effect on the young, who are the most likely to need a mortgage when buying a home, but it "also shifted the burden of homeownership from large down payment to greater mortgage payments" (Del Boca and Lusardi, 2003, 682).

By 1993, when the landslide changes in mortgage market had just been initiated, mortgage installments rose to as high as 52% of family income (Del Boca and Lusardi, 2003; Villosio, 1995). Since 1993, changes have had more impact, and Italian banks have also extended loan periods. But since prices have also increased, mortgage payments tend to be high for households who took out loans with a high LTV-ratio. Wider access to mortgage finance has enabled more households to become owner-occupiers, increasing competition for housing and thus increasing housing prices. This in return, may tempt, and has tempted, banks to loosen mortgage restrictions further (lower down payments, higher LTV-ratios, and loans for people without fixed employment). This mirrors developments in other countries where the loosening of mortgage restrictions made it possible for households to acquire more expensive properties, but also led to higher housing prices. The banks pursued a policy of cheap money; to "keep the market going," mortgage restrictions were loosened further (cf. Aalbers, 2005). The price boom(s) associated with the expansion of credit possibilities created a situation in which homeowners with outstanding mortgage debts also began to carry more risk. In other words, banks as well as households take on more risk. Furthermore, as elsewhere, the expansion of the mortgage market has included a new group of borrowers who carry higher risk than other groups.

Conclusion

European mortgage markets are quite different from one another in many respects. EU policies have not unified the European mortgage market; in most countries national lenders continue to dominate the market even though regulation itself has been internationalized to some extent. Globalization and Europeanization processes have been selectively absorbed and have led to both convergence and continued divergence. Path-dependent trajectories are highly important, but can sometimes be bypassed by global processes such as the development of secondary mortgage markets or downplayed by the entry of foreign firms. In Italy, for example, British and Dutch mortgage companies possess only a small market share and are dependent on local intermediaries and nationally defined rules of the game, but at the same time they have caused the restructuring of the Italian mortgage market in many ways: mergers and acquisitions, changes in the state regulation system, changes in the rules of the game and in rules of thumb, and changes in the mentality of lending and the related increased use of credit scoring techniques. Italy and the Netherlands are quite different in this respect: where foreign entry revolutionized the mortgage market in Italy, it had relatively little effect in the Netherlands. The Dutch mortgage market changed mostly from the inside; the Italian market from the outside.

The globalization of regulation remains partial, while the globalization of firms is limited but on the rise. In addition, the Basel regulations institutionalize and speed up convergence in credit risk management and solvency standards resulting in a flattening of the context of market regulation. Even though regulation is being more and more harmonized, many differences remain and are not easily overcome. Cultural differences, tax differences, and juridical differences remain. All this implies some further convergence of regulation, but not the creation of one European market. Deregulation and reregulation in both Italy and the Netherlands have created a vastly expanding mortgage market. This is like the U.S., Britain, and other countries that have enabled the growth of the mortgage market, but unlike Germany. Fueling the mortgage market has led to significant house price increases in all those countries. Yet, we see quite different patterns in the global financial crisis. In the U.S., and to some extent Britain, it was the unbounded growth of the mortgage market that led to the financial crisis that, in return, is affecting the mortgage market.

In the Netherlands and Italy, however, the national primary mortgage markets did not cause a financial crisis and that crisis is affecting these countries' mortgage markets only to some extent. First, subprime lending has not really taken off in the Netherlands and Italy, while subprime lending has been growing in Britain and was growing boundlessly in the U.S. Second, the U.S., and again to some extent Britain, are more dependent on the securitization of mortgage loans than the Netherlands and Italy. The credit crunch has frustrated mortgage securitization. Not only does the relative size of securitization make a big difference between these countries, but also the degree to which individual lenders are dependent on securitization to function. In the U.S. many lenders, in Britain some lenders, and in the Netherlands and Italy only a few lenders fully depend on securitization. In the Netherlands this applies to a few marginal, foreign lenders (ELQ, GMAC); the biggest mortgage lenders are general banks that only securitize part of their mortgage portfolio.[8] Some British lenders and many American lenders work according to an originate-and-distribute model in which all loans are securitized. Therefore, these lenders are hit hard by the faltering market for RMBS. As a result, the Dutch and Italian mortgage markets are hit much less by the financial crisis than are American and British mortgage lenders.

According to some statistics, the Dutch mortgage seems very risky with extremely high LTV, LTI, and mortgage-debt-to-GDP ratios that are comparable only to Denmark, but on the other hand the default rate, although rising, remains low in international terms. Italy, as we saw, presents the opposite picture with relatively low LTV, LTI, and mortgage-debt-to-GDP ratios, but with a structurally – not conjuncturally – high default ratio. The Dutch and Italian mortgage markets are very different, but there is no reason to believe they will be hit in the same way as the American and to some extent British mortgage markets. That does not rule out the possibility of house price decline – after all, both countries have seen rapid house price increases as a result of expanding mortgage markets – but since the structural factors underpinning the Dutch and Italian mortgage markets are hardly affected, a price decline of more than 10% seems unlikely. A sustained economic crisis will affect housing markets. U.S. levels of default and foreclosure seem unlikely in the Netherlands where, partly as a result of a restrictive urban planning regime, many regions still face housing shortages, and where the strong welfare state limits the number of people at risk of losing their job.[9] As the Dutch example illustrates well, a strong welfare state does not frustrate a strong financialization of markets, but may lower the risks that are inherent to financialization. In Southern European countries, like Italy, the family softens many risks of the market, but more households fall outside the risk absorption powers of the family than outside those of strong welfare states.

With the exception of the secondary mortgage market, the European financial landscape will remain one of different national mortgage markets that in some ways increasingly resemble each other. The creation of one mortgage market, however, is an illusion. The situation in Europe is fundamentally different from the U.S., where regulations may differ from state to state, but where the market is essentially organized at the federal level, while in Europe it is organized at the national level. Although some European countries such as the Netherlands, just like the U.S., have a system of "conforming loans" – in the Netherlands through the national mortgage guarantee, in the U.S. through Fannie Mae and Freddie Mac – there is no pan-European system of conforming loans and, despite recent calls for intensified European cooperation, it is unlikely that such a system will be created at any time soon because other differences between the organization of the different national markets are simply too big. We will, in other words, see the continuance of national varieties of residential capitalism. These capitalisms are not static, but dynamic: some of these dynamics are international, but others remain national.

Notes

1. Whitley (1998), although distinguishing more ideal-types, essentially does the same.
2. The selection of countries presented here largely depends on the availability of reliable and comparable data.
3. It must be noted that some of the small mortgage lenders, often from Britain or the U.S. have discontinued their activities in the Netherlands in 2007 and 2008 as a result of the financial crisis. This is for instance the case for ELQ, a subsidiary of Lehman Brothers that specialized in high-risk, jumbo and subprime mortgage products. ELQ had a market share of less than 1%.
4. GMAC, as a result of the mortgage market crisis, stopped granting new mortgages in the Netherlands in March 2008.
5. This was very common in the 1980s and early 1990s, but although funding for this has decreased in recent years, housing associations still buy deprived private rented housing.
6. Prices in Ireland, the Celtic tiger with its high economic growth in the 1990s, rose by 90% in the same period.
7. In particular the 1978 reform, which was meant to limit rent increases, but led to tenant evictions on the one hand and to underinvestment on the other.
8. The 30% drop in newly issued mortgage loans between October 2007 and October 2008 – which is mostly a result of the decline in refinancing loans not in first mortgages to buy a house – is about as large as the amount of newly issued mortgage loans that some general banks have securitized over the last two or three years.
9. And even if people lose their jobs, income decline will not be as rapid and severe as in weak welfare states. Moreover, the people most at risk of losing their job in the U.S. were often borrowers with subprime loans, while most of these people in the Netherlands live in social housing.

8
Political Framing in National Housing Systems: Lessons from Real Estate Developers in France and Spain

Julie Pollard

Introduction

In many Western countries, the desire for homeownership is understood as universal. A similar claim on the desire for property is common in the French and Spanish political spheres and in the media. During his campaign in 2007, French presidential candidate Sarkozy announced that the encouragement of owner-occupied housing would be his top housing priority and backed this up with mortgage interest tax deductions. Such political discourses have precedents within France and Spain. One famous slogan of the Franco regime was to transform a country of proletarians (*un país de proletarios*) into a country of homeowners (*un país de propietarios*) (Sambricio, 2003). In the 1970s, French President Valery Giscard d'Estaing advanced a political project to "make the French people own France" by making them homeowners, and "the French taste for property" has been a persistent idea within political rhetoric since the nineteenth century (Michel, 2006, 6). Should this desire be considered as citizens' wishes or as a political framing and a policy choice? Raising this question leads us to look at the connections between the players who structure the housing arena. More precisely, it presses us to consider the effects of decisions made by some players on others' preferences and choices. This chapter contributes to the examination of the influence of housing production configurations on people's so-called preferences. In other words, the chapter provides an investigation of which elements restrain and shape people's preferences for renting or owning their home.

Let's start with the frame of this chapter. The editors' introductory chapter suggests new ways of looking at housing politics. They suggest that two major ideas are inadequately taken into account. First, housing finance systems have an impact on people's political preferences. For instance, their preferences in taxation and public subsidies are biased by their housing tenure.[1] Second, as the contemporary international financial crisis demonstrates, housing politics are more and more responsive to global economic trends. The growing interdependence between national housing systems and the impact of transnational tendencies are shaking up national systems.[2] Understanding the "financialization" of everyday life and the role of housing markets have become crucial to grasp the evolution of housing issues. These observations lead them to criticize the typologies made to describe varieties of residential capitalism. They discuss the "varieties of capitalism" literature, which distinguishes liberal and coordinated market economies and Gøsta Esping-Andersen's typology, which establishes three Welfare State configurations – liberal, conservative, and social democratic. Because these approaches fail to take into account the major changes they consider, Schwartz and Seabrooke introduce two dimensions with which to differentiate "varieties of residential capitalism": owner-occupier rates and the level of mortgage debt to GDP.[3] With these two variables they propose a categorization based on four types: "corporatist market," "liberal market," "statist-developmentalist," and "familial." These configurations implicate three main stakeholders: the state, the citizens, and the financial market. Varieties of residential capitalism are examined by focusing on the demand side and emphasis is clearly placed on the citizens' viewpoint.

I suggest that we also need to focus on the supply side – more precisely by looking at real estate developers. This approach means concentrating especially on housing construction politics – and not on housing politics in general. The types of housing available and housing development both often come before people's preferences concerning housing. Why choose to focus on developers in order to grasp housing supply's dimensions? Real estate developers play a key role as they take initiative in building projects and will coordinate all firms and players involved in housing construction (banks, construction companies, notaries, architects, real estate agents, etc.). They are not always the only players in this role in all locations.[4] But in the main urban areas, where collective accommodation is the norm and where housing construction issues are particularly thorny and important, developers are absolutely key play-ers. For instance, developers (public and private together) build about 80% of the housing in the Paris and Madrid regions. People's choices are constrained by what the developers offer with respect to location and housing tenure. Housing production systems restrict people's choices at two levels. First, they are influenced, in an indirect way, by what the developers propose as housing. Second, they are influenced, in a direct way, by public incentives addressed to them to encourage them to rent or to buy their homes. For instance, the offers of rental housing do not come only from developers. They can come from private individuals renting one or several homes, too. In France, public policies favor pri-vate renting through significant tax exemptions. These tax exemption programs have been implemented since the beginning of the 1980s. The investor, who buys a new build home to rent it out, benefits from a tax break. In return, he engages to respect some criteria (in particu-lar, maximum level of rents).[5] These measures differ from the negative gearing to encourage investment into private rental markets described in the Australian and New Zealand systems (Mortensen and Seabrooke; Broome in this volume). In France, such policies are indeed mainly focused on new build housing. Their aim is to increase the housing stock, to support economic activities related to construction, and thus generate economic growth. There are no equivalent measures in Spain. These policies also have effects on housing production by developers, as they propose specific options that enable potential real estate investors to maximize their profits.[6]

Moreover, this perspective asks us to consider another way of look-ing at the effects of international pressure on housing. What are the effects of trends of internationalization on the national housing pro-duction systems? How far does financial control on housing challenge the organization, the structuring, and even the character of real estate developers? This approach makes it possible to question the two key ele-ments underlined in the book's introduction differently.

In many economic fields, focusing on the production side and on production firms seems to be self-evident and often constitutes the first direction investigated by scholars. But this is not the case in the hous-ing field. In France, investigations on housing are mainly restricted to social housing issues (Harloe, 1995; Lefebvre et al., 1991; Quilichini, 2001; Sala Pala, 2005, 2006; Simon, 2001; Zittoun, 2001). In Spain, this bias toward social issues related to housing also exists among sociolo-gists (Cortés Alcalá, 2005; Leal Maldonado, 2002, 2004a, 2004b, 2005). And the economists working on housing – clearly more numerous in Spain than in France – deal largely with public spending or with the effects of this sector on the whole national economy (Fernández Carbajal, 2004; López García, 2003, 2005; Naredo Pérez, 2004). Even research that focuses on housing production has paid little attention to private developers, but concentrates mainly on the role played by public developers (in France) or on the lack of public developers and on the role of the family in national housing systems (in Spain). This often leads a simplistic opposition between the free market housing sector (and players) and the public sector (or the sector supported by public players). Focusing on housing production and on the structuring of the production system provides a specific insight on housing issues. My approach shows the national embedding of so called "free market players." The aim of this chapter is to show that the tendencies that have been emphasized in the introductory chapter have very different impacts on the supply and demand sides. Looking at housing production systems requires the stressing of the continuity of national trends, even when looking at the private players.

My research is based on two case studies. I look at housing policies in France and in Spain. These two cases contrast markedly as regards levels of public intervention, aims of housing policies, and public structuring of the sector. In France, housing policies are characterized by a long tradition of state interventionism and remain largely centralized[7] – based on the idea of the need for social equity for all citizens within the national territory. Housing policies are, to a large extent, biased toward the area of social housing that is mostly rental housing. In Spain, housing policies are governed by regional administrations. The Autonomous Communities – *Comunidades Autónomas* – are responsible for the organization of town planning and housing in their area. The Spanish tradition of housing policies has been almost exclusively in favor of homeownership. Subsidized rented housing represents less than 1% of the stock.

In Section 8.1 I present the two housing systems set up after the Second World War in France and Spain. In Section 8.2 I emphasize the organization of the development supported by these systems. I will particularly highlight the role given to private developers and show how political institutions shape economic players' actions in both national contexts. I then question the current status (and the relative stability) of these systems, focusing on the place of different types of developers and on the types of housing they produce. In Section 8.3, I evaluate the impact of international variables on the production side: to what extent do they challenge the traditional systems?

8.1   The development of two housing production systems

The strengthening of private developers as an invisible aspect of the housing policies' institutionalization in France and Spain

The development of housing policies followed different paths in France and in Spain. However, the expansion of the number of private real estate developers has been favored in both countries by direct and indirect public support. Public support devoted to private developers was established after the First World War. At the end of the 1930s, policies to promote housing construction were initiated together with a range of measures taken to stimulate economic activity. But it is above all from the beginning of the 1950s that public authorities' intervention in the housing field sharply increased in scale in both France and Spain. In the context of a considerable lack of housing construction, political choices were taken and policy tools were decided and implemented, which have had a long-term impact on the sector. A few years after the Second World War, a consensus emerged among French political players about the need to boost housing construction and extend social housing production. At the end of the 1950s the Franco regime in Spain took strong measures to control urban planning and to eradicate shantytowns. One of the key aspects was the encouragement of private developers to the detriment of public ones. In both countries, public aid for developers significantly rose. This helped give this professional group a key position in housing construction. Thus, while they were fragmented, local, and unstable organizations in the first half of the twentieth century, private developers have become permanent, professionalized, and powerful players in both countries during its second half.

The role played by public, semipublic, or social developers is generally put at the heart of housing systems set up after the Second World War. These public and quasi-public developers seem to characterize the housing provision system. The expansion of the private real-estate sector and the role of public support in this expansion have thus far been less visible. Yet, the expansion in the numbers private developers, during the 30-year boom period after the Second World War, is closely linked to the growth of public aid. I propose a more inclusive perspective on housing production systems.

The aim of this first part is to present the two distinct configurations of housing systems that were developed in France and in Spain and to show how they have shaped the roles and status of all types of real estate developers.

France: Two housing production sectors

Housing policy in the 1950s is often presented as a story of social housing production (Heugas-Darraspen, 1994; Lefèbvre et al., 1991; Zittoun, 2001). Support of the social housing sector[8] encouraged the expansion of a specific and separate category of developers: the developers that specialized in social housing (*organismes de logement social*) – to simplify, I will call them "social developers." Social housing was – and still is – almost exclusively rental housing.

But housing policy after the Second World War also encouraged the expansion of a subsidized but private sector[9] (*secteur aidé*). This sector experienced great development until the 1960s and facilitated the growth of private developers.[10] This intermediate sector – sometimes called "sector of regulated mortgage loans and subsidies of the *Crédit Foncier de France*" – was established by the law of July 21, 1950, together with other measures to bolster housing construction. This subsidized sector, which stands between the social sector and the free market sector, had been already set up by the end of the 1930s,[11] but the policy procedures remained incomplete. More than the subsidies, the effectiveness of the procedures set up in 1950 rested on specific mortgage loans[12] (*prêts spéciaux*), which benefited from a state guarantee (Effosse, 2003). The aim of these measures was to compensate for the very low level of the free market housing production and to reduce the state budget, of which the social sector took up a large proportion. Thanks to this public support, developers could reduce their personal financial contribution to a project, with a low level of risk and a high return on investment. Sabine Effosse (2003) shows that this sector, which was considered provisional, was actually the driving force behind French housing construction after the Second World War. From 1950 to 1967, the subsidized sector contributed to the construction of about 1.8 million of housing units – that is to say, almost 40% of all housing units built. Only 26.5% of the housing built was social housing. And yet, the importance of the subsidized sector "was hidden by the importance taken by the social sector, which had become the leader sector at the end of the 1960s" (Effosse, 2003, 6).

Both housing sectors benefited from different kinds of public aid. Thus through the different subsidies offered to private and social developers, the state favored the creation and development of two separate housing segments. The first was a social one and the other was a subsidized one. The two types of developers, which corresponded to these two types of housing, were clearly separate.

This historical approach complicates the simplistic opposition between a social sector, into which the state would have put all its efforts, and a free market sector that would have developed in a totally autonomous way without any kind of public intervention. During this period, the free market sector was weak and played a very marginal role in housing construction. The growth of the subsidized sector enabled the strengthening of private developers who would later play a part in the free market sector.

Spain: The encouragement of a large protected sector

The Spanish Civil War destroyed a large share of the housing stock. A Ministry of Housing was created in the early 1940s to solve the problems of homeless people and shantytowns resulting from the war and from rural depopulation. The end of the 1950s saw a shift away from an autarkic development model toward a policy of economic openness (Cortés Alcalá, 2004; Llordén Miñambres, 2003; Vaz, 2004). Spain entered an era of economic development, modernization, and urban growth that lasted until the mid-1970s. This period is called the *Desarrollo* (Development). Céline Vaz (2004, 5) shows that the *Desarrollo* corresponds to a kind of "feverish urge to build." The consequence is that housing built during that time represents a significant part of the housing stock of Spanish cities. At the beginning of the 1990s, almost 55% of the existing housing stock had been built between 1941 and 1980. "The construction policy was intended both to stimulate the economy and to solve the housing shortage. Emphasis was placed on quantity not on quality" (Cortés Alcalá, 2004, 88).

The policy measures taken in the 1940s and then in the 1950s introduced successively different types of subsidized housing: *viviendas bonificables* in 1944, *viviendas de renta limitada* in 1954, and then *viviendas subvencionadas* in 1957. Despite variations in the naming, all of these types of housing corresponded to the same kind of public intervention. It aimed at encouraging construction by private developers through subsidies and tax exemptions. These programs have had mostly convergent effects. They contributed to the creation and development of a vast, more or less unified, subsidized housing category, called the protected housing sector (*vivienda protegida*). According to political discourses, this housing sector was supposed to perform some social functions, helping all people to become owners of their housing. In fact, the policies largely favored the middle and upper classes. Few solutions were implemented to solve the housing problems of the working class. The Spanish case can be characterized by a particularly important gap between discourses about the priority of helping working class people to become homeowners and practices – the public support of the creation of a subsidized sector with a very large "target population." In most of the measures taken, two options existed: the housing could be rented or bought; but the subsidies almost always favored buying. The majority of housing was therefore built for sale. The proportion of owner-occupied housing rose from 46% in 1950, through 57% in 1970, 78% in 1991, to 81% in 1999.

These subsidies encouraged massive investments by private developers in the protected housing sector. "Between 1957 and 1967, 83% of housing built in Spain received public financial support. However, whilst the state was the primary force driving residential construction, the direct provision of public housing never reached the levels seen in other Western countries" (Cortés Alcalá, 2004, 89). Private and public developers could benefit from public grants, but as a matter of fact public developers played a less and less significant role. Private developers became the leading players in the construction of protected housing. As Judith Allen (2006, 266) puts it, this system was grounded on clientlist political practices: "Franco brokered a deal with large contractors, based on a strong town planning system, which reduced risk and increased profits in return for their political support." Clientelism is essentially an exchange of services provided by the state in return for support for political parties (Ferrera, 1996).

As these programs continued in the following decades, they constituted incentives for substantial growth of the proportion of protected housing and this had a strong impact on housing construction. In particular, from the mid-1960s and during the 1970s, the construction level was closely linked to the construction of protected housing: in the mid-1970s, protected housing represented more than two-thirds of the total amount of housing built. This gave rise to the setting-up of a public bank that acted as guarantor for loans for protected housing (*Banco hipotecario de España*).

To conclude, the Spanish configuration established in the 1950s and stabilized during the following decades was based on the domination of private developers and on the domination of homeownership. The French configuration established in the 1950s was based on the coexistence of two types of developers: social developers and private ones and on the relative balance of two types of housing tenure: rental and ownership. This historical perspective enables us to underline how much the structuring and the growth of private developers were influenced by the state intervention. These observations contest the idea that a private development sector emerged only because of private demand.

8.2   How much do housing production systems shape people's choices?

Whether people are tenants or homeowners influences their political choices. But the reasoning is quite circular: at the same time as housing regimes influence people's political preferences, they partly result from national political framing. This section questions the current status of the French and Spanish housing development systems. Do the systems set up after the Second World War still have great resonance? To what extent do the current development systems reduce the character and limit the preferences of tenants, homeowners, and would-be homeowners? What are the roles of private developers in both countries?

It is possible to underline some general features of housing's political framing in both countries, without comparing the whole series of policy measures and tools. These features can be identified by looking at goals stated for the housing policies and by analyzing the legitimizing strategies of politicians to justify their aims. This does not mean that Spanish and French housing policies have been entirely uniform and stable since the 1950s. However, there have been continuities in the way housing issues have been grasped in each country since then. In particular, these continuities concern the connections between economic and social dimensions of housing policies in France as well as in Spain. The links between these two dimensions lie at the heart of the political framing of housing issues in both countries.

Before describing these configurations and showing how they shape housing development, I will examine the changes in of housing tenure in both countries. Today, in Europe, the share of households owning their homes varies considerably. The ratio of homeowners fluctuates from 43% in Germany and 50% in Sweden to 83% in Spain (and even more in some eastern countries, like Hungary, Romania, and Bulgaria). France is in the middle with 58% owner-occupation rates.

Table 8.1 compares the evolution of French and Spanish housing tenure from 1980 to 2007. The comparison of the ratio of homeowners to tenants (Table 8.1) reveals the durability of the differences between the two countries studied.[13] In Spain, rented housing has declined from 53% of the total in 1950 through 41% in 1960 (Leal Maldonado, 1992), to only 11% in 2007 (*Annuaire Eurostat, 2008*). In France,

Overall, the owner-occupied sector increased from 45% of the dwelling stock in 1970, to one household in every two in 1984, and reached

55% by 1999. Meanwhile, the private rented sector decreased slightly, from 22% in 1970 to 18.5% in 1992. The social rented sector represented 6% of total stock in 1963, jumped to 26% in the late 1960s, and then fell to 18% in the early 1980s and to 13.5% by 1991. (Stébé and Blanc, 2004, 102)

The data reveal that despite evolution toward an increase in the homeownership ratio, national specificities remain influential. How far can political framing explain these situations? How far does political framing influence the role and status of private developers?

France: The division between social and economic aspects of housing policies

In France, most of the government's public agenda on housing, and the media coverage, concern the social dimension of housing policies. The politicization of the housing issue is firmly fixed on the side of social issues. For instance, during the last five years, the events below, which

Table 8.1 Occupied dwelling stock by tenure (%), 1980–2007

	Tenure	France	Spain
1980	Rent	41	21
	Owner-occupation	47	73
	Other	12	6
1990	Rent	39	15
	Owner-occupation	54	78
	Other	7	7
1995	Rent	40	14
	Owner-occupation	54	80
	Other	7	6
2000	Rent	39	10
	Owner-occupation	55	84
	Other	7	6
2003	Rent	38	11
	Owner-occupation	56	82
	Other	6	7
2007	Rent	38	11
	Owner-occupation	58	83
	Other	4	6

Source: Housing Statistics in the European Union 2004 (2005), www.boverket.se, Annuaire Eurostat 2008.

have brought housing to the forefront of the media and/or political agenda, attest to it. Recent examples of events that attracted attention to the social stakes of housing issues are for instance: demonstrations during the winters of 2006 and 2007 led by an association called *Les enfants de Don Quichotte*, thorny debates concerning the national right to housing (*Droit au Logement Opposable*), and the emergence of safety issues after fatal fires in ancient Parisian residential blocks in September 2005. Thus, in France, housing policies are frequently limited to social housing policy. Social housing policy has undergone great changes in France since the 1950s. Michael Harloe (1995) uses the term "residualization" to sum up these changes. It indicates two main changes: a decrease in the scale of the policies carried out (state withdrawal and decrease in social housing provision) and the policies' focus on the most vulnerable people. As a result, the role of social developers in housing production as a whole has notably decreased.

But social housing policy is only one aspect of housing policies, as I have already demonstrated. Hélène Michel (2000) highlights that, in the 1980s, major changes occurred in housing policies in particular with regard to private property. She demonstrates how the passionate political debates concerning relations between tenants and owners have been lessening. According to her, the development of the other side of housing policies is linked to an evolution of the framing of housing issues. She writes:

> Addressing housing now corresponds to look after the good functioning of a market that engages a whole industry from the production till the renovation and renting and selling of housing. The administrative management in that domain becomes more and more technical. It necessitates the members of Parliament to specialize on that question, which at the same time loses its ideological dimension. (Michel, 2006, 15)

Housing policies cannot be reduced to one or other of these aspects: a highly politicized social policy or a completely technical economic policy. Rather, it seems important to insist on the distinction – but at the same time on the interdependence – between the economic and the social dimension. These two dimensions coexist in the political framing of housing issues. In France, housing policies were – and still are – characterized by a duality and a tension between social and economic policy objectives. This tendency was reinforced during the last decades. Public authorities developed both social housing strategies and policies to support home ownership or property investment. The housing development system still reflects this duality: the social side is dealt with by developers who specialize in social housing; the commercial side is in the hands of private real estate developers. Even if the perspective is quite different, this statement corresponds to the assumption of Pierre Bourdieu (2000) in his work on the single family housing market. According to Bourdieu, housing was one of the first policy areas to face social policy defenders and deregulation supporters in the 1970s. However, even if deregulation supporters have gained a dominant position, players promoting housing as a social right remain powerful. Explanations can be found in the institutional position of these players and in cognitive frames of housing issues.

Spain: The economic framing of housing

In the remnant Spanish welfare state, housing provision had little place. The Spanish system has been called "rudimentary" (Barlow and Duncan, 1994) or "familialism." It was characterized by narrow support for homeownership and by a low level of protection by the state. The family played a determining role. Judith Allen (2006, 251) demonstrates that families were not passive beneficiaries of housing policies but instead the family was – and still is – a social institution actively promoting its own housing welfare." Political scientists Ricard Gomá and Adelantado Gimeno show that housing has been an essential pillar of economic policies at all times since the inception of a housing policy (Gomá, 2000; Subirats, 2000). Depending on the context and on country, support of housing production can correspond to any of several aims. In Spain, the encouragement of economic activities has always been important. Emphasis on strong employment linkages and on other economic consequences of housing has long been at the forefront of political discourses. The dynamism of the sector during the first half of the 2000s – until 2006 – was one of the main factors of Spanish growth, which was about 3.9% in 2006 and 3.6% on average from 2000 to 2006 (Eurostat, 2008). This economic framing of housing policy went together with the key role allocated to private developers. Incentives to encourage private development were always at the heart of the government programs. This had repercussions on the kind of public assessments that occurred. Most of the time, evaluations centered on quantitative data, that is the amount of housing produced. Evaluations were done regardless of the use or the location of the housing being produced. Jesús Leal Maldonado (2005) shows the continuity of this economic framing of housing policies. He assumes that the two main features of the Spanish housing sector are the narrow incentives toward homeownership and the strong emphasis on high productivity of the sector/high levels of housing construction. According to him, these features are still predominant today as a consequence of 50 years of public interventions that weren't really called into question . He insists on the weakness of the social side of the policies. In 1988, more than 70% of tax exemptions were centered on the 30% of the households having higher rents. Setting limits for housing investments that are tax deductible has partly corrected these effects since then,[14] but social concerns remained secondary.

From a comparable angle, Luis Cortés Alcalá (2005) analyzes the meaning of "housing crisis" in the Spanish case. He shows that the image of the housing sector prevailing at the beginning of the 2000s is an image of tremendous dynamism. He argues however that if one shifts attention to the capacity of the Spanish system to provide housing for people during their whole life, the deep crisis of housing in Spain becomes obvious. To understand this crisis and its effects in a period of economic expansion, housing has to be seen as basic necessity not as an economic growth pillar (Cortés Alcalá, 2005). Jesús Leal Maldonado (2004b) quotes some results of national public opinion surveys to show that since the end of the 1990s, housing has become one of the most critical social issues in Spain. But instead of facing that crisis, housing policies have increased market tendencies. According to him, this is linked to the decrease of direct investment, the increase in tax exemption, and the fact that local authorities have given up the use of public land to promote protected housing. As far as housing is concerned, the Spanish case appears rather extreme. It seems that instead of a separation between economic and social dimensions as in the case of France, Spain is facing a domination of the economic dimension of housing issues. We could even say that social development stakes are subordinate to economic and commercial stakes of housing policies. This is a consequence of the political framing of housing issues and is also linked to the strong growth and employment effects of housing construction. Construction employed 10% of the active population – that is particularly important in a country that had historically high unemployment – and provided 12%–17% of Spanish GDP, about two times more than the European average.

Nevertheless, some recent changes have to be acknowledged. An independent Housing Ministry (*Ministerio de Vivienda*) – independent of the Ministry of Development (*Ministerio de Fomento*) that it was part of before – was created after the PSOE (*Partido Socialista Obrero Español*) came to power in 2004. It was interpreted by some nongovernment players as a first step to the recognition of housing as a social right. According to the editors' introductory chapter, Spain can be characterized as a familialist country. This does not, however, suggest the housing is not also viewed as a social right, but that the means of transferring housing is linked more to family relationships than in many liberal economies. Moreover, the new legislation on land use and planning that came into effect in July 2007 includes several measures to limit speculation on land and to encourage the construction of protected housing. Opinions about the possible implementation and effects of these measures are divided. However, it is obvious that to be efficient, such programs will have to make private developers an integral part of the plan. Indeed as they are almost the only contractors, the implementation of housing policies inevitably goes through them.

At the moment, Spain still can be characterized as a monotenural system, with the dominance of private developers over other players, the importance of economic stakes over social stakes, and strong preponderance of homeownership over rented homes.

8.3   How much do international changes challenge housing production systems?

The aim of this section is to question the scale and the effects of the trends toward internationalization on private real estate developers and thus on national housing production systems. How do developers integrate into the increasingly globalized system? Do changes on the supply and demand sides go along the same lines?

Some similar trends in both countries

Are both systems confronting similar pressures? This question is difficult to answer. However, some comparable changes are currently affecting both countries. Judith Allen (2006, p. 275) underlines one common change for European countries: "the global repositioning of the European economy means that virtually all European countries are facing the same pressures for more particularistic and personalized (targeted) welfare systems, within which the provision of housing for poorer groups is problematic." The growth in numbers of private developers in both countries can be seen as a counterpart of state withdrawal and/or repositioning regarding the social housing sector or issues. A growing part of housing policies thus involves state regulation of private developers.

Two other changes are particularly important as far as housing issues are concerned. First, moves toward decentralization must be underlined. In both countries, local governments have been playing growing roles since the beginning of the 1980s. In Spain, the Autonomous Communities are responsible for housing policies, as written in Article 148 of the Constitution of 1978. Spanish cities are also playing a growing role in the field of planning and housing. In France, housing policy remained formally centralized until 2004. But the discrepancy between this formal institutional stability throughout the 1980s and 1990s and the strong increase in the power of local authorities in that field during that period has to be pointed out. Indeed the decentralization of urban planning competencies, which took place in the early 1980s, contributed to the evolution of the sharing of responsibilities between state and cities in the housing field. In both countries, housing policy has become multilayered.

Second, a less visible move toward fiscalization of policy programs has to be highlighted. The role of fiscal tools has grown in France as well as in Spain. In France, when describing the evolution of public intervention, the substitution of housing subsidies oriented toward the supply side by subsidies oriented toward the demand side in 1977 is generally emphasized by researchers working on housing. But another significant change, the fiscalization of public intervention, is often forgotten. Tax exemptions and fiscal incentives aimed at private developers have existed since the beginning of housing policies in the 1930s, but this kind of intervention tends to replace others. In Spain, the situation is different. Fiscal policies have been the basis of housing policies since the 1970s. This importance grew in the 1980s and in the 1990s. The importance of fiscal regulation is a feature shared by the two countries despite their strong differences.

But more precisely, to what extent do internationalization variables directly affect housing productions systems? How far do private developers extend their activities into the international market?

Stability in the housing sector's structuring

Assumptions about internationalization of private real estate developers have to be looked at carefully. Even if developers communicate a great deal about their internationalization processes – or at least Europeanization process, the reality of internationalization does not correspond to the image they display. Developers' attempts at internationalization have rarely been successful (although some Spanish developers have recently invested in eastern European countries).[15]

Otherwise, foreign developers have great difficulty in carving out a place in other countries. A set of explanations can be proposed. First of all, their activities require detailed knowledge about town planning and construction procedures, which vary highly from country to country and sometimes even from region to region. For example, in Spain, each Autonomous Community has its own rules. Second, the developers need to master not only formal rules, but informal rules too. The range of informal rules is broad: from the architectural preferences of the city executives to knowledge of the players in power behind the scenes and the capacity to be in constant contacts with them. Awareness of these informal rules is particularly complex. Respecting these rules is crucial because developers remain reliant on local authorities, who have the power to give or refuse building permits. The formation of relationships with local authorities is particularly difficult and often requires long-term commitments in a town. Housing development entails the introduction of a new population or the residential settling of inhabitants. For local executives, new housing projects constitute therefore a very sensitive consideration. Most of the time, they are much more concerned about, for example, office developments.

Internationalization of developers is not impossible but it requires particular strategies. Three kinds of strategies prevail. The first is the redirection of the firm's activities, that is, toward developing offices instead of housing. The second consists of forming links with local developers (developers already present on the territory) or buying them. This method enables them to benefit from the land resources and/or sector and political networks of the local developer. The third option is a search for niches development possibilities, that is, to offer specific products that are not produced by local developers. All of these strategies remain marginal compared to the local and national activities of the French and Spanish developers.

Conclusion

This chapter analyzed changes in housing politics in France and Spain from the production – and most of all from the developers' – point of view. I have stressed how discussions of housing politics must deal with the supply side as well as the demand side, and that to understand supply we must investigate to the role of real estate developers. The relationships between the state, real estate developers, and citizens are highly political and operate in an environment where the political framing of housing as a social right or a means to wealth has a long history. This chapter has contrasted the French and Spanish experiences, and has highlighted the importance of real estate developers.

What about the current crisis and housing price busts in relation to France and, more dramatically, Spain? It is too soon to evaluate the precise impact of the current crisis on the housing development sectors. But it is already obvious that it reveals and reinforces national peculiarities. The crisis has made a much deeper impact on the Spanish housing sector. Since the fall of 2007, several Spanish developers, including some of the biggest ones, have collapsed. The spectacular bankruptcy of Martinsa-Fadesa in July 2008 demonstrates the sector's difficulties. Spanish banks are creating specialized real estate departments and shoring up developers' capital to prevent the sector's collapse. French developers are suffering shortfalls but nothing approximating the problems faced in Spain. In France public regulation attenuated the effects of the expansion of the real estate sector at the beginning of the 2000s, and is also now lessening the effects of the crisis. In France, the amount of empty new build housing is around 60,000 units, In Spain this figure is estimated to be about 800,000. Moreover, public-driven solutions for the sector are more likely to be implemented in France. For instance, at the time of writing, November 2008, negotiations were under way to make French social developers purchase empty housing built by private developers. No equivalent solution could be implemented in Spain. The way to forward is deeply contrasted: some French developers are already considering their prospects after the crisis, whereas Spanish developers are uncertain about their survival.

Notes

1. By housing tenure, I am referring to the occupant's status, that is to say whether the occupant of a given housing situation is a renter or an owner.
2. Following Judith Allen (2006, p. 272), we consider that housing systems are "conceived of as the complex of activities and practices which shape how people access housing."
3. These elements are indicators of decommodification of housing and of the presence of mortgage securitization.
4. In France, about 50% of housing developers are individual landlords. Insofar as single family detached houses are concerned, people are mostly building their own properties. In Spain, the proportion of individual landlords developing housing projects is about 20% of the whole housing production.
5. Depending on individual cases, the investor/landlord manages the property or delegates this role to the developer or an agency.
6. In France, the importance of the real estate investors among all developers' clients has been estimated as more than 50% of the housing sold in 2004.

7. Moves toward decentralization have nevertheless been occurring since 2004 (the Law of August 13, 2004).
8. In France, the term social housing indicates "a stock of rental housing owned by specialist organizations, mainly social developers and secondly companies with mixed public-private ownership" (Brun et al., 2002, 268).
9. Subsidized housing refers to housing that benefits from public aid but is not included in the category of social housing.
10. These measures have had a strong impact on the character of private developers. During the 1950s, the number of developers grew and the role of independent developers became much more important: at the beginning of the 1950s, only one developer in four was independent (most of them were part of real estate agents, construction firms, and property agents); ten years later half of developers were independent.
11. In accordance with the law of August 25, 1937.
12. These specific mortgage loans were not part of the measures taken in 1937.
13. It has to be specified that the comparisons are not totally reliable because of the mismatch the statistics at the European level. There is also a lack of common definitions between countries, for instance about what constitutes social housing.
14. Moreover, according to financial analysts, this tax exemption policy was far from neutral as regards price growth, with the developers taking it into account when they set the prices. So, these policies could have contributed to the rise of the house prices.
15. A report made by Madrid's private developers association (ASPRIMA, *Asociación de promotores inmobiliarios de Madrid*) states that Spanish developers have been attracted to these countries because of several factors: in particular their entry in the EU (in 2004 or 2007), their great growth potential, the level of inflation, and their interest rates.

9
Origins and Consequences of the U.S. Subprime Crisis
Herman M. Schwartz

Introduction: What went wrong at a macro level

The same dynamics driving the housing boom in the U.S. and elsewhere also drove the boom off the rails, producing the current global financial crisis. As in all booms, the bubble burst when the boom used up its fuel. Global disinflation, the recycling of U.S. trade deficits, and a ready supply of new buyers at the bottom of the U.S. housing ladder powered the boom. When these gave out, so did the boom. During the 1990s, U.S. multinational and retail firms offshored more and more labor intense production to low cost Asia, producing a flood of ever cheaper nondurable goods imports. Net, this lowered official inflation rates and thus the corresponding interest rates for mortgages. Simultaneously, European and Asian recycling of trade surpluses allowed U.S. arbitrage in global financial markets – the U.S. was able to borrow short term at low interest rates while investing overseas long term at higher rates of return. This also lowered interest rates for mortgages. Cheap mortgages lured millions of aspiring U.S. homebuyers onto the bottom rungs of the housing ladder. These new housing market entrants generated trillions of dollars of fictitious capital gains for incumbent homeowners, freeing them to move up the housing ladder and spend freely. As Schwartz (Chapter 2 of this volume) argued, the U.S. housing finance machine transformed these inputs into extra aggregate demand and thence into differential growth for the U.S.

But the very success of U.S. differential growth was what threw the housing growth machine from top gear into reverse gear. As social scientists might put it, the exhaustion of growth was an endogenous feature of growth itself. One of the most powerful fuels for disinflation was the reduction of prices for consumer nondurables through offshoring of labor intense production to Asia. This reduced cumulative nondurables inflation by 10% relative to services (Broda and Romalis, 2008; Broad and Weinstein, 2008). But on net, new homebuyers by definition tended to be lower income, lower skilled workers. The more that labor intense production moved offshore, the fewer potential housing market entrants there could be as incomes stagnated at the bottom. Initially the relatively high proportion of nondurable goods in the consumption package of those unskilled workers offset their falling real wages, as did falling interest rates on mortgages. Yet eventually the two blades of the scissors of falling wages and rising house prices had to meet, cutting one fuel line to the housing boom machine.

Second, successful offshoring of low wage manufacturing to China and other developing countries produced multiplier effects there, powering their economic growth but also creating new inflationary pressures. Given their initial low level of development, economic growth necessarily involved greater and greater calls on global raw material supplies, including, most importantly, oil. Development meant creating an entirely new infrastructure – roads, buildings, power generation, telecommunications – and thus huge energy intense inputs of cement, steel, and copper. All told, Chinese imports of oil, soybeans, and copper were about 30 times higher in 2008 than they were in 1995 (Jen and Bindelli, 2007). Developing nations' calls on global resources reversed the 1990s disinflation, forcing developed country central banks to raise interest rates in 2005. This cut a second fuel line.

Third, the very nature of housing and credit markets meant that the last entrants into the market would be the least creditworthy, making loans to them a risky proposition. From 1995 to 2005, the U.S. homeownership rate rose by roughly five percentage points from 65% to 70%, pushing the homeownership frontier out into the terra incognita of the uncreditworthy. Indeed, homeownership peaked in 2004, just as subprime loans shot up from about 7% of new mortgages to nearly 20%, indicating that nearly all creditworthy buyers had been "housed" (Harvard University Joint Center for Housing Studies, 2008). The majority of loans made in 2004–06 were of the subprime or "Alt-A" variety, indicating that borrowers were not creditworthy, lacked a down payment (purchase money), or were buying a wildly overpriced house relative to their income. These loans were generally at high and variable interest rates, making debtors vulnerable to any uptick in the reference rate for mortgages. Everyone understood that these buyers could not survive an increase in their mortgage interest rate. Thus these subprime loans were designed to be refinanced into lower, fixed rate loans after a few years of house price appreciation.

In short, by 2006, the housing boom had exhausted its inputs of new homebuyers, disinflation, and low interest rates. The housing-led differential growth machine then began to run backward, slowing the U.S. economy. Why did this produce a global financial crisis? The macroeconomic phenomena above were not disembodied, abstract flows. Instead they were channeled through a relatively small set of financial intermediaries who transformed global capital flows into mortgages and then back out into global financial markets as MBS and CDOs, a derivative largely based on MBS. Global financial firms devised what they thought was a relatively simple system for profiting from these trillion dollar flows. They created a carry trade in which they borrowed billions in short term money to buy their own apparently long term CDOs, profiting from the difference in interest rates. This carry trade was safe and profitable only if housing prices continued to rise. But when Chinese growth turned disinflation to inflation and the housing boom absorbed all the creditworthy buyers, housing prices turned and began a self-sustaining fall mirroring the earlier self-sustaining rise.

Falling prices threw the deceptively simple but extremely risky carry trade run by financial institutions into crisis. Inflation ticked up, draining cash from homeowners who already lacked sufficient income to service their mortgages. Interest rates ticked up, dampening and then reversing house price appreciation. Falling housing prices blocked the refinance off ramp for subprime buyers riding on the high interest rate highway. Thus subprime and Alt-A debtors began to default on their loans. Delinquency on all mortgages made in 2007 ran at three times the level for 2005 vintage mortgages, with 15% of 2007 subprime mortgages and 7% of Alt-A mortgages delinquent (Simon, 2008). With $1.6 trillion outstanding in MBS built on subprime and Alt-A mortgages, this threw highly leveraged financial firms into a crisis of their own making.

9.1   The crisis

The crisis emerged in slow motion in 2007 and 2008, presenting TV viewers with something not seen since the 1930s: desperate depositors queuing in front of large failed banks in Britain and the U.S. On September 14, 2007 depositors lined up outside the Northern Rock mortgage bank, Britain's eighth largest bank. Northern Rock had funded long term mortgages with short term borrowing on international markets, a version of the carry trade noted above. Within a few days, the Bank of England reversed its announced policy of nonintervention and supplied emergency loans to Northern Rock before ultimately nation-alizing it. Two months earlier, two German banks had also grounded, although less catastrophically, on the shoals of subprime mortgages. German banking authorities quickly orchestrated emergency bailouts and mergers for them. Japanese banks, while more stable, were not immune. Giant Nomura Bank's subprime losses in one quarter in 2007 amounted to roughly seven times its total cumulative profits on U.S. mortgages from 2002–06 (Morse, 2007), and Japanese banks had writ-ten off more than $12 billion by mid-2008.

Major U.S. banks were no less troubled from the summer of 2007 through mid-2008. In August, the Bank of America, perhaps at the behest of the Federal Reserve, bailed out Countrywide Financial Corporation. Countrywide was a key player in mortgage markets, originating nearly 10% of all new U.S. mortgages and handling payments on nearly 20% of all existing U.S. mortgages (including mine). In March 2008, the Fed provided an extraordinary credit guarantee so that J.P. Morgan could buy the failing Wall Street investment bank Bear Stearns, which had been crippled when its own subprime mortgage funds went bust. In July 2008, IndyMac, the largest originator of Alt-A mortgages in the U.S., went into FDIC receivership with $19 billion in liabilities, mak-ing it the largest bank failure (in constant dollars) in the U.S. since the Great Depression. Summer 2008 saw the mortgage giants Fannie Mae and Freddie Mac, which together guarantee about $5 trillion in U.S. mortgages, and insurance giant AIG all rescued from overt bankruptcy by a Federal capital injection amounting to 80% of their shares. Finally, in October 2008, finance ministries everywhere except Japan began nationalizing banks and guaranteeing deposits.

Global credit markets repeatedly jammed up in response to these events, fearful that opaque CDOs were tainted by increasingly default prone subprime mortgages, and that this would render their counter-parties insolvent. As of mid-2007, 56% of the global total of $1.3 trill-ion CDOs were backed by residential mortgages, mostly from the U.S. (Solomon, 2007). From summer 2007 onward, spooked central banks tried to reliquify global credit markets with unprecedented injections of cash that grew by an order of magnitude with each new credit freeze. In August 2007 alone the U.S. Federal Reserve Bank shoved $79 bill-ion into the U.S. banking system, and then in September 2007 made a surprisingly large 50 basis points (0.5%) cut in the Fed Funds rate, the rate at which it lets banks borrow from the Fed. The European Central Bank's (ECB) summer 2007 intervention was even larger, at €95 billion, although without a rate cut. Despite this, various parts of the global credit system froze up, as for example when trading temporarily ceased in Europe's $2.8 trillion covered bond market in November 2007.

Perceptions that these interventions were extraordinary soon slipped from memory as continuing problems forced the U.S. government and ECB into a series of even more unusual steps to rescue credit markets. In December 2007, the central banks of Europe, the U.S., Canada, and Switzerland effectively revived the 1960s Gold Pool by announcing that they would provide emergency liquidity to each other. This grew to nearly half a trillion dollars by late 2008. They also promised emergency liquidity on an auction basis to troubled banks, waiving virtually all of the usual rules about acceptable collateral. On this basis the ECB auctioned out nearly double its usual amount from December 2007 to October 2008 (ECB 2007; see also Bajaj and Norris, 2007). In January 2008, global stock markets sold off, prompting an emergency Federal Reserve Bank federal funds interest rate cut of 75 basis points or 0.75%. By March 2008, the Fed had set up three more special liquidity conduits to channel well over $400 billion dollars to troubled financial firms. For the first time this included not just the normal commercial banks but also investment firms, and for the first time the Fed accepted troubled MBS and CDOs as collateral. The Bank of England followed suit. By December 2008 the Fed had added five more credit facilities covering nearly every part of the financial sector and central banks had committed roughly $2.5 trillion in liquidity support to financial firms. And the scope of these interventions seemed likely only to expand going forward. What went wrong?

9.2   What went wrong at a micro level: Underlying causes

How did financial firms get themselves into such big trouble? Why did the Fed and ECB need to inject trillions of dollars and euros of new liquidity into the market? To understand both banks' difficulties and why they needed huge volumes of liquidity to get out of them, we need to delve into the seemingly complicated world of Structured Investment Vehicles (SIVs) holding MBS and CDOs. While SIVs and CDOs are conceptually complicated, the basic issues are very simple. Indeed, they boil down to a simple carry trade, as noted above. Put as simply as possible, banks used SIVs to borrow billions of dollars on a short-term (90–180 day) basis at low interest rates. The SIVs then turned around and invested those billions into what looked like long term securities – CDOs based on 30-year mortgages – paying higher interest rates. The raw material for most of these CDOs was the $1.6 trillion in subprime and Alt-A mortgages securitized from 2004 to 2007.

In principle, this kind of maturity mismatch – borrowing short term to invest long term – is very risky, and in practice, the fact that many of those mortgages went to high risk subprime and Alt-A borrowers increased those risks. The banks believed that they could avoid these risks for one simple reason: they believed that the maturity mismatch was more apparent than real. They thought that most of the adjustable rate mortgages behind the MBS and MBS-based CDOs their SIVs were buying would be refinanced after two years. This would allow banks' SIVs to repay their borrowed short term money before the macroeconomic environment turned against them. Banks did not believe that defaults might occur across the board rather than being contained to a few localities. To the banks' surprise, housing prices began falling in 2006, making it impossible for subprime and Alt-A borrowers to refinance their loans. Meanwhile, rising inflation made it more and more likely that these borrowers would outright default. Those defaults caused the market value of CDOs to plummet, causing the financial crisis when banks tried to roll over their short term loans and found that they could not do this.

Let's start with MBS in order to understand CDOs and then SIVs. Vanilla, pass through, MBS are reasonably safe vehicles for securitizing mortgages. Fannie Mae and Freddie Mac pioneered and dominated this market. They would package mortgages with somewhat similar interest rates, maturities, and credit risk into a huge pool with an average interest rate payout, maturity, and credit risk. Investors bought a percentage of that MBS pool to get a *pro rata* share of principal and interest payments from the pool. Fannie and Freddie, acting as loan servicers, would "pass through" these payments to investors. If the pool experienced a 1% default rate, then all buyers of that pool experienced a 1% loss on their share of the pool. To get a different interest rate, maturity, or level of risk investors would need to buy a different MBS. Unlike more complicated derivatives, the mortgages in a pass through MBS stayed intact, allowing the MBS bond holders or the servicer to identify and foreclose the defaulter. A defaulting mortgage only affected its own MBS pool, and conversely investors in that pool could foreclose defaulting homeowners without affecting other MBS pools.

Default (credit risk) on conforming mortgages in pass through MBS historically was lower than 0.5%. The mortgages going into these vanilla MBS had to conform to Fannie Mae's and Freddie Mac's underwriting standards – thus the adjective "conforming" in conforming mortgage.

These standards required a potential homebuyer to possess a good credit rating, to document that their total postmortgage debt payments would consume no more than 34% of their gross household income, to make a substantial down payment (usually over 10% and typically 20%), and (as of 2007) to borrow less than $417,000. Furthermore, conforming mortgages could not go to multifamily units with more than four apartments.

This low default rate earned Fannie and Freddie's MBS an AAA (investment grade) rating from the credit rating agencies, and allowed them to insure payment to investors at a low cost, usually less than 25 basis points (0.25%). Indeed, the real risk with a vanilla MBS was not credit risk *per se*, but rather that debtors would exercise their right to prepay the mortgage by refinancing or accelerating principal payments, and thus effectively "call" the bond. Vanilla MBS in many ways are a classic product of the Bretton Woods, or Fordist, era welfare state. They socialized the risks in providing housing finance, implicitly homogenized the returns to investors, favored debtors (because principal prepayment was costless), and homogenized borrowers to a middle class family model buying and occupying a single family home.

By contrast, private label MBS and CDOs are much more a product of the post-Fordist era. They took mortgages from nonconforming households (in all senses), allowed investors to speculate and earn differential returns, and shifted risks to debtors. Almost by definition, most of the mortgages going into the pool of non-GSE MBS were nonconforming. If those mortgages had been conforming, they would have been offered to Fannie Mae or Freddie Mac on account of their superior insurance and servicing costs. While not all nonconforming mortgages are subprime, almost all carry greater risks than do prime, conforming mortgages. The risk of default for subprime mortgages is roughly five to six times that for prime mortgages.

Why would anyone buy a security backed by such mortgages with such a high rate of default? How did such securities attract AAA credit ratings? Private label MBS did not offer investors a *pro rata* share of payments from a given pool of mortgages. Instead, bankers took a pool of nonconforming mortgages, sliced them into different CDOs, and then assigned each CDO a specific legal priority (seniority) over the underlying flow of payments from the pool. Regardless of which mortgages made interest payments or principal prepayments, those payments were assigned first to the CDO with the highest legal priority (so-called "super senior" tranches). This legal priority in claiming cash from the flow of payments is precisely what made some CDOs look low risk, even though the underlying mortgages might be subprime. Nearly all of the mortgages in the pool would have to default for the super senior tranche to remain unpaid. Once the highest tranche has been paid, the next highest tranche would receive payments, and so on. Each subsequent tranche thus had to wait on the tranche(s) above to take its share of payments. An investor's return from a CDO depended on their legal seniority in the chain of claims attached to the original pool of mortgages.

CDO thus were synthetic products containing bits and pieces of various mortgages. A defaulting mortgage could thus affect many different CDOs, and a specific set of CDO investors could not foreclose without affecting other CDOs. The logic behind mixing different mortgages into a wide range of CDOs was to limit the risk from any single default. What mixing did, though, was allow one defaulter to contaminate many CDOs. This prompted the widespread "salmonella in the sausage" metaphor about bad CDOs. And in fact, the rate of default on Baa rated CDOs (the very bottom of investment grade) was approximately ten times the default rate on similarly rated corporate bonds (Calomiris, 2007).

Having manufactured an AAA rated CDO bond from subprime dross, banks could then move this CDO debt off their books and into their so-called structured investment vehicles (SIVs). Banks created SIVs as off balance sheet investments, which meant that banks didn't have to back the SIVs with their own regulatory capital or reserves. Holding mandatory reserves for regulatory purposes decreases banks' profitability. SIVs allowed banks to avoid this regulatory drag on earnings. Banks did back up their SIVs with emergency lines of credit, though, and this is important later in this drama.

SIVs allowed banks to use leverage to maximize their profits. CDOs by themselves were not necessarily problematic. The combination of CDOs and SIVs, however, was toxic for the entire financial system. The simplest way to understand an SIV is to imagine it as a bank run mutual fund for big investors. The bank and some big investors would create and capitalize an SIV with their own money. This constituted the equity base for the SIV. The SIVs would then leverage their equity by borrowing anywhere from 10 to 14 times its equity in the form of short and medium term money in commercial capital markets. SIVs did this by issuing short term debt, so-called Asset Backed Commercial Paper (ABCP) that matured in 90–180 days. SIVs would have to refresh, or reborrow this money every time the 90–180 day term came up. The SIVs used this borrowed short term money to buy AAA rated CDOs. The organizations lending short term money to SIVs counted on the CDOs to provide collateral in the event of a default by the SIV. Global ABCP offerings doubled to $1.2 trillion annually, in 2004–07, based on increased demand from SIVs (Tett and Davies, 2007).

How did the SIV make money? The banks' SIVs basically had the same credit rating as the CDOs, so banks could not profit from an interest rate spread based on apparent creditworthiness. Instead banks used SIVs to engage in a carry trade, borrowing short term cash to invest in nominally long term CDOs. SIVs were profiting from the spread created by the *apparent* maturity difference between the long term CDOs that they held, and the short term and medium term ABCP they issued to fund purchases of those CDOs. Longer term debt generally carries higher interest rates than short term debt, and longer term CDOs did yield higher interest, not least because subprime mortgages paid higher interest. And the SIV magnified this difference in returns to its equity holders through the massive leverage noted above. This leverage was the source of great risk and great profits. By leveraging 10 to 14 times, SIVs could turn their own very small equity investment into very large profits. The entire benefit of the spread between short and long term rates fell into equity holders' hands.

Banks and their SIVs were insouciant about their apparent and large maturity mismatch. Their insouciance derived from their belief that their nominally "long term" CDO assets were in reality short term debt, despite being backed by nominally 30 year mortgages. Usually the mortgages backing a vanilla MBS mature in seven to ten years on average, but some amortize the full 30 years. By contrast, most of the mortgages going into the CDOs were 2/28 ARMs. That is, the relatively low initial interest rate lasted two years, and then for the next 28 years the interest rate would reset annually or biannually. Everyone, banks and buyers alike, expected that these mortgages would be refinanced in year two before the ARM reset to a higher interest rate. Subprime and Alt-A homebuyers taking out 2/28 mortgages did so in the belief that house prices rising at a 5%–10% annual clip would soon give them the equity they needed to qualify for a conforming, fixed rate mortgage at a lower interest rate. Banks believed that buyers' refinancing would spare them from defaults when interest rates reset upward on these mortgages. Instead, they would have cash in hand to return to their own ABCP creditors. And if those lenders refused to roll over SIVs' ABCP before refinancing occurred, SIVs believed they could use their emergency credit lines from their parent banks

Table 9.1 Cumulative write-downs and credit losses on subprime mortgages and MBS, at August 2008, $ billions, by nationality of bank

	Write-down and loss	Capital raised
US banks	243.4	172.9
Belgian, Dutch and Swiss banks	73.1	43
British banks	64.9	59.3
German banks	56.1	26.3
French banks	23.3	25.3
Asian and Mideast banks	21.7	19.7
Other European banks	9.8	2.3
Canadian banks	9.6	2.8
Total	**501.1**	**352.9**

Source: Yalman Onaran, 'Banks' Subprime Losses Top $500 Billion in Writedowns,' Bloomberg 12 August 2008, http://www.bloomberg.com/apps/news?pid=20601087&sid=a8sWOn1Cs1tY&

to shield them from any forced liquidation of the CDOs they owned, while they awaited the inevitable refinances that would quickly retire the CDO.

The investors in SIVs thus thought they had set up a basic carry trade, issuing apparently AAA rated short term paper while actually investing in not-really-long-term, not-really-AAA creditworthy instruments that paid out long term interest rates with no apparent risk. As long as housing prices kept rising, there would be no problem. Except that housing prices did not keep rising. Table 9.1 lists the losses that had ensued by August 2008, just before the wave of government nationalizations and bank failures.

9.3   What went wrong: Proximate causes

The essence of the current crisis is that banks and borrowers alike needed continued 10% annual housing price appreciation to bring their bets into the money. But the very arrival of subprime borrowers signaled the end of house price appreciation. The supply of creditworthy new and trade-up buyers was exhausted, which is why banks began offering loans to less creditworthy households. No new buyers meant that housing prices could not continue to rise indefinitely, yet the only available new buyers were people who could not actually afford their mortgages.

We can disaggregate the sources for this bad bet on the banks' side. Three things went awry in the SIVs' CDO gamble: excessive faith in mathematical models; reliance on historical default data behind those models; and a belief that housing prices would always rise. As new, over-the-counter, tailormade, and complicated derivatives, CDOs could not be valued in a public, liquid market. The regulatory agencies and the ratings agencies allowed SIVs and investment banks to value CDOs based on their internal models. This was so-called Level 3 pricing under the Financial Accounting Standards Board (FASB) Statement #157 promulgated in September 2006. Level 1 pricing involves marking to market, when a security can be valued using a recent sales price for the exact same security in public, ongoing trades. Level 2 pricing involves using publicly available data on similar but not exact copies of the derivative to guestimate – using a model – prices for relatively illiquid securities with no recent history of trades and thus no price quotes. Level 3 "marking to model" involves pure guesswork. The model says a unique derivative is worth a certain amount, and without any trades or public data, who is to say otherwise? (Finance industry wags call this "marking to make believe" because of the obvious conflicts of interest.) Marking to model instead of marking to market allowed SIVs to accumulate imprudently large quantities of essentially illiquid CDOs. But what if these models were wrong? What if these models underestimated the probability of forced sales of many illiquid CDOs, rather than a gradual liquidation?

Second, and worse, the historical data behind those models did not reflect the radical change in the underlying population of subprime borrowers. The ratings agencies and the investment banks had used data on subprime default rates in the 1990s to justify their assessment of current risks. But the population and environment behind these data changed in the 2000s. In the 1990s, subprime mortgages constituted a small, niche product in the mortgage market, with default rates that were in the low single digits. Subprime mortgages provided a legitimate way for people with damaged but improving credit or who had varying or cash income to get into the housing market. At a price of course – banks charged higher interest rates to reflect the lack of documented income or a weak credit score. Banks carefully screened subprime borrowers precisely because they were bad credit risks whose defaults would land on banks' own balance sheets. Moreover, an environment of gently rising housing prices helped 1990s subprime borrowers to refinance themselves into lower interest rate mortgages after a few years. All this mitigated 1990s default rates for subprime mortgages.

The influx of new, effectively unmodeled subprime borrowers after 2003 rendered retrospective default models inaccurate, as did the end of house price appreciation. First, mortgage brokers rather than banks screened subprime borrowers. Brokers made money by originating mortgages, not by holding them to term, and earned more money if a buyer could be lured into a large, high interest rate mortgage. With no credit risk, brokers had incentives to market as many dodgy mortgages as they could. Brokers made loans to otherwise uncreditworthy "NINJAs" who had "No Income, No Job and no Assets." The historical data also did not capture a subtle shift from using subprime as an instrument for borrowers with damaged credit to using subprime and Alt-A for good credit borrowers who wanted to borrow much, much more than they could afford in order to buy the granite kitchen counter equipped McMansion that defined the "good life." 1994 saw only $34 billion in subprime originations, mostly through banks; 2004–06 subprime originations averaged over $600 billion annually, mostly through brokers and specialist lenders (Credit Suisse, 2007). The connection to the similar $600 billion jump in the ACBP market should be obvious.

This set up the third problem in the SIV CDO gamble: what if housing prices failed to rise annually at double digit rates? Subprime and Alt-A borrowers were betting that continuously rising housing prices would bail them out of their ARM before the first interest rate reset. They contracted for 100% financing, at a higher than prime interest rate, because they did not expect to be paying that rate forever. Instead, if housing prices continued to rise 10% or more annually, then after two years our erstwhile subprime borrower would find themselves with 20% equity in their house and qualify for a lower fixed interest rate conforming 30-year mortgage. They could thus refinance their house before the reset seriously affected their finances. And reset they must, because 78% of all subprime mortgages originated in 2006 were 2/28 ARMs (Credit Suisse, 2007).

What if no new creditworthy buyers entered the market to release owners' unrealized equity and allow those owners to trade up? Then overstretched borrowers would not have 20% equity and would not be able to refinance into a conventional mortgage at lower interest rates. Instead, they would face a crippling interest rate reset that might force them into default. And this is exactly what happened in late 2006 and 2007. The rising tide of subprime mortgages met a sudden rise in interest rates as the Fed tried to reduce inflationary food and fuel price pressures. Housing prices softened. Suddenly refinance was impossible and the most recent subprime borrowers, who were most reliant on rising prices to bail them out, began to default at rapidly rising rates. Whereas only 4% of all 2004 vintage securitized subprime loans were in default after nine months, 10% of 2006 vintage loans and 16% of 2007 vintage subprime loans were in default after nine months. The reversal of housing price appreciation plus the prior change in subprime borrower behavior turned the Level 3 mark to model into pure make believe. SIVs were holding dross, not AAA rated assets. But they still owed billions of dollars in ABCP collateralized by those CDOs, and every three to six months those ABCP loans had to be refinanced.

As rising mortgage defaults percolated up into SIVs' CDOs, those SIVs found it harder and harder to raise cash to refinance their own ABCP, as defaults compromised the value of their collateral. SIVs had three options for repaying maturing ABCP: liquidate their CDOs, borrow new money to repay older ABCP debts, or use their emergency credit lines. But who would put up new money? Most banks were already invested in SIVs, so they all knew that defaults were rising and thus that these CDOs were potentially worthless. Who would buy CDOs knowing that double digit declines in value might happen? The supply of hapless Norwegian villages or teachers' pension funds was not infinite. Instead SIVs turned to their patron banks for emergency loans. This put those banks into a difficult position, as they did not have enough cash to cover their own SIVs' needs.

Banks could not go into the open market to borrow either, because who would lend to them? Even if other banks were not similarly caught short, those banks had good reason to suspect that any CDOs offered as collateral might dramatically fall in value. Indeed, banks were so worried about counterparty risk – the risk that a bank that borrowed from them might default – that they stopped lending to other banks against nearly all kinds of collateral. This fear produced the massive credit crunches of August and November 2007, and March and July–October 2008. The market rejected CDOs backed by student and automobile loans, and stopped offering cash in the Auction Rate Securities market on which many municipalities relied. The market's rejection of CDOs caused the nominal value of SIVs to drop $150 billion from July 2007 to December 2007, while ABCP issues declined $400 billion in the same period (Tett and Davies, 2007).

Banks thus had to begin bringing their SIVs back onto their books, defeating the whole purpose of SIVs in the first place. Bringing SIVs back on the books reduced the profitability from investing in CDOs because banks had to set aside regulatory capital for them. This requirement also had huge negative macroeconomic consequences. Bringing

SIVs on board and setting aside capital would force banks to reduce their other forms of lending, because they would have insufficient capital under the Basel II standards relative to their outstanding lending. (Banks must hold sufficient capital to offset the possibility that loans going bad might force the bank into bankruptcy.) And the problems extended beyond the banks themselves, because the near collapse of the ABCP market affected the ability of nonfinancial businesses to issue ABCP to meet their ongoing obligations while waiting on payment from sales of their goods.

Banks once more had committed the fallacy of composition, believing that they could coin money from undercapitalized SIVs without experiencing any systemic risks or creating new behaviors in the market that might alter the behaviors on which they based their models. But investments that are safe for one bank alone are not necessarily safe for all of them. As banks piled into the CDO and ABCP markets, they exhausted the supply of credible subprime and Alt-A borrowers and reliable mortgage brokers. This changed the environment that had made CDOs a rational investment in the first place. Once housing prices stopped being on fire, all the assumptions behind SIVs' leveraged speculation in CDOs disappeared and capital markets froze. Banks could not solve their own problems, so they turned to the state.

9.4 Government intervention and the renationalization of the mortgage market

As in prior financial crises, the U.S. Federal Reserve and Treasury initially took the lead, although by October 2008 it was Britain that acted most decisively. As in prior crises the initial U.S. responses reflected an initially optimistic understanding of the crisis. The Fed initially assumed that banks were fundamentally solvent, that most CDO assets were fundamentally good, and thus that the greatest danger was from a panic sale of CDOs that might bring down banks and the financial system. Thus the initial interventions were relatively small, even if they seemed extraordinary at the time, and centered on liquidity. Aside from Britain's *de facto* nationalization of Northern Rock, the August 2007 interventions all took the form of extra liquidity for banks. Central banks extended cash to banks to enable them to make good on their emergency lines of credit to their SIVs. Central banks assumed that markets would soon accurately price CDOs, enabling them to trade and thus enabling banks to do business with one another again and fund their SIVs with other people's money. Some of this money came from the partial recapitalization of major banks and bond dealers by Sovereign Wealth Funds. These funds provided roughly $70 billion of the $260 billion of new capital core U.S. financial institutions needed in 2007 and 2008.

But five successively larger spikes in the so-called TED spread signaled that more and more credit markets were locking up. Each TED spike triggered new and larger central bank and finance ministry interventions (see Table 9.2). The TED spread measures the gap between the three-month Treasury bill and a three-month Eurodollar loan at LIBOR, the rate that banks charge each other. The TED spread reflects banks' assessment of other banks' creditworthiness and thus their guess about the probability of bank failures. During the ten years prior to the crisis, this so-called TED spread averaged about 42 basis points. In each crisis, the TED spread shot up well above this, hitting nearly 250 basis points in August 2007, 220 basis points in November 2007, just over 200 basis points in March 2008, 150 basis points in July 2008, and well over 400 in September–October 2008.[1] These spreads resemble the usual spread between developed and developing country public debt.

Central bank and finance ministry interventions fell into three broad categories that eventually addressed all three broad problems banks always face: liquidity, capital adequacy, and deposit stability. Banks were unable to borrow from each other because of counterparty risks, and thus ultimately unable to lend either long or short term to the real economy. Defaults on MBS threatened to wipe out banks' capital, triggering cascading defaults through counterparty risk and calls on credit default swaps, as well as declining share values for banks. Depositors ran for safer places like government bonds, forcing banks to curtail not just long term but also short term lending. Governments responded at first only with emergency liquidity injections that soon became routine. When this failed they sought to alleviate mortgage distress and thus damage to bank balance sheets. This soon turned into stealth or outright nationalization of financial institutions whose capital had evaporated. Finally governments began offering unlimited guarantees to depositors. Each step was intended to address a specific part of the crisis. Each step seemed unprecedentedly large at the start yet soon looked small relative to later interventions. Each round of crisis expanded not only the dollar size of each intervention but also its application to new areas of the financial system. Each, at the time of writing, seems unlikely to be unwound any time soon. Let's start with liquidity injections, which were intended to keep banks solvent and lending.

Table 9.2 Central bank and finance ministry interventions, August 2007–October 2008

Date	Institution	Amount / Action	Institution	Amount / Action
August 2007	US Federal Reserve	$62 billion	European Central Bank (ECB)	€156 billion
	Bank of Canada	CAD 1.64 billion	Bank of Japan	¥1 trillion
	Reserve Bank of Australia	AUD 4.95 billion	Swiss National Bank (SNB)	SFr 2–3 billion
	Monetary authority of Singapore	SGD 1.5 billion (c. $1 billion)		
December 2007	Federal Reserve Bank	$30 billion term auction facility	Federal Reserve, ECB and Swiss National Bank	$90 billion currency swap arrangement
	Bank of Canada	CAD 3 billion		
May 2008	US Federal Reserve	$200 billion term securities lending facility and primary dealer credit facility	ECB, SNB	Extra $10 billion and $2 billion into currency swap pool
September 2008	US Federal Reserve	Term auction facility increased to $75 billion	European Central Bank	$20 billion per month extra into currency swap pool
	US Federal Reserve	Term securities lending facility auctions become weekly	US Treasury	De facto nationalization of Fannie Mae, Freddie Mac and AIG
	G-7 plus Swiss central banks	$427 billion currency swap arrangement		
October 2008	G-7 plus Australian, Swedish and Swiss central banks	Coordinated 0.5% rate cut, October 2008	Denmark, Germany, Iceland, Ireland, UK, US	Deposit insurance caps, raised, removed, or extended to new classes of deposits
	OECD Finance Ministries: Loan guarantees	Austria: €85 billion France: €320 billion Germany: €400 billion Italy: €20 billion Netherlands: €200 billion Spain: €100 billion US: $700 billion	OECD Finance Ministries: Bank recapitalizations	Germany: €80 billion France: €40 billion UK: $64 billion US: $250 billion

Source: Author's compilation from contemporaneous news reports and central bank press releases.

Financial firms' immediate problem in mid-2007 was the absence of any open market that might set a value on CDOs, and the fear that such a market might value them at levels that would imply crippling writeoffs. Central banks thought the problem was limited to mortgage securities. The first interventions thus provided liquidity to banks in unusual volumes so they could absorb those CDOs onto their books without actually having open market transactions. The Fed and the ECB coordinated what they thought would be a once-only $200 billion plus global liquidity injection in August 2007, lending cash against the usual collateral or treasuries and Agency (Fannie Mae, Freddie Mac) bonds.

The rising tsunami of mortgage defaults and foreclosures in the fall of 2007 prompted a dawning recognition that resetting interest rates on ARMs in 2008–09 would throw many more mortgages into default. This combined with the difficulties in disentangling exactly which mortgages comprised the highly opaque CDOs on banks' books to throw suspicion on other synthetic assets built from car loans, student loans, and corporate receivables. In other words, not just fear of more bad debt, but more bad debt everywhere. Consequently, the entire ABCP market began drying up again in the late fall of 2007 as private firms refused to lend to each other. The collapse of the Auction Rate Securities market, a parallel ABCP market funding municipalities, triggered a new round of intervention (Iley, 2008).

This time, central banks changed the rules governing the kind of collateral they would accept, and began accepting private label residential and commercial MBS in exchange for the liquid government debt they loan to banks. Normally, the U.S. Federal Reserve only accepts Treasury bonds and Agency (Fannie Mae, Freddie Mac, and Ginnie Mae) bonds as collateral. The Fed's vehicle for this intervention was the $30 billion Term Auction Facility (TAF) in December 2007. Initially, TAF allowed banks access to cash on a 28-day rather than overnight basis, and its $30 billion was an order of magnitude larger than typical open market operations. TAF disciplined banks by forcing them to bid for funds. This marketlike mechanism steered cash to the banks with the biggest problems, but in an opaque way that reduced the possibility of a run on those banks. By August 2008, $200 billion of TAF cash was available on an 84-day basis.

TAF soon spawned similar facilities for nondepository banks. At the third TED spike in March 2008, the Fed created two new facilities that accepted novel forms of collateral, and permitted open market operations on a 28-day basis (Federal Reserve Bank). The Term Securities

Lending Facility of March 2008 allowed banks to use non-Agency MBS as collateral against Treasury bonds and cash. The Fed also created a parallel fund for broker dealers (nonbank entities authorized to do business with the Fed), the Primary Broker Dealer Facility.

TED spike four and Bear Stearns' collapse provoked the Fed to begin accepting all kinds of asset backed securities, including AAA rated but suspect CDOs, at the discount window under a Term Securities Lending Facility expanded to $200 billion (Federal Reserve Bank 2008a). Thus from August 2007 to July 2008, the share of Treasury bonds on the Federal Reserve Bank's balance sheet fell from 90% to just over 50% as banks and brokers sought liquidity to meet their obligations. Finally in September 2008 the Fed announced it would also begin backing depository banks' purchases of commercial paper (ABCP) through the ABCP Money Market Mutual Fund Liquidity Facility and guaranteeing nonfinancial firms' commercial paper through the Commercial Paper Funding Facility. By September 2008, the Fed was providing about $1.6 trillion in liquidity support to the U.S. and foreign financial systems, through 12 different facilities.

The ECB similarly auctioned off funds in late December 2007, providing over €130 billion net at a 4.21% interest rate. This was higher than normal for the ECB's open market operations, but much lower than the prevailing LIBOR. The volume transacted was also the largest ECB auction since the ECB began operations. From summer 2007 through August 2008, the average ECB open market auction involved twice as much cash as did the auctions from 1999 to summer 2007. In December 2007, the major central banks also agreed to swap currencies to allow European borrowers with dollar liabilities to have access to dollars through channels that would not disrupt credit markets. This facility was expanded several times. Then in October 2008 the major central banks did a coordinated rate cut.

These interventions failed to resolve the problem, because by 2008 banks saw the problem not as a liquidity crisis but rather as a solvency crisis. They did not believe their counterparties were safe given that no one really knew the quantity and quality of bad CDOs, MBS, and CDS poisoning a given counterparty's books. (And indeed, the auction of Lehman Brothers' assets postbankruptcy revealed huge losses on these instruments.) Thus banks choked off lending to each other, and in doing so began choking off credit to the real economy.

Consequently central bank intervention began shifting from liquidity provision to efforts to shore up banks' capital base. This took two forms. First, central banks tried to prop up housing prices, so as to limit foreclosures and prevent panic selling of foreclosed properties. This would help banks to avoid losses on deteriorating MBS and CDO that would force them to take writeoffs against their capital. Research suggested that falling housing prices were a primary cause of foreclosure. This intervention took two forms. New regulations and programs aimed at limiting or preventing interest rate resets on ARMs that might drive recent buyers into delinquency. This helped resolve bank's collective action problem around foreclosure – if all delinquent mortgages were liquidated, home prices would collapse, yet no bank could forebear while other banks foreclosed.

In the second loss mitigation effort, U.S. public lending agencies ramped up their provision of capital for resale into mortgage markets, in order to keep sales from collapsing as banks ran away from mortgage lending. The U.S. Federal Home Loan Banks as well as Fannie Mae and Freddie Mac once more became the primary sources of U.S. mortgage finance. Overall the FHLBs provided nearly $750 billion to banks in the third quarter of 2007, helping total lending by the FHLBs in 2007 to rise by nearly $350 billion as compared with 2006 (FHLB; Iley, 2008). This reversed the privatization of mortgage finance characterizing the long 1990s. In 2007 Fannie Mae and Freddie Mac absorbed billions of dollars of Alt-A mortgage backed securities, bringing them to 11% of Fannie Mae's total book by June 2008 (Hagerty, 2008). In addition, governments intervened directly in some mortgage contracts to force small writedowns that would keep those mortgages current. When these two efforts at loss mitigation failed, central banks had to step in and directly recapitalize banks by buying shares or outright nationalizing firms.

Conclusion

No economic boom goes on forever. The housing boom had exhausted its core inputs by 2005. Disinflation turned to inflation as Chinese wages began rising and, more important, prices for foods and fuels jumped to unprecedented levels. Cheap mortgage finance exhausted the supply of new housing market entrants needed to enrich housing market incumbents, and banks increasingly made loans to borrowers with little hope of ever making payments on what were increasingly large debts.

The bursting of the housing bubble need not have had disastrous consequences for the financial system. But it did, precisely because the entire global financial system had mortgaged itself to the fortunes of the housing market by abetting the bubble. Banks' huge profitability rested on their ability to disguise a simple but highly leveraged carry trade in which they borrowed money short term to buy their own seemingly long term MBS and CDOs via off balance sheet SIVs. Banks' bad bets went awry when housing prices began falling, taking CDOs and SIVs with them.

Politically this crisis may mark the high tide of the neoliberal erosion of the institutional structural of the Bretton Woods era Keynesian welfare state in the U.S. Neoliberal deregulation came late to housing. Until the 1990s, housing finance had effectively been nationalized and regulated via the effective monopoly that the giant government sponsored enterprises (GSE), Fannie Mae and Freddie Mac, had over the securitization of mortgages. During the 1990s, private MBS securitization and the creation of nonvanilla MBS undermined the GSE's monopoly and accentuated the risks of borrowing for homeowners and lending for the beneficial owners of MBS. Housing related risk was desocialized, particularly after 2002, when nonagency MBS began gaining significant market share. The Bush (junior) administration abetted this expansion of private sector market share by relaxing regulatory standards and suggesting that Fannie Mae and Freddie Mac reduce their presence in the market.

The crisis has renationalized and denationalized U.S. housing finance. By denationalization I do not mean privatization. The crisis has effectively destroyed private issuers of MBS, with private MBS issues declining to zero in the third quarter of 2007 and most minor players in bankruptcy. The major players lack the credibility and capital to reenter this business. This leaves only the government sponsored enterprises–Freddie and Fannie plus the FHLBs–standing as large scale purchasers of raw mortgages and producers of credible MBS (Iley, 2008; Paletta, 2008). In the last half of 2007, these three institutions generated nearly all of the new credit in the U.S. market. The FHLB supplied capital to mortgage lenders on the one side, while Fannie and Freddie absorbed and packaged mortgages on the other side. The GSEs' role will only expand. This shift of mortgage origination and securitization back to the GSEs constitutes the renationalization of U.S. housing finance. The denationalization involves the continued sale of U.S.-generated MBS to foreign central banks (Setser, 2008).

Note

1. Bloomberg Financial, available at http://www.bloomberg.com/apps/cbuilder?ticker1=.TEDSP:IND, date accessed January 15, 2009.

10
Conclusion: Residential Capitalism and the International Political Economy

Herman M. Schwartz and Leonard Seabrooke

Introduction

In August 2007 the global economy hit an iceberg composed of mortgage debt. $600 billion in U.S. subprime mortgages comprised the visible part of that iceberg, but several trillion dollars of mortgage and other assets packaged into CDOs constituted the invisible part of the iceberg. Like the *Titanic*, the global economy took on water slowly, but steadily, and over the following 13 months the rivets began popping off the financial system. One by one the bulkheads of off balance sheet entities called SIVs gave way, spilling negative financial liquidity into the investment banking compartments behind them and thence to commercial banks and insurance companies. Governments hastily moved banks to the front of the lifeboat queues, while pondering what to do about homeowners in steerage who were underwater on their mortgages. As with the *Titanic*, there had been abundant warnings that the market value of the housing collateral backing securities was well out of line with historic norms, yet no one seemed to doubt that houses provided riskless collateral for all manner of novel securities.

The academic literature on comparative and international political economy was also largely blind to housing's political and macroeconomic significance. Out of thousands of papers listed in the paper archive for the August 2008 American Political Science Association annual meeting, only one paper MBS or CDOs, and only a handful mention housing or securitization in some significant way.[1] Discarding errant references to the U.S. House of Representatives and "securitization" as a military rather than financial concept leaves behind a few papers mostly dealing with the provision of low income housing from a public policy point of view. The number of articles published in political science journals on unemployment insurance considerably outnumbers that on housing finance. Although prominent scholars like Francis Castles and Gøsta Esping-Andersen have written on the political consequences of housing policy and housing finance, these issues are largely relegated to political science's periphery, or to disciplines like geography and urban sociology (see for example Aalbers, 2006; Gotham, 2006).

This volume rectifies this deficiency by advancing four major arguments. The first is foundational: the original debate between Jim Kemeny (1980) and Francis Castles (1998) opened up an important line of inquiry into the nature of modern capitalist economies and welfare states, even if majority of scholars took the path more trod. Similarly, the majority focus on unemployment insurance and pensions in isolation from housing overshadowed Esping-Andersen's (1985) analysis of social democratic parties' efforts to use housing policy as a political tool to cement middle class loyalty to the welfare state. But the Kemeny-Castles debate and Esping-Andersen's early contribution offer important insights into modern politics. These arguments need to be periodized and updated given the secular change in homeownership levels and innovations in mortgage finance. In particular, while Castles and Kemeny largely focused on homeowners' tax preferences, widespread homeownership and indebtedness also affects inflation preferences.

Second, housing and housing finance play a largely unrecognized role in aggregate demand formation and equally important in relative demand formation across OECD societies. The VOC literature correctly stresses the microeconomic consequences flowing from different clusters of institutions that ameliorate coordination problems for firms (Hall and Soskice, 2001). VOC is the lineal descendant of a series of analyses originating with Andrew Shonfield's *Modern Capitalism* (1965). Like VOC, Shonfield showed that institutional diversity mattered, but unlike VOC, Shonfield's major concern was how institutions mattered for macroeconomic outcomes, including stability and growth. Though Shonfield did not consider housing finance, the chapters in this volume show that disinflation flowed through housing finance institutions to generate growth. The public or quasi-public nature of housing finance institutions everywhere made them explicitly political (see Seabrooke, 2008). We do not see our emphasis on housing finance as contradicting VOC or denying the salience of its various studies. Rather, our "varieties of residential capitalism" approach seeks to return to Shonfield's focus on macroeconomic outcomes at a time when growth and stability no longer seem assured, and when financial structures are changing rapidly.

Third, a concern for macroeconomic outcomes leads logically to two questions of periodization concerning housing's political and economic role. Houses clearly played different roles in each of what can be loosely styled the Bretton Woods period and the neoliberal period commencing after the admittedly arbitrary breakpoint of the 1979 Thatcher-Volcker monetarist revolution. In the Bretton Woods period, homes and housing finance were a channel for economic growth originating elsewhere. Psychologically and politically, houses were homes – inert, immobile, and illiquid – during Bretton Woods. In many OECD member countries strong state support for home ownership also formed an important component of the postwar social compact that helped to legitimize market-based economies. This compact provided various forms of income security, enabling the vertical extension of property rights, and in some cases increasing social mobility for households across both middle and lower income thresholds.[2]

But by the 1990s, the neoliberal period, houses had become assets – apparently live, cashable, and liquid – in countries with liberal housing finance systems. This transformation had both psychological/phenomenological and financial aspects. Financially, housing finance systems became an independent source of aggregate demand. Phenomenologically, the shift from home to asset aided in the shift of political identities from citizen to market player. The increased commodification of housing also helped to drive a wedge between the interests of existing home owners and new or possible future entrants to the housing market, breaking down the social cohesion that emerged under the earlier period of broad-based home ownership (see Broome, this volume). Much as conservative parties desired, commodification fostered a realignment in political behavior after the Bretton Woods era, by shifting some voters at the margin toward a more conservative politics (cf. Blyth, 2008, 394–5).

Finally, we must address the central role housing finance plays in the current crisis. Defaults on mortgage debt clearly triggered the global crisis. But did mortgages alone cause the crisis? The underlying causes for the crisis clearly lay in an excessive reliance on credit and asset growth for demand creation in rich countries on the one hand, and in an excessive reliance on external demand by developing countries committed to a dollar exchange rate peg on the other. Houses became the central focus of the financial system's problems precisely because they were the primary source of consumption growth in the more dynamic OECD economies, and because they were the last remaining pillar of the old welfare state where privatization or marketization could plausibly occur. As many of the chapters in this volume suggest, some governments also sought to sustain housing booms for their own political ends and redefined national economic growth models in the process.

This concluding chapter addresses each issue, mustering evidence from the preceding chapters.

10.1 Welfare trade-offs

The chapters in this volume show that the "welfare trade-off" identified by Kemeny (1980) and Castles (1998) persists, especially with respect to overt public pensions, although publicly mandated and/or tax privileged private pensions muddy the picture. But there is no obvious one-for-one correspondence either between pension spending and homeownership or between total public spending and homeownership. Instead, there are at least four distinct patterns. Each reflects a different form of state intervention rather than the absence or presence of the state. Where the state does not provide housing or pensions through its own organizations, it substitutes quasi-public institutions or large targeted tax-based subsidies. And as Pollard shows in this volume, the action is sometimes on the supply side rather than the demand side.

The chapters here by Watson, Broome, Tranøy, and Mortensen and Seabrooke show a strong and continuing trade-off between homeownership and state spending in the liberal housing economies and Norway. Citizens in the traditional liberal housing economies have chosen to use residential property as means of storing wealth over the income life cycle, while paying less tax and thus relying less on the state for social support (including housing). At various points in time, the state in those societies validated this choice by granting income tax relief to mortgage interest, supplemented by tax sheltered private pensions. Up until the housing crash of 2007–08, these societies had both high intergenerational inequality and high interclass inequality. These societies remain the poster children for the Castles and Kemeny arguments. Relatively low taxation permits a broad swath of the population to buy houses. Simultaneously the relatively low public pension and the ongoing shift away from defined benefit private pensions increasingly induces them to do so as a substitute for retirement income.

But it would be a mistake to think that this constitutes some kind of state passivity or policy vacuum. In fact, in all our liberal housing economies, including Norway and especially the U.S., the state has constructed an elaborate set of institutions supporting homeownership. In the U.S., these encompass not only the tax deductions for owner-occupier mortgage interest that Chris Howard (2006) labels part of the U.S. "hidden welfare state." A panoply of public policies support widespread homeownership, and thus alleviate pressure for more robust public pensions. First and foremost among these policies was the creation of Fannie Mae and Freddie Mac as quasi-public financial firms with an implicit government guarantee that was validated in the summer of 2008. This permitted the "Frannie" twins to float trillions of dollars in MBS on a very thin capital base. In turn, this made possible the very buyer/debtor friendly dominance of callable, fixed interest rate, no recourse loans that dominate the U.S. market, in contrast to nearly every other market (see Table 1.1). Frannie lowered interest rates for consumers by permitting the banks that actually originated mortgages to remove interest rate risk from their balance sheets. Frannie's MBS constituted a fairly consistent one-third of the U.S. private securities market from the mid-1990s onward, energizing a transactions oriented financial sector.

Lower interest rates and abundant land mean that the U.S. historically has had relatively low mortgage debt in relation to its level of homeownership, when compared to other OECD member countries. While work within IPE typically assumes extreme indebtedness in the U.S., this was not the case for housing indebtedness alone until the explosion of housing prices after 2001. (And U.S. consumer debt figures are also misleading in that much credit card debt reflects "convenience debt" that is extinguished on a monthly basis as consumers substitute temporary credit for cash payment; cf. Montgomerie, 2007.) If we were to assess who is subprime and who is not according to the criterion of housing related debt, then the Dutch, the Danes, the British, the Irish, and many Australians and New Zealanders would have a rude shock based on their relatively larger mortgage debt. In turn, and in marked contrast to most of the Nordic countries, the U.S. has much greater emphasis on building individual and familial wealth through housing. Unsurprisingly, the housing elements of the U.S. welfare state favor everyone but the "poor" and are justified normatively by their positive association with images of entrepreneurship and self-reliance (Seabrooke, 2006). Tranøy's and Watson's chapters show how similar dynamics are emerging in Norway despite its more comprehensive formal welfare state, and in Britain despite its postwar tradition of public housing. And as Mortensen and Seabrooke show in this volume, Australian housing was similarly caught up in individual efforts to build wealth, while in the Danish case individuals were able to rack up world-beating levels of personal indebtedness because of the welfare state and close association with communal forms of ownership.

In these systems intergenerational wealth transfers reinforce wealth inequality, because people with robust private pensions also typically have robust savings and more expensive houses and, often, more houses period. This reinforces existing wage market trends toward greater inequality and suggests that wealth transfers may push Norway away from its current, relatively flat wealth distribution. Similarly, the near total liberalization of residential property finance in New Zealand has led to a significant *decline* in home ownership as the lower-middle and working classes have been squeezed out by upper class and foreign investors, calling into question the adequacy of New Zealand's flat rate old age pension (Broome, this volume). Seabrooke has characterized the Australian case as one in which the "old eat the young" because the tax system heavily favors those over age 55. And in Britain, an even more inadequate pension system is now matched to rising negative equity for many young homeowners. Within these systems intergenerational equity concerns have the potential to produce struggles from "younger outsiders against older insiders" in a manner that may challenge conservative politics (Blyth, 2008, 400). Of course, the rich young may also choose to side with the rich old and replicate conflicts that fall upon more traditional class lines.

The pattern in liberal housing economies contrasts with that in the high taxation, corporatist countries, Denmark, Netherlands, and Germany. There, high levels of national wealth have not automatically led to widespread property ownership. Only about half of households own property in each. But the state provides generous social support in old age in addition to a wide range of social support. Take, for example, Denmark – which has a liberalized housing finance system and not only Europe's biggest residential property based bond market but one that relative to GDP dwarfs that in the U.S. In Denmark strong tax breaks support property ownership. But what makes these tax breaks attractive is the high level of taxation – the individual upper marginal tax rate is 63%, while the majority pays around 45%. These rates make housing all the more attractive as an investment vehicle, even taking into consideration subsidies for renters (Mortensen and Seabrooke, this volume). But these high tax levels also fund a generous and more egalitarian welfare state than the one in the U.S. or most liberal housing economies.

Danish citizens both expect and give normative blessing to different regulations, oversight, and tax incentives or breaks favoring housing, but without much sense that home ownership can potentially create intergenerational inequalities that will erode support for that welfare state. This may be so because the tax breaks on housing have shifted several times in the past 30 years. During the late 1980s, the withdrawal of tax concessions for mortgage debt temporarily crippled the housing market and created widespread negative equity, although largely for well-to-do Danes. Danish homeowners assimilated this experience more thoroughly than contemporary Britons, whose memories of negative equity in the early 1990s evaporated in the heat of the post-2000 housing bubble. But the pain of Denmark's late 1980s recession contributes to political parties' current unwillingness to raise property taxes or claw back the current tax concessions. Yet housing's contribution to Danish inequality is currently offset by the relatively low level of homeownership and the massive upward mobility created by high quality public education and health care systems. Mortensen and Seabrooke note a significant trend toward well-to-do parents purchasing private property for their children during the Danish housing boom. Although this could crowd out property access for less well-off children through higher prices, intergenerational equity problems are mild compared to liberal housing economies. In all our corporatist systems, buffers limit the long-term potential for wealth inequalities as compared to the liberal systems, where wage and ownership inequalities are self-reinforcing.

What about systems in which the state spending is skewed toward pensioners as a class, as in Italy and the other familialist systems? Here newly formed households face both taxation to support the old and an illiquid housing market that until recently required large down payments and provided only short-term mortgages (Aalbers, this volume). As Castles and Ferrara (1996) have forcefully argued, Southern European welfare states defy the normal housing versus pension trade-off only by constraining public spending on other welfare programs or by running up massive deficits. (Uzuhashi, 2003 suggests that Japan shows some of the same features.) The first option involves upward intergenerational transfers favoring pensioners or the exclusion of noncore workers from pension schemes. Noncore workers, including migrant workers in other countries, find themselves facing the pension-housing trade-off characteristic of liberal housing economies, but without the easy access to housing credit typical of the liberal system.

Here the family and the black economy play a key role in housing provision. Families use housing as a tax-opaque vehicle for intergenerational

wealth transfers that equilibrate government spending across generations and core/noncore workers, albeit in a highly uneven way. Families
pool both monetary and physical resources for the generation entering the housing market, albeit after very long sojourns in the paren-
tal house. This self-help tradition contributes to this group's second
evasion of the usual trade-off: lower tax receipts. A substantial share
of the housing supply in Italy is not properly registered, magnifying
the effects of the black economy and migrant remittances (Castles and
Ferrara, 1996, 178, 182–3). Much housing is built illegally, without planning permission, and with black market labor. Recent liberalization of
Italian and Spanish mortgage rules may change this pattern by making
mortgage money more accessible than it has been, although the 2008
bust will make lenders (and securitizers) cautious.

Finally politics in the statist-developmentalist systems also continue
to echo Castles' predicted trade-off, but with different overtones. In
these societies, homeowners are a small share of the population, and
mortgage debt and mortgage interest payments are relatively low as a
share of personal income. The state provides a robust basic public pension and compels workers to join secondary schemes. Unlike the funded
and largely voluntary secondary schemes in the liberal housing economies, the French and Japanese schemes are essentially PAYGO. Sweden
is an important variation on this, though, with a partially funded
secondary pension, and Finland's system has some funded elements.
The flow of private pension money thus cannot support an expansion of housing and housing debt the way it does in the liberal housing economies, where much private pension funding is recycled into
MBS. Instead, these systems have relatively high levels of state owned
housing – particularly Sweden – which allows the state considerable
control over the volume of capital allocated to housing.

Intergenerational transfers are thus much more straightforward in
the statist systems, with the state shifting money from young to old
via taxation, rather than the more opaque and unequal transfer via the
housing market in liberal market systems. This permits much greater
amelioration of poverty, although the Japanese system is somewhat
regressive. Large scale provision of public housing in all but Japan
reduces financial pressures on lower income retirees, while increasing tax pressure on the young. Like the liberal housing economies, the
statist-developmentalist ones exhibit a clear trade-off, but unlike them
the state is heavily involved in constructing housing. This largely takes
the form of rental units, as Pollard shows for France (this volume), and
as demonstrated in Sweden's *miljonprogrammet* (which built more than

1,000,000 apartments and houses in one decade). In Japan, companies built a considerable portion of the housing stock in the new industrial towns that merged after the Second World War. Although this differs from the other models, it is consistent with the overall pattern of Japanese occupational and company provided welfare, keeping in mind that the state's control over finance meant it stood behind major firms. Similarly, Japanese public pensions were also smaller than expected because elderly Japanese often cohabit with their adult children, passing along ownership of the house as the children's reward for providing care (Uzuhashi, 2003).

In all of these systems housing institutions reflect social norms as much as state welfare institutions. The critical interaction is really between the form and level of housing indebtedness, not homeownership *per se*, and the form and level of welfare system spending. States confronted individuals with a set menu of public benefits, including disguised or overt subsidies for housing, and individuals then made the best of their situation. Thus, generally, it is not surprising that individuals responded to these incentives by buying more or less housing, using the resources available to them. Here the VOC literature is correct to stress the importance of complementarities. Public pensions and housing go together in the same way that private housing and pensions do.

In a more particular case, U.S. subprime borrowers were perfectly rational – at an individual level – in trying to build assets or wealth over their income life cycle knowing that they could not rely on state welfare in old age. The key issue in the liberal housing economies is whether the quality of state regulation or support from public or quasi-public mortgage institutions (QPMIs) assures access to housing on a sustainable basis when only a public basic pension is available. The U.S. did this well for many years, while British politicians and banks clearly mismanaged the shift from the coherent match of public housing and pensions to private housing and pensions. Just so, Norwegian cooperative owners were perfectly rational in trying to seize control of the capital gain created by inflation and economic growth even though this in effect undermined state finances. One wonders if this would have been possible without oil revenues.

The capacity of QPMIs to fuse private capital and public values depends on how they are regulated and the extent of community support for them (expressed through protest or otherwise). The main mechanism is the definition of what constitutes creditworthiness. Just as welfare state eligibility criteria reflected and reinforced moral principles regarding ideal behavior, creditworthiness reflects ideal behavior, the "ideal" household composition and appropriate household roles. Government support for housing thus generates specific "normal" kinds of families. For example, the U.S. Frannies are permitted to securitize or purchase only mortgages that are considered "conforming" under their charter. The definition of "conforming" has changed over the past decades, largely in the direction of providing greater access to mortgage credit for lower income and minority groups, including the purchase of subprime MBS (Stuart, 2003). Despite this, the conditions constituting mortgages as conforming largely matched the ideal suburban family type.

Much the same occurred in other countries. As Aalbers reports in this volume, Dutch banks until recently did not count a spouse's income toward debt-to-income ratios for mortgages. This discouraged female labor market participation in favor of a "normal" vision of families built around stay at home mothers. Similarly the vast majority of Swedish apartments built in the million apartments program were oriented toward a model family of two adults and two children. The state's overwhelming role in structuring housing choices and the relationship between this and the financial system points us in two directions. The first, taken up in Section 10.2, is the relationship between housing and economic growth and stability. The second, taken up in Section 10.3, is the relationship between state institutions and the broader population's practices and attitudes toward housing.

10.2 Demand formation

State structuring of housing markets also structured family types and specific demands for pension regimes. This leads logically to a consideration of the specific institutional bases that match supply and demand in the macroeconomy. Housing and housing finance systems played two distinct roles during the past 50 years. During the original Bretton Woods system, collective bargaining institutions assured that supply and demand would grow in tandem. Explicit deals linked increases in productivity to increases in pay (Boyer, 1990; Eichengreen, 2007). Although there is evidence that these corporatist deals impeded growth in the second period, there is no doubt that they put a floor under wages and thus mattered for macroeconomic stability and outcomes in the earlier Bretton Woods era (Kenworthy, 2002; Schwartz, 2009). The expansion of public sector and other forms of sheltered employment during Bretton Woods similarly put a floor under aggregate demand, stabilizing private investment with its huge multiplier effects. Capital controls and tight regulation of finance assured that local firms had access to cheap finance for that investment. Finally the enormous U.S. economy served as a global buyer of last resort when production outpaced local demand.

Although housing was an important source of demand in the Bretton Woods era, it was positioned toward the end of the causal chain. Stable and rising wages enabled people to buy houses and consumer durables on credit, often at low interest rates in real terms, which in turn fed back into stably rising aggregate demand. In Northern Europe, states built housing to ameliorate the shortfalls of the 1930s and 1940s, as with the Swedish million apartments program noted above. This high level of public involvement suggests that housing was not an autonomous source for the increase in people's ability to consume, but rather that rising wages and government organized spending energized demands for ever better housing, which then powered a second round of growth. This was true even for the U.S., where highway construction, the Frannies' support for 30-year mortgages, and the newly expanding service sector facilitated suburban housing. Macroeconomic balance between supply and demand emerged from wage formation and government spending. This favored growth while accepting some future risk of inflation.

The unraveling of the Bretton Woods system in the 1970s broke the institutional links connecting aggregate supply and demand. The institutions linking wages to productivity, and balancing supply with demand, all came under assault in the 1980s and 1990s. In the U.S., businesses broke the link between pay and productivity by shifting production offshore and breaking unions. In Europe, firms exposed to world trade joined with fiscal bureaucrats troubled by rising public debt to undo the automatic links between public and private sector pay (Schwartz, 1994). While European firms could not explicitly break the pay-productivity link, they sought greater world market shares by negotiating local wage restraint with their unions. These actions created a growing gap between supply and aggregate demand. We do not go as far as Robert Brenner (2006) in arguing that massive surplus capacity characterized the entire period after the 1970s. But wages and particularly wages in the bottom 60% of the U.S. population clearly lagged behind productivity after 1980 and especially after 1990. Wage restraint in Northern Europe had similar effects, albeit distributed more evenly across wage earners. On the other side of the equation, developing country industrialization based on low wages and exports increased global supply faster than global demand, aggravating this gap.

What then led to renewed growth in the 1990s? Certainly a wave of innovations first planted in the 1970s and 1980s came to fruition in the 1990s: the internet; supply chain management; mobile telephony. These underlay the shared growth impulses in Europe/Japan and the U.S. during the 1990s, and showed up in the large contribution of Solow's residual to productivity growth. But these also aggravated the imbalance between supply and demand, as they were often capital conserving and boosted profits, not wages. They also aggravated downward pressure on wages in developed countries by enabling an even faster shift of production to low wage areas. While the resulting backwash of cheap imports initially improved real incomes in the 1990s, by the end of the 1990s they were a significant contributor to job destruction in manufacturing (Broda and Romalis, 2008; Broda and Weinstein, 2008).

Ultimately demand increasingly emerged from the interaction of disinflation and housing finance structures in the liberal housing economies (Schwartz, this volume). Financial deregulation enabled homeowners – as distinct from wage earners – to access otherwise illiquid assets. Access to housing linked credit, like home equity loans or the illusion of increased savings that home equity created, permitted or induced people to spend more freely. Housing based credit became the source of new aggregate demand. First and foremost among the newly liquid assets was housing equity. As Schwartz argues, the structural features of U.S. style housing finance systems translated disinflation into new aggregate demand by letting people access and spend their rising home equity and by abetting rising home prices. By contrast, the rich countries with more repressed housing systems had to rely on external demand for much of their growth. Tapping into housing wealth, now understood as an asset rather than a dwelling or a substitute for a robust pension, became one new way of generating aggregate demand in the absence of stably rising wages.

The institutional structures supporting aggregate demand in the Bretton Woods era carried with them a risk of self-sustaining inflation. Explicit links between last year's inflation rates and current wage gains meant that prior inflation was automatically incorporated into current inflation rates. Wage bargaining institutions thus automatically amplified any large scale price shock. In this case, the disequilibrating oil price shocks of the 1970s arose endogenously from the very success that the Bretton Woods institutions had in stabilizing and raising working class incomes to the point where they too could buy cars. This in turn put excessive pressure on the oil supply.

The institutional structures supporting aggregate demand in the contemporary period did not incorporate this kind of inflation risk. Indeed, these institutional structures required continued disinflation to work well, because disinflation boosted asset prices, including of housing, by lowering nominal interest rates. Continued consumption required rising asset prices and continued access to those assets through new credit creation. New aggregate demand thus required new debt, with that debt secured against assets whose upward revaluation in turn rested on the debt financed consumption. Rising debt levels created the danger that any shortfall in demand might trigger a cascade of falling asset prices. If demand fell short in one sector, the subsequent fall in asset prices there might trigger falling asset prices in many sectors as weak demand spread to other sectors. In this case, the shock emerged endogenously from rising house prices.

Higher prices initially enabled more consumption, as mortgage equity withdrawal (Schwartz, Chapter 2, this volume) and massive speculation in buy-to-let homes (Watson; Mortensen and Seabrooke; Broome, in this volume) flowed through into home renovation and other sectors. But continuously rising prices eventually put considerable stress on new buyers. These buyers resorted to adjustable rate (variable rate) subprime mortgages in order to afford their purchase. As interest rates reset on these mortgages, buyers found themselves unable to make payments (Schwartz, 2009). Mortgage defaults in subprime led to defaults first in the rest of the housing market and then in other markets. By early 2009 more U.S. prime mortgages were in foreclosure than subprime. This created a self-reinforcing collapse of consumption and the assets that both supported and were validated by that consumption. The process of demand creation based on access to and spending from housing wealth obviously rested on a set of legal and organizational structures permitting and promoting this kind of behavior. But it also rested on a massive shift in people's attitudes toward housing. This is the topic of Section 10.3. How did normative attitudes and ideas about housing as a social right or a means to wealth change through boom and bust?

10.3   Everyday limits of housing policy change

Many of the contributors to this volume speak of people's views about the degree to which they believe housing is a social right or means to wealth. The patterns behind our varieties of residential capitalism emerge not only from how the state and market institutions frame housing as a policy issue, but also from changing popular attitudes and behaviors that sometimes produce unintended consequences and/ or impulses for policy change. The relationship between how the state frames housing and how ordinary people change their expectations and behavior is reciprocal. As suggested in "economic constructivist" literature, politicians and economic elites can use "ideas as weapons" during a period of uncertainty to create institutional change (Blyth, 2002), while "everyday politics" among the broader population can also provide clear signals on the limits of social and economic change (Broome, 2009; Hobson and Seabrooke, 2007; Seabrooke, 2007). Both top down and bottom up dynamics can be found in our varieties of residential capitalism.

For example, Watson (this volume) highlights how the British government pushed financial literacy schemes that sought to transform citizens into responsible savers in an increasingly individualized asset-based welfare society. In this climate housing prices had to be maintained at a high level and were viewed as critical to national economic growth, while responsibility for access to housing was increasing placed on the individual within a discourse of self-responsibility. From a different angle Pollard (this volume) discusses how housing policy in France was framed as a nonpolitical and administrative problem while in Spain it was framed as a familial concern with priority over other social issues. France's paternalistic state locked it into automatically helping private developers when the crisis hit. By contrast, the familial frame employed to legitimize the Spanish property boom pushed private developers to form alliances with banks rather than government when the boom went bust. More generally, while housing policies may be framed by governments in particular ways, the response from the population can also be anticipated.

Gradual transformations in broad popular attitudes set everyday limits to changes in housing markets. As housing markets are intimately related to welfare systems, how states favor some social and economic groups through housing policy will generate resistance and a transformation in expectations and behavior among disfavored groups. Because housing policy is necessarily a form of social control, a "citizen-recipient-consumer becomes eternally grateful and resentful" toward housing and welfare provision (Chua, 2003, 84). This is especially the case when developments in housing markets are not accordance with social norms. For example, Mortensen and Seabrooke (this volume) discuss how egalitarian politics can be seen in both the Australian and Danish housing markets, but with very different outcomes. In the Australian case egalitarian politics is perceived as the social need for a "fair go" in being able to acquire owner-occupied property at a reasonable price. In the Danish case egalitarian politics initially meant equal opportunity to housing as a social right and then, increasingly, as access to property that could be used to store wealth. The crisis of housing affordability in the Australian case was constructed not only around economic pressures but a broad perception that the property boom was violating fundamental social norms. Such frustrations evolved into formal political support for the Australian Labor Party. In the Danish case one prominent example of everyday politics in reaction to the property boom came through the privatization of the housing cooperative associations. This process was permitted by the state but really took place in thousands of housing board meetings, where those present voted to revalue where they lived at free market rather than social prices.

As many of the chapters in this volume demonstrate, property booms have challenged long established norms on whether housing within a society should be considered as a social right or a means to wealth. Rapid transformations in how citizens consider housing markets will now be tested and longer established norms may reemerge. In other cases, the extent of asset redistribution during the boom period may mean that a return to a preboom form of residential capitalism is impossible. In such cases we would expect intergenerational and class-based conflicts to become more prominent if governments choose not, or are unable, to respond to everyday politics.

10.4   The current crisis and housing finance

The global financial crisis of 2007–08 might make much of this volume seem retrospective. The scale and breadth of the crisis had moved well beyond the housing sector as 2008 drew to a close. Does this diminish our claim about the significance of housing for international and comparative political economy? And does it change our claims about housing as a political force? The chapters above suggest that the current crisis only reinforces the importance of looking at housing finance systems and their relationship to politics. Housing related debt was and remains one of the largest classes of assets. The weight of housing in a typical budget means that housing continues to interact strongly with both pension systems and perforce state budgets.

Clearly excessive investment in housing and excessive faith in housing prices and thus the collateral behind housing debt was just one manifestation of a broader phenomenon of asset price inflation in the 1990s and 2000s. It might be argued that had liquidity not flowed into housing, it would have gone somewhere else, inflating asset values there. And indeed, in the 1990s the more obvious bubble was in equities and in particular any equities that could plausibly claim to be a play on some profitable use of Internet technologies. Yet the sheer size of housing assets relative to all assets meant that housing inevitably would certainly be central to any crisis and probably also causal for that crisis. MBS generated by the Frannies accounted for a solid one-third of all U.S. private debt securities after the early 1990s, and one-quarter even if marketable U.S. Treasury debt is included. The proportion is even higher in Denmark. It is doubtful that a second equities bubble could have emerged so soon after the Internet bubble, and equally so the 1997 Asian Crisis dampened any speculative bubble in emerging market debt securities.

This left only MBS as a bubble vehicle. While the share of MBS is naturally lower in countries with limited securitization, banks there are directly exposed to mortgage debt carried on their own books, as well as to any tainted MBS acquired from U.S. banks. Steep falls in housing prices in France, Ireland, and Spain, as well as the grinding erosion of German house prices stresses banks in all these countries. If the OECD economies are to recover quickly, the market or state has to generate some solution to the current imbalance between income and obligations in the housing market. In particular, home prices have to recover to a nominal (though not real) level close to the nominal value of the mortgages written against them.

The Internet related equities bubble of the 1990s ultimately generated less demand (and less damage) than housing, even in the 1990s. Retrospective analysis suggests that everywhere in the OECD, consumers have a higher propensity to spend unrealized housing wealth than they do unrealized capital gains on equities (Ludwig and Sløk, 2002). Housing wealth, and thus spending, was greatest in the liberal systems, but also significant in some of the statist countries and two of our three corporatist systems. In the U.S., net mortgage equity withdrawal averaged $300 billion per year in the 1990s before jumping to nearly $1 trillion per year in 2001–05 (Greenspan and Kennedy, 2007, 9, 17). By contrast, the Bush administration's first big stimulus in the spring of 2008 amounted to only $150 billion in a much larger economy, and a mooted EU-wide fiscal stimulus late in 2008 came in at about €200 billion (about $256 billion at prevailing exchange rates). On the other side of the crisis, housing related payments will continue to absorb much household income in the liberal systems, constituting a drag on growth.

Equally so, the structural features animating the political economy of housing will change markedly in the next few years. The simultaneous decline in all asset classes in nearly all countries leaves housing's proportional share unchanged. But the decline in asset prices calls into question the viability of the housing ownership/pension trade-off in the liberal housing economies. Governments everywhere will face larger deficits from the 2008 recessions and what will probably shape up as a slow recovery. But in the liberal systems, mortgage payments now last into retirement in many cases. At the same time, while private pension plans' exposure to bad MBS was fairly limited, the bulk of second tier pension assets were in equities, whose value has fallen sharply. These simultaneous falls undermine the entire rational for substituting houses for robust public pensions. In the self-help familialist systems, the loss of export growth has already stressed public finances. While housing payments will not be a drag on pensioners, states may revisit the issue of pension reform. The corporatist systems face similar difficulties.

As the crisis worsened in the winter of 2008–09 finance ministries in the United States and Europe moved closer to full nationalization of the formal banking sector. What was not clear was whether this would shift housing finance back to the national models prevailing under Bretton Woods. As our country chapters show, those models generally treated housing as something closer to a social right, while restricting homeowners' ability to treat houses as assets. Much will depend on the larger political reaction to the insecurity and loss of wealth from financial crisis of 2007–09 and its related recessions.

The crisis has had one beneficial effect. Many of the intergenerational inequities that had accumulated over the past two decades are now partially dissipated. The typical "Nth" new labor market entrant once faced the prospect of buying historically expensive housing for shelter and equally expensive equities for pension purposes from the typical "Nth" retiring worker, while simultaneously funding that worker's pension via payroll taxes. Houses and equities are now priced at more reasonable levels, assuming that the "Nth" new worker can find a job.

All these considerations point to the issue of macroeconomic complementarities we raised above and in the introductory chapter. While the VOC literature stresses microeconomic complementarities, the current crisis is macroeconomic in nature, not microeconomic. Microeconomic reforms cannot help much at this time. Instead, as the prior sections noted, governments need to promulgate new institutions that generate wages adequate to validate housing prices and thus the financial pyramid erected on top of those housing assets, as well as capable of absorbing supply. Some of this may come from a readjustment of exchange rates that shifts demand in trade surplus countries toward their domestic markets. China is an obvious suspect here. But the European economies that restrain wages and also repress their housing finance systems are also part of the problem. In the liberal housing economies the current crisis will undoubtedly dissuade people from consuming via expanded debt for some time, at least when they are faced with a choice. For that matter, the finance sector has drastically cut back credit to consumers.

Conclusion: Homes alone?

We have provided a rear view mirror on a set of institutions and politics that unquestionably have already changed substantially and will continue to change in the next few years. Residential property markets must be included as a major causal driver of the outcomes that comparative and international political economy are concerned with. Not only is the family home *the* store of wealth for citizens in the OECD and a place where people spend an enormous amount of time, but residential property markets matter for understanding ongoing processes of commodification and decommodification, and growth and crisis, in capitalist economies. Residential property's imbrication in financial markets means that changing attitudes toward how housing is used financially tell us much about the degree of risk that people are willing to accept, and the degree to which they have become willing participants in the extension of specifically market risks into everyday life. The shift in homeowners' perceptions of houses as literal and figurative shelter in old age toward houses as a perpetual ATM or cashpoint machine is a telling indicator about changing attitudes toward houses and their role in society and the economy.

Residential property also stands at the center of the worst financial crisis in the history of modern capitalism since the 1930s Depression; it could plausibly end up as the worst crisis since the industrial revolution. Existing studies of disembodied financial flows and of international efforts to regulate global finance largely missed the elephant in the financial zoo. These studies focused attention on flows to the Asian tigers, or efforts by the lions (the big commercial banks), hyenas (hedge funds), and jackals (investment banks) to evade their zookeepers – prudent central banks and regulators – and feast on consumers who typically lacked the agility of antelope. The normally placid elephants in the mortgage market attracted no attention, despite their size. Yet these elephants have now trampled the financial vegetation on which all depend for growth.

The connections and complementarities between residential property finance and pensions, local government tax bases, and economic growth suggest that comparative and international political economy should attend more to this part of global credit markets. Pensions constitute the largest or second largest public expenditure in all rich OECD economies. Housing constitutes one of the biggest components of household budgets and of capital expenditure. In various ways each matters greatly for economic growth, and the two are tightly coupled. We have shown that four distinct regimes link housing finance to pensions and intergenerational equity. Each regime has its own combination of homeownership levels, and scale and type of mortgage debt. These combinations produce fairly distinct political phenomena, though the contributors here have only begun to sketch out these combinations. We hope we have convinced others to take on some of the work of further fleshing out these arguments.

Notes

1. Search performed at http://convention3.allacademic.com/one/apsa/apsa08/ on November 6, 2008; the sole paper mentioning MBS and/or CDOs was from one of the authors of this chapter.
2. Our thanks to Jane Zavisca for stressing this point.

Bibliography

Aalbers, M.B. (2003) "Pressure and Suction on Housing Markets," *European Journal of Housing Policy,* 3(1): 61–81.

Aalbers, M.B. (2005) "'The Quantified Customer', or How Financial Institutions Value Risk," in P. Boelhouwer, J. Doling, and M. Elsinga (eds.) *Home Ownership: Getting In, Getting From, Getting Out* (Delft: Delft University Press), pp. 33–57.

Aalbers, M.B. (2006) "The Geography of Mortgage Markets," Amsterdam Institute for Metropolitan and International Development Studies Working Paper, Amsterdam.

Aalbers, M.B. (2007) "Geographies of Housing Finance: The Mortgage Market in Milan, Italy," *Growth and Change,* 38(2): 174–99.

Aalbers, M.B. (2008) "The Financialization of Home and the Mortgage Market Crisis," *Competition & Change,* 12(2): 148–69.

Abdelal, R. (2007) *Capital Rules: The Construction of Global Finance* (Cambridge, MA: Harvard University Press).

"ABS Stats: First Time Buyers Return," *Broker News,* January 14, 2009.

Aftenposten (2008) "Aret meglerne forsvant" ["The Year the realtors disappeared"] December 29, 2008.

Age, The (2003a) "The Great Australian Illusion," August 5, 2003.

Age, The (2003b) "Treasury head warns of housing 'bubble,' then backpedals," September 17, 2003.

Age, The (2007) "Australian dream fades as cost sends some to ghetto," July 30, 2007.

Allen, J. (2006) "Welfare Regimes, Welfare Systems and Housing in Southern Europe," *European Journal of Housing Policy,* 6 (3): 251–77.

Allen, J., Barlow, J., Leal, J., Maloutas, T., and Padovani, L. (2004) *Housing & Welfare in Southern Europe* (Oxford: Blackwell).

Andreotti, A., Benassi, D., and Bernasconi, M. (2000) "Comparative Statistical Analysis at National, Metropolitan, Local and Neighbourhood Level," *Italy / Milan and Naples. URBEX Series 5* (Amsterdam: Amsterdam Study Centre for the Metropolitan Environment).

Andrew Morse, (2007) "Nomura to Close US Mortgage Business," *Wall Street Journal,* October 15.

Annaniassen, E. (1996) "Markedet Slippes løs. 1982–1990," in *Tidene skifter. Boligsamvirkets historie i Norge,* 3: 42–85.

Arbaci, S. (2002) "Patterns of Ethnic and Socio-Spatial Segregation in European Cities: Are Welfare Regimes Making a Difference?" in M.L. Fonseca, J. Malheiros, N. Ribas-Mateos, P. White, and A. Esteves (eds.) *Immigration and Place in Mediterranean Metropolises* (Lisbon: FLAD Luso-American Foundation), pp. 83–115.

Argy, F. (2003) *Where to From Here? Australian Egalitarianism Under Threat* (Sydney: Allen and Unwin).

Audas, R. and MacKay, R. (1997) "A Tale of Two Recessions," *Regional Studies,* 31(9): 867–87.

Australian Bureau of Statistics (2007) "2006 Census QuickStats," http://www.censusdata.abs.gov.au/

"Australian Dream Fades as Cost Sends Some to Ghetto," *The Age*, July 30, 2007.

Australian Senate (2008) "A Good House Is Hard to Find: Housing Affordability in Australia," Select Committee on Housing Affordability in Australia, June 2008 (Canberra: Commonwealth of Australia).

Australian Taxation Office (2007) *Taxation Statistics, 2005–06* (Canberra: Australian Taxation Office).

Australian, The (2007) "Super Way to Pay just 15pc Tax," June 9, 2007.

Australian, The (2009) "Lenders axe reverse mortgages," January 23, 2009.

Australian Treasury (2004) "A More Flexible and Adaptable Retirement Income System," available at: http://demographics.treasury.gov.au/ (Canberra: Australian Treasury).

Ave, G. (1996) *Urban Land and Property Markets in Italy* (London: UCL Press).

Badcock, B. (2004) "Global Exposure and Auckland's Housing Market," *Urban Policy and Research*, 22(1): 59–68.

Bajaj, V., and Norris, F. (2007) "Central Bankers to Lend Billions in Credit Crisis," *New York Times*, December 13, 2007.

Bale, T. (2003) "Pricking the South Sea Bubble: From Fantasy to Reality in Labour-led New Zealand," *Political Quarterly*, 74(2): 202–13.

Ball, M. (2005) *RICS European Housing Review 2005* (Conventry: Royal Institute of Chartered Surveyors).

"Bank Deposits Guaranteed for 3 Years," *Sydney Morning Herald*, October 12, 2008.

Barlow, J. and Duncan, S. (1994) *Success and Failure in Housing Provision: European Systems Compared* (Oxford: Pergamon).

Barth, E., Moene, K., and Wallerstein, M. (2003) *Likhet Under Press* (Oslo: Gyldendal Akademisk Forlag).

Bates, R.H., Greif, A., Levi, M., Rosenthal, J.-L., and Weingast, B.R. (1998) *Analytic Narratives* (Princeton, NJ: Princeton University Press).

Bay, A. H. (1985) *Boligstatus og stemmegivning eller; Boligpolitikkens betydning for høyrebølgen*, Unpublished Cand. Polit thesis, University of Oslo: Department of Political Science.

Beer, A., Kearins, B., and Pieters, H. (2007) "Housing Affordability and Planning in Australia: The Challenge of Policy Under Neo-liberalism," *Housing Studies*, 22(1): 11–24.

Bernardi, F. and Poggio, T. (2004) "Home-Ownership and Social Inequality in Italy," in K. Kurz and H.P. Blossfeld (eds.), *Home Ownership and Social Inequality in Comparative Perspective* (Stanford: Stanford University Press), pp. 187–232.

Berry, M. and Dalton, T. (2004) "Housing Prices and Policy Dilemmas: A Peculiarly Australian Problem?" *Urban Policy and Research*, 22(1): 69–92.

Bieling, H.-J. (2006) "EMU, Financial Integration and Global Economic Governance," *Review of International Political Economy*, 13(3): 420–48.

Blyth, M. (2002) *Great Transformations* (Cambridge: Cambridge University Press).

Blyth, M. (2003) "Same as It Never Was: Temporality and Typology in the Varieties of Capitalism," *Comparative European Politics*, 1(2): 215–25.

Blyth, M. (2008) "The Politics of Compounding Bubbles: The Global Housing Bubble in Comparative Perspective," *Comparative European Politics* 6(3): 387–406.

Boelhouwer, P., Haffner, M., Neuteboom, P., and de Vries, P. (2004) "House Prices and Income Tax in the Netherlands: An International Perspective," *Housing Studies*, 19(3): 415–32.

Borio, C. (1995) "The Structure of Credit to the Non-government Sector and the Transmission Mechanism of Monetary Policy: A Cross-Country Comparison," *BIS Working Papers*, 24.

Bostic, R., Gabriel, S., and Painter, G. (2005) "Housing Wealth, Financial Wealth, and Consumption: New Evidence from Micro Data," unpublished paper, University of Southern California.

Bourdieu, P. (2000) *Les structures sociales de l'économie* (Paris: Seuil).

Boyer, R. (1990) *The Regulation School: A Critical Introduction* (New York: Columbia University Press).

Bradley, Grant (2008) "Property Prices Dip 6.8 per cent in Year," *New Zealand Herald*, November 10, available online at www.nzherald.co.nz/property/news/article.cfm?c_id=8&objectid=10542078 (accessed December 19, 2008).

Brenner, R. (2006) *The Economics of Global Turbulence* (London: Verso).

Broda, C. and Romalis, J. (2008) "Inequality and Prices: Does China Benefit the Poor in America?" unpublished paper, University of Chicago, March 2008.

Broda, C. and Weinstein, D. (2008) "Exporting Deflation? Chinese Exports and Japanese Prices," unpublished paper, University of Chicago.

Broker News (2009). "ABS Stats: First Time Buyers Return," January 14, 2009.

Brook Cowen, P.J. (1998) "Neo-liberalism," in R. Miller (ed.) *New Zealand Politics in Transition* (Auckland: Oxford University Press), pp. 341–9.

Broome, A. (2006) "Setting the Fiscal Policy Agenda: Economic News and Election Year Tax Debates in New Zealand," *Law in Context*, 24(2): 60–77.

Broome, A. (2009) "Money for Nothing: Everyday Actors and Monetary Crises," *Journal of International Relations and Development*, 12(1): 3–30.

Broome, A. and Seabrooke, L. (2007) "Seeing Like the IMF: Institutional Change in Small Open Economies," *Review of International Political Economy*, 14(4): 586–601.

Brotherhood of St. Laurence (2003) "Abolish negative gearing to ease low-cost housing crisis" 7.07.2003, http://www.bsl.org.au/main.asp?PageId=243.

Brun, J., Driant, J.-C., and Segaud, M. (2002) *Dictionnaire critique de l'habitat et du logement* (Paris: A. Colin).

Buckle, M. and Thompson, J. (1995) *The UK Financial System: Theory and Practice* (second edn.) (Manchester: Manchester University Press).

Burns, J. and Dwyer, M. (2007) *New Zealand Household Attitudes Towards Savings, Investment, and Wealth: Phase One* (Wellington: Reserve Bank of New Zealand), available online at www.rbnz.govt.nz/research/econresearch/3198451.pdf (accessed April 15, 2008).

Cafruny, A.W., and Ryner, M. (eds.) (2003) *A Ruined Fortress? Neoliberal Hegemony and Transformation in Europe* (Lanham, MD: Rowman & Littlefield).

Calomiris, C.W. (2007) "Not (Yet) a 'Minsky Moment'," unpublished paper, October 5, Columbia University.

Campbell, J.L. (2004) *Institutional Change and Globalization* (Princeton, NJ: Princeton University Press).

Campbell, J.L. and Pedersen, O.K. (2007) "The Varieties of Capitalism and Hybrid Success: Denmark in the Global Economy," *Comparative Political Studies*, 40(2): 307–32.

Campbell, J.L. and Pedersen, O.K. (eds.) (2001) *The Rise of Neoliberalism and Institutional Analysis*, (Princeton, NJ: Princeton University Press).

Case, K.E., Quigley, J.M., and Shiller, R.J. (2001) "Comparing Wealth Effects: The Stock Market Versus the Housing Market," National Bureau of Economic Research Working Paper 8606, http://www.nber.org/papers/w8606.

Casini, M. (1995) *Il Credito Immobiliare* (Milano: Banca d'Italia).

Castles, F.G. (1985) *The Working Class and Welfare* (Sydney: Allen and Unwin).

Castles, F.G. (1998) "The Really Big Trade-off: Home Ownership and the Welfare State in the New World and the Old," *Acta Politica*, 33(1): 5–19.

Castles, F.G. (2002) "Developing New Measures of Welfare State Change and Reform," *European Journal of Political Research*, 41(5): 613–41.

Castles, F.G. and Ferrera, M. (1996) "Home Ownership and the Welfare State: is Southern Europe Different?" *South European Society and Politics*, 1 (2): 163–85.

Castles, F.G. and Mitchell, D. (1992) "Identifying Welfare State Regimes: The Links Between Politics, Instruments and Outcomes," *Governance*, 5(1): 1–26.

Catte, P., Girouard, N., Price, R., and André, C. (2004) "Housing Markets, Wealth and the Business Cycle," OECD Economics Department Papers, No. 394, OECD Publishing.

Chua Beng Huat (2003) "Housing Provisions and Management of Aspirations," in R. Forrest and J. Lee (eds.) *Housing and Social Change: East-West Perspectives* (London: Routledge).

Chiuri, M.C. and Jappelli, T. (2002) *Financial Market Imperfections and Home Ownership: A Comparative Study* (Salerno: CSEF, University of Salerno).

Clapham, D. (2006) "Housing Policy and the Discourse of Globalization," *European Journal of Housing Policy*, 6(1): 55–76.

Coates, D. (2005) *Prolonged Labour: The Slow Birth of New Labour Britain* (Basingstoke: Palgrave Macmillan).

Cole, I. and Etherington, D. (2005) "Neighbourhood Renewal Policy and Spatial Differentiation in Housing Markets: Recent Trends in England and Denmark," *European Journal of Housing Policy*, 5(1): 77–97.

Coleman, A. (2007) "Credit Constraints and Housing Markets in New Zealand," *Discussion Paper Series DP2007/11*, Reserve Bank of New Zealand.

Committee on the Global Financial System (2006) "Housing Finance in the Global Financial Market," CGFS Papers, No. 26.

Conley, D. and Gifford, B. (2006) "Home Ownership, Social Insurance, and the Welfare State," *Sociological Forum*, 21(1): 55–82.

Corbridge, S., Thrift, N., and Martin, R. (eds.) (1994) *Money, Power and Space*, (Cambridge: Blackwell).

Cortés Alcalá, L. (2004) "Spain: High-Rise as Urban Phenomenon," in R. Turkinton, R. Van Kempen, and F. Wassenberg (eds.), *Housing and Urban Policy Studies* (Deft: Deft University Press).

Cortés Alcalá, L. (2005) "La crisis de la vivienda," *Documentación social*, 138: 81–100.

Costello, P. (1999) "A New Business Tax System," Australian Treasury, press release September 21, http://www.treasurer.gov.au/DisplayDocs.aspx?pageID=&doc=pressreleases/1999/058.htm&min=phc.

Council of Mortgage Lenders (2000) *UK Will Continue to Lead Mortgage Securitisation in Europe* (London: Council of Mortgage Lenders).

Council of Mortgage Lenders (2005) *UK Housing Review 2004/2005* (London: Council of Mortgage Lenders).

Cox, K.R. (ed.) (1997) *Spaces of Globalization: Reasserting the Power of the Local* (New York: Guilford).

Credit Suisse (2007) *Mortgage Liquidity du Jour*, March 12.

Cronin, J. (2004) *New Labour's Pasts: The Labour Party and Its Discontents* (Harlow: Pearson).

Crouch, C. (2005) "Models of Capitalism," *New Political Economy*, 10(4): 439–56.

Dagbladet (2007) "Barna får bolighjelp" ["Offspring is helped with housing"], August 2, 2007.

Dalziel, P. (1997) "The Reserve Bank Act," in B. Roper and C. Rudd (eds.), *State and Economy in New Zealand* (Auckland: Oxford University Press), pp. 74–90.

Dalziel, P. (2002) "New Zealand's Economic Reforms: An Assessment," *Review of Political Economy*, 14(1): 31–46.

Dalziel, P. (2007) "Housing, Monetary Policy and Economic Development in a Small Open Economy," paper presented at the New Zealand Association of Economists Annual Conference, Christchurch, June 27–29, 2007.

Danish Ministry of Taxation (2006) "Price Statistics," July–December 2005 (May 2006 version), cited from Lunde, J. (2006) "Københavnerpriser, andelsbolig-fordele, 'penge over bordet' og Århushistorier," mimeo, Department of Finance Copenhagen Business School, September 2006.

Danish National Bank (2007) *Monetary Review, 4th Quarter 2007* (Danmarks Nationalbank: Copenhagen).

Danmarks Nationalbank (2007) *Monetary Review, 4th Quarter 2007*. Danmarks Nationalbank: Copenhagen.

Danmarks Statistik, available from www.statistikbanken.dk/BYGV33

Davidson, A., Sanders, A., Wolff, L.-L., and Ching, A. (2003) *Securitization: Structuring and Investment Analysis* (Hoboken, NJ: Wiley Finance).

de Bruin, A. and Flint-Hartle, S. (2003) "A Bounded Rationality Framework for Property Investment Behaviour," *Journal of Property Investment and Finance*, 21(3): 271–84.

De Nederlandse Bank (2000) *Het bancaire hypotheekbedrijf onder de loep. Rapport over de ontwikkelingen op de hypotheekmarkt in de periode 1994–1999 gebaseerd op onderzoek naar de hypothecaire kredietverlening bij Nederlandse financiële instellingen* (Amsterdam: De Nederlandse Bank).

de Veirman, E. and Dunstan, A. (2008) "How do Housing Wealth, Financial Wealth and Consumption Interact? Evidence from New Zealand," *Discussion Paper Series DP2008/05*, Reserve Bank of New Zealand.

Debelle, G. (2008) "A Comparison of the US and Australian Housing Markets," address to the "Sub-prime Mortgage Meltdown" Symposium, Flinders University of South Australia, Adelaide, Australia, May 16.

Del Boca, D. and Lusardi, A. (2003) "Credit Market Constraints and Labor Market Decisions," *Labour Economics*, 10: 681–703.

Det Økonomiske Råd (Danish Economic Council) (2006) Dansk Økonomi, forår 2006 (Copenhagen: Det Økonomiske Råd).

"Denmark Unveils $18 bln Bank Loan Package," Reuters Online, http://www.reuters.com/article/marketsNews/idUSLI53099420090118, accessed January 21, 2008.

Dieter, H., Seabrooke, L., andTsingou, E. (2009) "The Global Credit Crisis and the Politics of Financial Reform," GARNET Policy Brief No. 8, January.

Doling, J. (1997) *Comparative Housing Policy: Government and Housing in Advanced Industrialized Countries* (Houndmills: Macmillan).

Doling, J. and Ford, J. (eds.) (2004) *Globalisation and Home Ownership: Experiences in Eight Member States of the European Union* (Delft: DUP Science, Housing and Urban Policy).

Drahos, P. and Braithwaite, J. (2001) "The Globalization of Regulation," *The Journal of Political Philosophy*, 9(1): 103–28.

Drew, A., Karagedikli, Ö., Sethi, R., and Smith, C. (2008) "Changes in the Transmission Mechanism of Monetary Policy in New Zealand," *Discussion Paper Series DP2008/03*, Reserve Bank of New Zealand.

Dumenil, G. and Levy, D. (2004) "Neo-Liberal Income Trends," *New Left Review*, 30: 105–33.

Dupois, A. and Thorns, D.C. (1996) "Meanings of Home for Older Home Owners," *Housing Studies*, 11(4): 485–501.

Easton, S. and Gerlach, R. (2005) "Interest Rates and the 2004 Australian Election," *Australian Journal of Political Science*, 40(4): 559–66.

Eccleston, R. (2004) *The Thirty Year Problem* (Sydney: Australian Tax Research Foundation).

Effosse, S. (2003) *L'invention du logement aidé en France: l'immobilier au temps des Trente Glorieuses* (Paris: Ministère de l'économie, des finances et de l'industrie).

Eichengreen, B. (2007) *The European Economy since 1945: Coordinated Capitalism and Beyond* (Princeton, NJ: Princeton University Press).

Ellis, L. (2006) "Housing and Housing Finance: The View from Australia and Beyond," Reserve Bank of Australia Research Discussion Paper, RDP 2006:12, Canberra.

Engelen, E. (2003) "The Logic of Funding European Pension Restructuring and the Dangers of Financialisation," *Environment and Planning*, A35: 1357–72.

Engelhardt, G.V. (2005) *Housing Trends among Baby Boomers* (Washington DC: Research Institute for Housing in America).

Erhvervs- og Byggestyrelsen (2006) "Analyse af andelsboligsektorens rolle på boligmarkedet," 71, 99, http://www.ebst.dk/file/4156/analyse-andelsbolig markedet.pdf.

Erhvervsbladet (2008) "Dansk Byggeri skriger på hjælp," November 21, 2008.

Esping-Andersen, G. (1985) *Politics against Markets: The Social Democratic Road to Power* (Princeton, NJ: Princeton University Press).

Esping-Andersen, G. (1990) *The Three Worlds of Welfare Capitalism* (Princeton, NJ: Princeton University Press).

European Central Bank (2004) *European Mortgage Markets* (Frankfurt am Main: European Central Bank).

European Central Bank (2007) "Open Market Operations" available online at http://www.ecb.int/mopo/implement/omo/html/20070090_all.en.html, date accessed January 3, 2009.

European Mortgage Federation (1994) *Annual Report* (Brussels: EMF).

European Mortgage Federation (2001) *Key Figures* (Brussels: EMF).

European Mortgage Federation (2003) *Hypostat 2003* (Brussels: EMF).

European Mortgage Federation (2005) *Hypostat 2004* (Brussels: EMF).

European Mortgage Federation (2007) *Mortgage Finance Gazette* (Brussels: EMF).
European Mortgage Federation (2008) *Hypostat 2007* (Brussels: EMF).
European Securitisation Forum (2006) *ESF Securitisation Data Report. Winter 2006* (London: European Securitisation Forum).
Evans, L., Grimes, A., Wilkinson, B., and Teece, D. (1996) "Economic Reform in New Zealand 1984–1995: The Pursuit of Efficiency," *Journal of Economic Literature*, 34(4): 1856–902.
E24 (2009) "Lysning i desember: Fallet bremser," 2 January 2009. Accessed at http://e24.no/eiendom/article2845553.ece
Fannie Mae (2003) *Annual Report* (Washington, DC: Fannie Mae).
Federal Home Loan Bank, Office of Finance at http://www.fhlb-of.com/issuance/statisticsframe.html.
Federal Reserve Bank (2004) Flow of Funds, Washington, DC: Federal Reserve Bank, on-line database.
Federal Reserve Bank press release, May 2, 2008, http://www.federalreserve.gov/newsevents/press/monetary/20080502a.htm.
Fellowes, M. and Mabanta, M. (2007) "Borrowing to Get Ahead and Behind: The Credit Boom and Bust in Lower-Income Markets," *Brookings Institutions Survey Series*, May 2007.
Ferguson, G. (1994) *Building the New Zealand Dream* (Palmerston North: Dunmore Press).
Fernández Carbajal, A. (2004) "Veinticinco años de política de vivienda en España (1976–2001): Una visión panorámica," *Información Comercial Española. Revista de Economía*, 816: 145–61.
Finlayson, Alan (2008) "Characterizing New Labour: The Case of the Child Trust Fund," *Public Administration*, 86(1): 95–110.
Ford, J. and Wilcox, S. (1998) "Owner Occupation, Employment and Welfare: The Impact of Changing Relationships on Sustainable Home Ownership," *Housing Studies*, 13(5): 623–38.
Forum Group on Mortgage Credit (2004) *The Integration of the EU Mortgage Credit Markets* (Brussels: European Commission).
Freddie, Mac (2005) *Annual Report* (McLean, VA: Freddie Mac).
Froud, J., Leaver, A., and Williams, K. (2007a) "New Actors in a Financialised Economy and the Remaking of Capitalism," *New Political Economy*, 12(3): 339–47.
Froud, J., Leaver, A., Williams, K., and Zhang, W. (2007b) "The Quiet Panic about Financial Illiteracy," in L. Assassi, A. Nesvetailova, and D. Wigan (eds.) *Global Finance in the New Century: Deregulation and Beyond* (Basingstoke: Palgrave Macmillan).
Gamble, A. (1988) *The Free Economy and the Strong State: The Politics of Thatcherism* (London: Macmillan).
Ganghof, S. and Eccleston, R. (2004) "Globalisation and the Dilemmas of Income Taxation in Australia," *Australian Journal of Political Science*, 39(3): 519–34.
Generale, A. and Giorgio, G. (1996) "Il recupero dei crediti: costi, tempi e comportamenti delle banche," *Banca d'Italia Temi di Discussione* 265.
Gentle, C., Dorling, D., and Cornford, J. (1994) "Negative Equity and British Housing in the 1990s: Cause and Effect," *Urban Studies*, 31(2): 181–99.
Germain, R. (1997) *The International Organization of Credit* (Cambridge: Cambridge University Press).

Girouard, N. and Blöndal, S. (2001) "House Prices and Economic Activity," OECD Economics Department Working Papers, No. 279 (Paris: OECD Publishing).

Girouard, N., Kennedy, M., van den Noord, P., and André, C. (2006) "Recent House Price Developments: The Role of Fundamentals," OECD Economics Department Working Papers, No. 475 (Paris: OECD Publishing).

Giuliodori, M. (2005) "The Role of House Prices in the Monetary Transmission Mechanism Across European Countries," *Scottish Journal of Political Economy*, 52(4): 519–43.

Gomá, R. and Adelantado Gimeno, J. (2000) "La política de vivienda," in J. Adelantado Gimeno (ed.) *Cambios en el estado del bienestar: políticas sociales y desigualdades de España* (Icaria: Universitat Autònoma de Barcelona).

Gotham, K. (2006) "The Secondary Circuit of Capital Reconsidered: Globalization and the U.S. Real Estate Sector," *American Journal of Sociology*, 112(1): 231–75.

Gourevitch, P. and Shinn, J. (2005) *Political Power and Corporate Control* (Princeton, NJ: Princeton University Press).

Gourinchas, P.-O. and Rey, H. (2005) "From World Banker to World Venture Capitalist: US External Adjustment and the Exorbitant Privilege," NBER Working Paper 11563, National Bureau of Economic Research.

Grady, J. and Weale, M. (1986) *British Banking 1960–1985* (London: Macmillan).

Green-Pedersen, C. (2002) *The Politics of Justification* (Amsterdam: Amsterdam University Press).

Greenspan, A. and James K. (2007) "Sources and Uses of Equity Extracted from Homes," Finance and Economics Discussion Series, 2007 (20), Board of Governors of the Federal Reserve System (US).

Greenspan, A. and Kennedy, J. (2005) "Estimates of Home Mortgage Originations, Repayments, and Debt On One-to-Four-Family Residences," FEDS Paper 2005 (41).

Grepinet, P. (2006) *La crise du logement: des chiffres pour comprendre, des pistes pour agir* (Paris: l'Harmattan).

Gruis, V. and Nieboer, N. (2007) "Government Regulation and Market Orientation in the Management of Social Housing Assets: Limitations and Opportunities for European and Australian Landlords," *European Journal of Housing Policy*, 7(1): 45–62.

Guiso, L. and Jappelli, T. (2002) "Private Transfers, Borrowing Constraints, and Timing of Homeownership," *Journal of Money, Credit and Banking*, 34(2): 315–339.

Hacker, J. (2004) "Privatizing Risk without Privatizing the Welfare State: The Hidden Politics of Social Policy Retrenchment in the United States," *American Political Science Review*, 98(2): 243–60.

Hacker, J. and Pierson, P. (2002) "Business Power and Social Policy," *Politics & Society*, 30: 277–325.

Hacker, J.S. (2006) *The Great Risk Shift: The Assault on American Jobs, Families, Health Care and Retirement – and How You can Fight Back* (New York: Oxford University Press).

Hagerty, James (2008) "Fannie Mae Loss of $2.3 Billion Exceeds Forecast," *Wall Street Journal*, August 9, http://online.wsj.com/article/SB121818529773923803.html.

Hall, P. and Franzese, R. Jr. (1998) "Mixed Signals: Central Bank Independence, Coordinated Wage Bargaining and European Monetary Union," *International Organization*, 52(3): 505–36.

Hall, P.A. and Soskice, D. (2001) "An Introduction to Varieties of Capitalism," in P.A. Hall and D.W. Soskice (eds.), *Varieties of Capitalism* (Oxford: Oxford University Press), pp. 1–66.

Hall, P.A. and Thelen, K. (2008) "Institutional change in varieties of capitalism," *Socio Economic Review*: forthcoming, http://ser.oxfordjournals.org/cgi/content/full/mwn020.

Hall, Stuart (1983) "The Great Moving Right Show," in Stuart Hall and Martin Jacques (eds.) *The Politics of Thatcherism*, London: Lawrence and Wishart.

Hargreaves, B. (2007) "What Do Rents Tell Us about House Prices?," Paper Presented at the Pacific Rim Real Estate Society Conference, Fremantle, January 21–24, 2007, available online at www.prres.net/papers/Hargreaves_Rents_and_House_Prices.pdf (accessed April 20, 2008).

Harloe, M. (1995) *The People's Home? Social Rented Housing in Europe and America* (Oxford: Blackwell).

Hardt, J. (1998) "European Integration: Prospects for the Mortgage Lending Industry," Council of Mortgage Lenders Housing Finance, Brussels: European Mortgage Federation.

Harvard University Joint Center for Housing Studies (JCHS) (2008) *The State of the Nation's Housing* (Cambridge, MA: Harvard University JCHS).

Hay, C.S. (1996) "Narrating Crisis: The Discursive Construction of the 'Winter of Discontent'," *Sociology*, 30 (2): 253–77.

Hay, C.S. (2006) "What's Globalization Got to Do with It? Economic Interdependence and the Future of European Welfare States," *Government and Opposition*, 41(1): 1–22.

Hay, C.S. (2008) "Good Inflation, Bad Inflation: The Housing Boom, Economic Growth and the Disaggregation of Inflationary Preferences in Britain and Ireland," paper presented at the Political Economy of the Subprime Crisis Workshop, University of Warwick, September 18/19, 2008.

Hay, C.S. and Rosamond, B. (2002) "Globalization, European Integration, and the Discursive Construction of Economic Imperatives," *Journal of European Public Policy*, 9(2): 147–67.

Hemerijck, A. (2002) "The Self-Transformation of the European Social Model(s)," in G. Esping-Andersen (ed.) *Why We Need a New Welfare State* (Oxford: Oxford University Press), pp. 173–213.

Heugas-Darraspen, H. (1994) *Le financement du logement en France* (Paris: La documentation française).

Hirst, P. and Thompson, G. (1996) *Globalization in Question* (Oxford: Polity).

HM Treasury (2000) *Building Long-Term Prosperity for All: Pre-Budget Report*, (London: HM Treasury).

HM Treasury (2001a) *Saving and Assets For All: The Modernisation of Britain's Tax and Benefit System, Number Eight* (London: HM Treasury).

HM Treasury (2001b) *Delivering Saving and Assets: The Modernisation of Britain's Tax and Benefit System, Number Nine* (London: HM Treasury).

HM Treasury (2003) "Child Trust Fund Proposals Published," www.hm-treasury.gov.uk.

HM Treasury (2006) *Pre-Budget Report 2006* (London: HM Treasury).

HM Treasury/Inland Revenue (2003) *Detailed Proposals for the Child Trust Fund* (London: Her Majesty's Stationery Office).

Hobson, J.M. and Seabrooke, L. (eds.) (2007) *Everyday Politics of the World Economy* (Cambridge: Cambridge University Press).

Hollingsworth, J.R. and Boyer, R. (eds.) (1997) *Contemporary Capitalism: the Embeddedness Institutions* (Cambridge: Cambridge University Press).

Holmes, F. (2004) "The Quest for Security and Welfare in New Zealand: 1938–1956," *IPS Policy Paper* 19 (Wellington: Institute of Policy Studies), available online at http://ips.ac.nz/publications/files/debc1acc5ec.pdf (accessed April 15, 2008).

House of Representatives, Standing Committee on Economics, Parliament (2008) "Competition in the Banking and Non-Banking Sectors," of the Commonwealth of Australia. Available at: http://www.aph.gov.au/house/committee/economics/banking08/report/Fullreport.pdf.

Howard, Christopher (2006) *The Welfare State Nobody Knows* (Princeton, NJ: Princeton University Press).

Howell, C. (2003) "Varieties of Capitalism: And Then There Was One?" *Comparative Politics*, 36(1): 103–24.

Hudson, R. (2003) "European Integration and New Forms of Uneven Development. But Not the End of Territorially Distinctive Capitalism in Europe," *European Urban and Regional Studies*, 10(1): 49–67.

Iley, Richard (2008) "Going with the Flow, Again," BNP Paribas 14 January.

Indovina, F. (2005) "Appunti sulla questione abitativa oggi," *Archivio di Studi Urbani e Regionali*, 82: 15–50.

International Financial Services (2006) *Securitisation* (London: International Financial Services).

International Monetary Fund (2008) *World Economic Outlook, April 2008* (Washington, DC: IMF).

Iversen, T. (1998) "Wage Bargaining, Central Bank Independence, and the Real Effects of Money," in *International Organization*, 52(3): 469–504.

Iversen, T. (2005) *Capitalism, Democracy, and Welfare* (Cambridge: Cambridge University Press).

James, C. (1998) "The Policy Revolution 1984–1993," in R. Miller (ed.) *New Zealand Politics in Transition* (Auckland: Oxford University Press), pp. 13–24.

Jonung, L. (2008) "Lessons from Financial Liberalisation in Scandinavia," *Comparative Economic Studies*, 50(4): 564–98.

Kemeny, J. (1980) "Home Ownership and Privatisation," *International Journal of Urban and Regional Research*, 4(3): 372–88.

Kemeny, J. (2005) "'The Really Big Trade-Off' between Home Ownership and Welfare: Castles' Evaluation of the 1980 Thesis, and a Reformulation 25 Years on," *Housing, Theory, and Society*, 22(2): 59–75.

Kemp, P.A. (2000) "The Role and Design of Income-Related Housing Allowances," *International Social Security Review*, 53(3): 43–57.

Kenworthy, L. (2002) "Corporatism and Unemployment in the 1980s and 1990s," *American Sociological Review*, 67(3): 367–88.

Kohler, M. and Roster, A. (2005) "Property Owners in Australia: A Snapshot," Reserve Bank of Australia Research Discussion Paper, RDP 2005–3, Canberra.

Langley, P. (2006) "Securitising Suburbia: the Transformation of Anglo-American Mortgage Finance," *Competition & Change*, 10(3): 283–99.

Langley, P. (2008) *The Everyday Life of Global Finance* (Oxford: Oxford University Press).

"L'Europe en chiffres," (2008) *Annuaire Eurostat*, p. 566.

Leal Maldonado, J. (1992) *Informe para una nueva política de vivienda* (Madrid: Ministerio de Obras Públicas y Transportes).

Leal Maldonado, J. (2002) "Segregación social y mercados de vivienda en las grandes ciudades," *Revista Española de Sociología*, 2: 59–75.

Leal Maldonado, J. (2004a) "El diferente modelo residencial de los países del sur de Europa: el mercado de viviendas, la familia y el Estado," *Arxius de sociologia*, 10: 11–37.

Leal Maldonado, J. (2004b) "Housing Policy against Social Housing in Spain," paper presented at the ENHR Conference, Cambridge, July 2–6.

Leal Maldonado, J. (2005) "La Política de Vivienda en España," *Documentación Social*, 138: 63–80.

Lefebvre, B., Mouillart, M., and Occhipinti, S. (1991) *Politique du logement, cinquante ans pour un échec* (Paris: L'Harmattan).

Leigh, A. (2006) "Political Economy of Tax Reform in Australia," *Public Policy*, 1(1): 52–60.

Levine, R. (1997) "Financial Development and Economic Growth: Views and Agenda," *Journal of Economic Literature*, 35(2): 688–726.

"Lenders axe reverse mortgages," *The Australian*, January 23, 2009.

Llordén Miñambres, M. (2003) "La política de vivienda del régimen franquista: nacimiento y despegue de los grandes constructores y promotores inmobiliarios en España, 1939–1960," in Sanchez Recio, G. and Tascon Fernandez, L. (eds.) *Los empresarios de Franco: política y economía en España, 1936–1957* (Barcelona: Crítica), pp. 145–70.

López García, M.-A. (2003) "Políticas de vivienda: eficiencia y equidad," *Papeles de Economía Española*, 95: 226–41.

López García, M.-A. (2005) "La fiscalidad como instrumento de la política de vivienda," *Economistas*, 23(103): 116–29.

Low, S., Sebag-Montefiore, M., and Dübel, A. (2003) *Study on the Financial Integration of European Mortgage Markets* (London/Brussels: Mercer Oliver Wyman/European Mortgage Federation).

Ludwig, A. and Sløk, T. (2002) "Impact of Changes in Stock Prices and House Prices on Consumption in OECD Countries," IMF Working Paper 02/01.

Lunde, J. (2005) "The Owner-occupiers' Capital Structure during a House Price Boom: Does Negative Equity Exist as a Permanent Feature in the Danish Housing Market?" Working Paper 2005-3, Department of Finance, Copenhagen Business School.

Lunde, J. (2007) "Distributions of Owner-occupiers' Housing Wealth, Debt and Interest Expenditure Ratios as Financial Soundness Indicators," Working Paper 2007-1, Department of Finance, Copenhagen Business School.

Lunde, J. (2008) "The Housing Price Downturn and its Effects," Working Paper 2008-1, Department of Finance, Copenhagen Business School.

MacKenzie, D. (2006) *An Engine, Not a Camera: How Financial Models Shape Markets* (Cambridge, MA: MIT Press).

Malpass, P. (1996) "The Unravelling of Housing Policy in Britain," *Housing Studies*, 11(3): 459–70.

Malpass, P. (2008) "Housing and the New Welfare State: Wobbly Pillar or Cornerstone?" *Housing Studies*, 23(1):1–19.

Martin, I. (2008) *The Permanent Tax Revolt: How the Property Tax Transformed American Politics* (Stanford: Stanford University Press).

McConnell, M.M., Peach, R.W., and Al-Haschimi, A. (2003) "After the Refinancing Boom: Will Consumers Scale Back Their Spending?" *Current Issues in Economics and Finance*, 9(12): 1–7.

McLeay, E.M. (1984) "Housing as a Political Issue: A Comparative Study," *Comparative Politics*, 17(1): 85–105.

McLeay, E.M. (1992) "Housing Policy," in J. Boston and P. Dalziel (eds.) *The Decent Society? Essays in Response to National's Economic and Social Policies* (Auckland: Oxford University Press), 169–85.

Memery, C. (2001) "The Housing System and the Celtic Tiger: The State Response to a Housing Crisis of Affordability and Access," *European Journal of Housing Policy*, 1(1): 79–104.

Merrett, S. and Gray, F. (1982) *Owner-Occupation in Britain* (London: Routledge).

Mezzetti, P., Mugnano, S., and Zajczyk, F. (2003) *Large Housing Estates in Italy. Overview of Developments and Problems in Milan, RESTATE report 2d* (Utrecht: Faculty of Geosciences, Utrecht University).

Michel, H. (2000) *Propriété, propriétaires: politiques publiques et groupes d'intérêt dans le secteur immobilier en France* (Paris: Thèse de doctorat de science politique, EHESS).

Michel, H. (2006) *La cause des propriétaires: État et propriété en France, fin XIXe-XXe siècle* (Paris: Belin).

Mingione, E. and Nuvolati, G. (2003) "Urban Development Programmes in Italy. National Institutional Innovation and European Programmes," in P. de Decker, J. Vranken, J. Beaumont, and I. van Nieuwenhuyze (eds.) *On the Origins of Urban Development Programmes in Nine European Countries* (Antwerp: Garant), pp. 101–17.

Mishra, A. and Daly, K. (2006) "Where Do Australians Invest?" *The Australian Economic Review*, 39(1): 47–59.

Montgomerie, Johnna (2007) "The Logic of Neo-liberalism and the Political Economy of Consumer-Debt Led Growth," in S. Lee and S. McBride (eds.) *Neo-Liberalism, State Power and Global Governance* (Dordrecht, Netherlands).

Morrison, P.S. (2007) *On the Falling Rate of Home Ownership in New Zealand*, research paper for Centre for Housing Research Aotearoa New Zealand, available online at www.chranz.co.nz/pdfs/falling-rate-home-ownership-in-nz.pdf, date accessed April 28, 2008.

Mosley, L. (2003) *Global Capital and National Governments* (Cambridge: Cambridge University Press).

Muellbauer, J. (2007) "Housing, Credit and Consumer Expenditure," Federal Reserve Bank 31st Economic Policy Symposium, Jackson Hole, WY, August 2007, pp. 33–4.

Murphy, C. and Harley, R. (2003) "Housing Affordability Hits a Low," *Australian Financial Review*, 29 July, p. 8.

Murphy, L. (1996) "Whose Interest Rates? Issues in the Development of Mortgage Backed Securitization," *Housing Studies*, 11(4): 581–99.

Murphy, L. (2000) "A Profitable Housing Policy? The Privatization of the New Zealand Government's Residential Mortgage Portfolio," *Regional Studies*, 34(4): 395–99.

Naredo Pérez, J.-M. (2004) "Perspectivas de la vivienda," *Información Comercial Española. Revista de Economía*, 815: 143–54.

NATSEM (2008) "Wherever I Lay My Debt, That's My Home: Trends in Housing Affordability and Housing Stress, 1995–96 to 2005–06," AMP/NATSEM Income and Wealth Report, Issue 19, NATSEM, University of Canberra.

Neuteboom, P. (2003) "A European Comparison of the Costs and Risks of Mortgages for Owner-Occupation," *European Journal of Housing Policy*, 3(2): 155–71.

Neuteboom, P. (2004) "A Comparative Analysis of the Net Cost of a Mortgage for Homeowners in Europe," *Journal of Housing and the Built Environment*, 19(2): 169–86.

New Zealand Herald (2008) "National's Rescue Package Puts it in the Fast Lane," October 28, 2008.

New Zealand Treasury (2008) "Guarantees," available online at www.treasury. govt.nz/economy/guarantee (accessed December 19, 2008).

Nomisma (2002) *Prospects in the Italian Real Estate Market* (Bologna: Nomisma).

Nothaft, F.E. (2004) "The Contribution of Home Value Appreciation to US Economic Growth," *Urban Policy and Research*, 22(1): 23–34.

NOU (1989) 1 *Penger og kreditt i en omstillingstid.*

NOU (1992) 30 *Bankkrisen.*

Nuvolati, G. and Zajczyk, F. (1990) *Il problema casa nell'area metropolitana milanese. Tendenze del mercato immobiliare, modelli residenziali e qualità della vita.* Rapporto Cimep (Milano: IreR).

Nykredit (2008) *Danish Covered Bonds* (Copenhagen, Nykredit).

O'Brien, R. (1992) *Global Financial Integration: The End of Geography* (London: Pinter).

Ohmae, K. (1990) *The Borderless World: Power and Strategy in an Interdependent Economy* (New York: Harper).

Organisation for Economic Cooperation and Development (1995) *Securitisation: An International Perspective* (Paris: OECD).

Organisation for Economic Cooperation and Development (2004a) *Economic Survey – Netherlands 2004* (Paris: OECD).

Organisation for Economic Cooperation and Development (2004b) *OECD Economic Outlook No. 75*, preliminary edition (Paris: OECD).

Organisation for Economic Cooperation and Development (2005a) OECD Factbook, http://www.sourceOECD.org.

Organisation for Economic Cooperation and Development (2005b) *OECD Economic Outlook No. 78*, preliminary edition (Paris: OECD).

Organisation for Economic Cooperation and Development (2005c) *Housing Finance Markets in Transition Economies* (Paris: OECD).

Organisation for Economic Cooperation and Development (2006) *OECD Economic Surveys – Denmark* (Paris: OECD).

Øvald, C.B. (2007) "Budskapet som forsvant. Når statsbudsjettet blir sendt i reprise," *Samtiden* 3: 78–89.

Peck, J. and Theodore, N. (2007) "Variegated Capitalism," *Progress in Human Geography*, 31(6): 731–72.

Pierson, C. (1998) *Beyond the Welfare State? The New Political Economy of Welfare* (Cambridge: Polity).

Polanyi, Karl (1944 [1957]) *The Great Transformation: The Political and Economic Origins of Our Time* (Boston: Beacon Press).

Pollard, S. (1992) *The Development of the British Economy, 1914–1990* (fourth edn) (London: Edward Arnold).

Pontusson, J. (2005) *Inequality and Prosperity* (Ithaca: Cornell University Press).

Porter, M.E. (1990) *The competitive advantage of nations* (London: Macmillan).

Quilichini, P. (2001) *Logement social et décentralisation* (Paris: LGDJ).

Realkreditrådet (2008) "Realkreditrådet korrigerer ejendomsprisstatistikken," January 30, 2008, http://www.realkreditraadet.dk/Nyt_-amp_presse.aspx?M= News&PID=0&NewsID=37

"Regeringen: Mere boligskat udelukket," DR Nyheder, November 24, 2005, www. dr.dk/Nyheder/Politik/2005/11/24/131500.htm.

Renaud, B. and Kim, K.-H. (2007) "The Global Housing Price Boom and Its Aftermath," *Housing Finance International*, 22(2): 3–15.

Research New Zealand (2007a) "More Public Spending Preferred Over Tax Cuts," Media Release, October 29.

Research New Zealand (2007b) "Rising Interest Rates Worrying Kiwis," Media Release, October 1.

Research New Zealand (2007c) "Significant Support for Capital Gains Tax on Investment Properties," Media Release, March 1.

Reserve Bank of Australia (1996) *Submission to the Financial System Inquiry,* September 6, 1996, Occasional Paper 14. Canberra: Reserve Bank of Australia.

Reserve Bank of Australia (2005) *Financial Stability Review,* March 2005. (Canberra: Reserve Bank of Australia).

Reserve Bank of Australia (2006a) *Financial Stability Review,* March 2006. (Canberra: Reserve Bank of Australia).

Reserve Bank of Australia (2006b) *Financial Stability Review,* September 2006. (Canberra: Reserve Bank of Australia).

Reserve Bank of Australia (2008a) *Financial Stability Review,* March 2008. (Canberra: Reserve Bank of Australia).

Reserve Bank of Australia (2008b) *Financial Stability Review,* September 2008. (Canberra: Reserve Bank of Australia).

Reserve Bank of New Zealand (2007) *Mortgage Interest Levy, A Detailed Option,* Wellington: Reserve Bank of New Zealand, available online at www.rbnz.govt. nz/monpol/about/2950448.html (accessed April 25, 2008).

"Reuters Online (2009) "Denmark unveils $18 bln bank loan package," available at http://www.reuters.com/article/marketsNews/idUSLI53099420090118. Accessed January 21, 2009.

Rex, J. (1973) *Race, Colonialism and the City* (London: Routledge and Kegan Paul).

Richards, A. (2008) "Some Observations on the Cost of Housing in Australia," Reserve Bank of Australia Bulletin, address at the Economic and Social Outlook Conference, The Melbourne Institute, Melbourne, March 27.

Rosamond, Ben (2005) "Globalisation, the Ambivalence of European Integration and the Possibilities for a 'Post-Disciplinary EU Studies,'" *Innovation: The European Journal of Social Science Research*, 18(1): 25–45.

Royal Institution of Chartered Surveyors (2007) *RICS Housing Accessibility and Affordability Update for Great Britain* (London, RICS).

Rudd, C. (2005) "Welfare Policy," in R. Miller (ed.) *New Zealand Government and Politics* (Auckland: Oxford University Press), pp. 418–27.

"Rudd outlines housing plan," *Sydney Morning Herald*, October 16, 2007.

Ruth Simon (2008) "Mortgages Made in 2007 Go Bad at a Rapid Clip," *Wall Street Journal*, August 9.

Sala Pala, V. (2005) "Le racisme institutionnel dans la politique du logement social," *Sciences de la société*, 65: 87–102.

Sala Pala, V. (2006) "La politique du logement social au risque du client ? Attributions de logements sociaux, construction sociale des clients et discriminations ethniques en France et en Grande-Bretagne," *Politiques et management public*, 24(3): 77–92.

Salet, W.G.M. (1999) "Regime Shifts in Dutch Housing Policy," *Housing Studies*, 14(4): 547–57.

Salomon, F. (2007) "What's a CDO?," available at http://www.portfolio.com/interactive-features/2007/12/cdo

Salverda, W. (2005) "The Dutch Model: Magic in a Flat Landscape?" in U. Becker and H. M. Schwartz (eds.) *Employment "Miracles,"* Amsterdam: Amsterdam University Press: 39–64.

Sambricio, C. (2003) *Un siglo de vivienda social (1903/2003)* (Madrid: Ministerio de Fomento).

Sassen, S. (2001) *The Global City: New York, London, Tokyo* (second edn) (Princeton, NJ: Princeton University Press).

Saunders, P. (1986) *Social Theory and the Urban Question* (second edn) (London: Routledge).

Scanlon, K. and Whitehead, C. (2004) *International Trends in Housing Tenure and Mortgage Finance* (London: Council of Mortgage Lenders).

Schmidt, V.A. (2003) "How, Where and When does Discourse Matter in Small States' Welfare State Adjustment?" *New Political Economy*, 8(1): 127–46.

Schoon, N. (2001) *The Chosen City* (London: Taylor and Francis).

Schwartz, H. and Becker, U. (2005) "Introduction: Miracles, Mirages, and Markets," in U. Becker and H.M. Schwartz (eds.) *Employment "Miracles"* (Amsterdam: Amsterdam University Press), pp. 11–38.

Schwartz, H.M. (1994) "Small States in Big Trouble: State Reorganization In Australia, Denmark, New Zealand, and Sweden in the 1980s," *World Politics*, 46(4): 525–55.

Schwartz, H.M. (2001) "The Danish 'Miracle': Luck, Pluck or Stuck?" *Comparative Political Studies*, 34(2): 131–55.

Schwartz, H.M. (2006) "Explaining Australian Economic Success: Good Policy or Good Luck?" *Governance*, 19(2): 173–205.

Schwartz, H.M. (2009) *Subprime Nation: American Economic Power, Global Capital Flows and Housing* (Ithaca: Cornell University Press).

Scott, A. (1998) *Regions and the World Economy: The Coming Shape of Global Production, Competition, and Political Order* (Oxford: Oxford University Press).

Seabrooke, L. (2001) *US Power in International Finance: The Victory of Dividends* (Basingstoke: Palgrave Macmillan).

Seabrooke, L. (2006) *The Social Sources of Financial Power: Domestic Legitimacy and International Financial Orders* (Ithaca: Cornell University Press).

Seabrooke, L. (2007) "The Everyday Social Sources of Economic Crises: From 'Great Frustrations' to 'Great Revelations' in Interwar Britain," *International Studies Quarterly*, 51(4): 795–810.

Seabrooke, L. (2008) "Everyday Politics and Quasi-Public Institutions in the International Financial Order," mimeo, International Center for Business and Politics, Copenhagen Business School, March.

Setser, B. (2006) "The Deterioration in the US Income Balance Has Just Begun," 26 September 2006. Available at http://blogs.cfr.org/setser/2006/09/26/the-deterioration-in-the-us-income-balance-has-just-begun/.

Setser, Brad (2008) "Brazil Backstops the Treasury Market, Russia Backstops the Housing Market, and China Backstops Flows through London," 17 January at http://www.rgemonitor.com/blog/setser/238328/.

"SF skifter kurs og freder boligskatten", Børsen. November 7, 2007.

Sheng, Y.K. and Kirinpanu, S. (2000) "Once Only the Sky was the Limit: Bangkok's Housing Boom and the Financial Crisis in Thailand," *Housing Studies*, 15(1): 11–27.

Sheridan, T.J., Manley, J., MacDonald, C., and Flynn, B. (2002) "Sliding Scale of Support: Government Intervention in Housing," *Housing Studies*, 17(2): 337–47.

Sherry, Senator Nick (2008) "The Australian ABS: The Way Forward," keynote address to the Australian Securitisation Forum, November 28, 2008. Available at: http://minscl.treasurer.gov.au/

Shiller, R. (2000) *Irrational Exuberance* (Princeton, NJ: Princeton University Press).

Shonfield, A. (1965) *Modern Capitalism: The Changing Balance of Public and Private Power* (New York: Oxford University Press).

Simon, P. (2001) "Les discriminations raciales et ethniques dans l'accès au logement social," *Fondations*, 13: 113–21.

Singer, David (2007) *Regulating Capital: Setting Standards for the International Financial System* (Ithaca, NY: Cornell University Press).

Sironi, A. and Zazzara, C. (2003) "The Basel Committee Proposals for a New Capital Accord: Implications for Italian Banks,"| *Review of Financial Economics*, 12(1): 99–126.

"Slut med forældrekøb for at score kassen," *Politiken*, July 16, 2007.

Smith, D. (1992) *From Boom to Bust: Trial and Error in British Economic Policy* (London: Penguin).

Soros, G. (2008) "Denmark Offers a Model Mortgage Market," *Wall Street Journal*, October 10, A15.

Stamsø, M.-A. (2008) "Housing and the Welfare State in Norway," *Scandinavian Political Studies*, 31(4): 1–26.

Statistics New Zealand (1998) *New Zealand Now: Housing*, 30 November 2007. Available online at www2.stats.govt.nz/domino/external/pasfull/pasfull.nsf/0/4c2567ef00247c6acc256b6d0002826e/$FILE/housing.pdf, accessed April 24, 2008.

Statistics New Zealand (2007) *QuickStats About Housing: 2006 Census*, available online at www.stats.govt.nz/NR/rdonlyres/2471D004-399D-472D-95DA-9020B30C9386/0/quickstatsabouthousingrevised2.pdf, date accessed April 24, 2008.

Statistics New Zealand (2008) *Economic Indicators*, available online at www.stats.govt.nz/economy/economic-indicators/default.htm, date accessed December 19, 2008.

Statistics Norway (2007) Levekårsundersøkelsen 2007. Boforhold. http://www.ssb.no/emner/05/03/bo/tab-2008-07-15-01.html

Stébé, J.-M. and Blanc, M. (2004) "France: From Dreams to Disillusion," in R. Turkinton, R. Van Kempen and F. Wassenberg (eds.) *Housing and Urban Policy Studies* (Delft: Delft University Press).

Stephen Jen and Luca Bindelli (2007) "AXJ as a Source of Global Disinflation and Inflation," Morgan Stanley Global Economic Forum, November 30, at http://www.morganstanley.com/views/gef/archive/2007/20071130-Fri.html (last accessed 1 December 2007).

Stephens, M. (2000) "Convergence in European Mortgage Systems Before and After the EMU," *Journal of Housing and the Built Environment*, 15(1): 29–52.

Stephens, M. (2003) "Globalization and Housing Finance Systems in Advanced and Transition Countries," *Urban Studies*, 40(5–6): 1011–26.

Storper, M. (1997) *The Regional World: Territorial Development in a Global Economy* (New York: Guilford).

Stuart, G. (2003) *Discriminating Risk: The U.S. Mortgage Lending Industry in the Twentieth Century* (Ithaca, NY: Cornell University Press).

Stuart, I., Badcock, B., Clapham, A., and Fitzgerald, R. (2004) "Changing Tenure: Housing Trends, Financial Deregulation and Housing Policy in New Zealand Since 1990," *Housing Finance International*, 18(4): 3–10.

Subirats, Joan and Gomá, Ricard (dirs.). *Políticas públicas en España : contenidos, redes de actores y niveles de gobierno*. Barcelona : Ariel, 1998.

Sunley, P., Martin, R., and Nativel, C. (2006) *Putting Workfare in Place: Local Labour Markets and the New Deal* (Oxford: Blackwell).

"Super Way to Pay just 15pc Tax," *The Australian*, June 9, 2007.

Sydney Morning Herald (2002) "The Young are Growing up Poor," September 19, 2002.

Sydney Morning Herald (2007) "Rudd outlines housing plan," October 16, 2007.

Sydney Morning Herald (2008a) "Bank deposits guaranteed for 3 years," October 12, 2008.

Sydney Morning Herald (2008b) "Too late to help some borrowers in arrears," December 30, 2008.

Taylor, J. and Bradley, S. (1994) "Spatial Disparities in the Impact of the 1990–92 Recession: An Analysis of UK Counties," *Oxford Bulletin of Economics and Statistics*, 56(4): 367–82.

Tett, Gillian and Davies, Paul (2007) "Out of the Shadows: How Banking's Secret System Broke Down," *Financial Times*, 16 December at http://www.ft.com/cms/s/0/42827c50-abfd-11dc-82f0-0000779fd2ac.html.

"The Great Australian Illusion," *The Age*, August 5, 2003.

"The Young are Growing up Poor," *Sydney Morning Herald*, September 19, 2002.

Thorns, D.C. (2000) "Policy Review: Housing Policy in the 1990s – New Zealand A Decade of Change," *Housing Studies*, 15(1): 129–38.

Thorns, D.C. (2006) "The Remaking of Housing Policy: The New Zealand Housing Strategy for the 21st Century," *Housing Finance International*, 20(4): 20–8.

"Too Late to Help Some Borrowers in Arrears," *Sydney Morning Herald*, December 30, 2008.

Tosi, A. (1987) "La produzione sociale della casa in proprietà: Practiche familiari, informale, politiche," *Sociologia e ricerca sociale*, 22: 7–24.

Tosi, A. (1990) "Italy," in *International Handbook of Housing Policies and Practices*,. W. van Vliet (ed.) (New York: Greenwood), 195–220.

Tosi, A. and Cremaschi M. (2001) "Housing Policies in Italy," IMPACT working paper. Vienna: The Interdisciplinary Centre for Comparative Research in the Social Sciences (ICCR).

Trade Council of the Danish Ministry of Foreign Affairs (2007) "The Danish Housing Market at the End of a Boom," *FOCUS Denmark*, 3: 14. Available from: http://www.netpublikationer.dk/UM/8425/pdf/Screen_Focus_Denmark.pdf (last accessed 1 November 2008).

Tranøy, B.S. (2000) "Losing Credit! The Politics of Liberalisation and Macro-Economic Regime Change in Norway 1980–1992(99)," PhD dissertation, Department of Political Science, University of Oslo.

US Bureau of Labor Statistics (2004) *Consumer Expenditure Survey 2004.*

US Department of the Treasury (2005) *Report on Foreign Holdings of US Portfolio Securities* (Washington, DC).

US Department of the Treasury (2007) *Report on Foreign Holdings of US Portfolio Securities* (Washington, DC).

Uzuhashi Takafumi (2003) "Japanese Model of the Welfare State: How Has It Changed during the 'Lost Decade' of the 1990s," *Japanese Journal of Social Security Policy*, 2(2): 1–11.

Van Dusseldorp, A.M. (2003) "Actuele ontwikkelingen op de hypothekenmarkt," in *Het 8e', Nationale Hypothekencongres.*

Van Leuvensteijn, M. (2003) "Collateral requirements and market power in the Dutch mortgage market," *CPB report 2003/4*, Den Haag: CPB Netherlands Bureau for Economic Policy Analysis.

Vaz, C. (2004) *Mémoire de DEA* (Université de Paris X-Nanterre: UFR Histoire).

Villosio, C. (1995) "Mercato del credito, proprietà della casa, risparmio delle famiglie," *Annali della Fondazione Einaudi*, 29: 213–248.

Wachtel, H.M. (1986) *The Money Mandarins: The Making of a Supranational Economic Order* (New York: Pantheon).

Wagner, R. (2005) "En model for de danske ejerboligpriser," Arbejdspapir nr. 1/2005, Økonomi og Erhvervsministeriet, København.

Waldfogel, J. (2004) "A Cross-National Perspective on Policies to Promote Investments in Children," in A. Kalil and T. DeLeire (eds.) *Family Investments in Children's Potential: Resources and Parenting Behaviors That Promote Success* (London: Routledge).

Warnock, F.E. and Warnock, V.C. (2006) "International Capital Flows and U.S. Interest Rates," *FRB International Finance Discussion Paper*, 840.

Whitehead, C. (1998) "Are Housing Systems Converging within the European Union," in M. Kleinman, W. Matznetter, and M. Stephens (eds.) *European Integration and Housing Policy*, pp. 19–31.

Whitley, R. (1998) "Internationalization and Varieties of Capitalism: the Limited Effects of Cross-National Coordination of Economic Activities on the Nature of Business Systems," *Review of International Political Economy*, 5(3): 445–81.

Wilding, P. (1997) "The Welfare State and the Conservatives," *Political Studies*, 45(5): 716–26.

Wilson, S. (2006) "Not My Taxes!: Explaining Tax Resistance and its Implications for Australia's Welfare State," *Australian Journal of Political Science*, 41(4): 517–35.

Wójcik, D. (2002) "Cross-border Corporate Ownership and Capital Market Integration in Europe: some Evidence from Portfolio and Industrial Holdings," *Journal of Economic Geography*, 2(4): 455–91.

Wood, G. and Capie, F. (1996) "Debt, Deflation and Economic Policy," *Review of Policy Issues*, 2(1): 15–26.

Wulff, M.N.N. and Maher, C. (1998) "Long-Term Renters in the Australian Housing Market," *Housing Studies*, 13(1): 83–98.

Yates, J. (2003) "'The More Things Change'? An Overview of Australia's Recent Home Ownership Policies," *European Housing Policy*, 3(1): 1–33.

Young, Audrey (2008) "Govt Acts to Keep Savings Safe," *New Zealand Herald*, October 13, available online at www.nzherald.co.nz/nz-election-2008/news/article.cfm?c_id=1501799&objectid=10537235&pnum=0 (accessed December 19, 2008).

Zittoun, P. (2001) *La politique du logement 1981–1995: Transformations d'une politique publique controversée* (Paris: L'Harmattan).

Zysman, John (1983) *Governments, Markets and Growth* (Ithaca, NY: Cornell University Press).

Index